Uncovering Your Personal Animal Totem

Darlene D Stout

Copyright © 2013 Darlene D Stout
All rights reserved.

ISBN: 0615809545
ISBN-13: 9780615809540

To all my beloved animals on both sides of the veil that have been a significant part of my soul's growth. You have been such tremendous master teachers for me. Your gifts of healing, solace, magic, and playfulness only scratch the surface when it comes to your extraordinary essence around me.

To my mom, Nora, my first human spiritual teacher and devoted supporter. Thank you for your exceptional love and sometimes-tested patience as we navigated our sacred contract in this life. Most of all, thank you for your continued powerful and kindred messages from beyond.

Also, my immense gratitude to my devoted spirit guides, who never stop amazing me with your wonderful, enchanting guidance and joy. This book would not have been possible without your steadfast support and guidance. I am eternally grateful for the delightful experiences you present to me each moment, and I thank you enormously with honor and reverence.

CONTENTS

Introduction ix

Part I: Preparing to Meet Your Totem Animals 1

Chapter 1: Getting Started 3
    Suiting Up 3
    Getting the Right Vibe 4
    Prospecting 4
    Creating Space 5
    Setting Up Sacred Space 6
    Chakras 6
    Timeline 8

Chapter 2: Signs along the Way 11
    What I Am Is What I Am 12
    It's All in Your Head 12
    It Is What It Is 14
    Sign, Sign, Everywhere a Sign 15

Chapter 3: A Picture Is Worth a Thousand Words 17
    Grasping Archetypes 17
    Finding Your Waldo 18
    Looks Can Be Deceiving 19
    On Your Mark, Get Set, Go 21

Chapter 4: Taking Your Wheels for a Spin 23
    Test-Driving Your Wheels 24
    Going Round and Round 25
    Embracing the Road 25
    Care and Maintenance of Your Wheels 26

Chapter 5: Somewhere over the Rainbow 27
    Brown—Foot Chakra 28
    Red—Root Chakra 29
    Orange—Sacral Chakra 29
    Yellow—Solar Plexus Chakra 30
    Green—Heart Chakra 30
    Blue—Throat Chakra 31
    Indigo—Third Eye Chakra 31
    Purple—Crown Chakra 33

Chapter 6: Your Travel Itinerary 35
    Planning Tips 35
    What to Take Along 36
    Where to Travel 36
    Traveling Alone and with Others 37
    Capturing Your Travel 37

Chapter 7: Setting the Ground Rules 39
    The Five Ground Rules 39
    How to Accessorize Your Journey 45
    Meeting the Inhabitants 48

Part II: Making Friends with Your Animal Totems 51

Chapter 8: Foot Chakra 53
    Uncovering Your Foot Chakra Totem Animal 53
    What Is a Foot Chakra? 54
    Let's Get Physical 55
    Honoring Your Feet 56
    The Foot Chakra Totem 58
    Connecting with Your Foot Totem 61
    Welcoming Your Foot Totem Animal 62

Chapter 9: Root Chakra 65
    Uncovering Your Root Chakra Totem Animal 65
    What Is a Root Chakra? 66
    Let's Get Physical 75
    Honoring Your Root 77
    The Root Chakra Totem 78
    Connecting with Your Root Totem 82
    Welcoming Your Root Totem Animal 83

Chapter 10: Sacral Chakra 85
- Uncovering Your Sacral Chakra Totem Animal 85
- What Is a Sacral Chakra? 86
- Let's Get Physical 88
- Honoring Your Sacral 93
- The Sacral Chakra Totem 94
- Connecting with Your Sacral Totem 96
- Welcoming Your Sacral Totem Animal 97

Chapter 11: Solar Plexus Chakra 101
- Uncovering Your Solar Plexus Chakra Totem Animal 101
- What Is a Solar Plexus Chakra? 102
- Let's Get Physical 104
- Honoring Your Solar Plexus 107
- The Solar Plexus Chakra Totem 109
- Connecting with Your Solar Plexus Totem 113
- Welcoming Your Solar Plexus Totem Animal 114

Chapter 12: Heart Chakra 117
- Uncovering Your Heart Chakra Totem Animal 117
- What Is Heart Chakra? 118
- Let's Get Physical 119
- Honoring Your Heart 121
- The Heart Chakra Totem 123
- Connecting with Your Heart Totem 127
- Welcoming Your Heart Totem Animal 129

Chapter 13: Throat Chakra 133
- Uncovering Your Throat Chakra Totem Animal 133
- What Is a Throat Chakra? 134
- Let's Get Physical 135
- Honoring Your Throat 138
- The Throat Chakra Totem 140
- Connecting with Your Throat Totem 143
- Welcoming Your Throat Totem Animal 146

Chapter 14: Third Eye Chakra 149
- Uncovering Your Third Eye Chakra Totem Animal 149
- What Is a Third Eye Chakra? 150
- Let's Get Physical 151
- Honoring Your Third Eye 154

    The Third Eye Chakra Totem 155
    Connecting with Your Third Eye Totem 159
    Welcoming Your Third Eye Totem Animal 160

Chapter 15: Crown Chakra 163
    Uncovering Your Crown Chakra Totem Animal 163
    What Is a Crown Chakra? 164
    Let's Get Physical 165
    Honoring Your Crown 168
    The Crown Chakra Totem 169
    Connecting with Your Crown Totem 173
    Welcoming Your Crown Totem Animal 175

Part III: All Together Now 179

Chapter 16: Working Together with Your Motley Crew of Critters 181
    Anchors Aweigh! 182
    Ahoy, There! 183
    How Guidable Are You? 184
    Plane Sailing 185

Chapter 17: What Your Motley Crew of Critters Can Do for You 187
    Like, Duh! 187
    Who's Your Totem? 188
    What Goes Around, Comes Around 188
    Wake Up and Smell the Coffee 189
    I Can See Clearly Now 189
    Hallelujah, It's a Healing! 190
    Abracadabra! 191
    Sometimes You Just Gotta Let It Go 191
    If You Play Your Cards Right 193

Chapter 18: Afterthoughts 195
    Afterword 196
    The End 199

Tips, Tricks, and Divine Wisdom 201
Meditation 203

INTRODUCTION

When I was a child, I was always intrigued by animals and nature. I felt that each creature I encountered spoke to me on some deep and profound level far beyond how we humans communicate. Throughout my childhood I was always on safari, trying to capture the essence of wild creatures so I could learn more about the wonders of their mysterious and exclusive secret world. Every animal I encountered seemed to speak to me in a way that stirred my soul. Trying to persuade them to become a part of my world was my utmost ambition as I followed them deeper into their world. When I wasn't able to connect with them physically, I could feel their invisible life forces accompanying me as I traveled through my day. When I couldn't be a part of their physical world, I took them with me energetically through my internal world. I can still remember getting annoyed looks from my mom as she tossed the grocery bags onto the backseat where I sat surrounded by my invisible wildlife friends. "Hey, watch out for my bear!" I'd exclaim as she'd roll her eyes and summon me to load the bags. I was always looking for an opportunity to be in the wilderness, whether pitching tents in the yard or building forts or tree houses—it was my opportunity to connect with animals and nature and to be a part of their powerful forces that brought me such wonder, peace, and tranquility.

Deep down inside I always knew I would work for spirit and with animals. However, I never really knew just how amazingly that would take form. It wasn't until years later that I would discover that those energetic animal seeds planted in me during my childhood would also be the amazing stepping stones to an extraordinary sacred dimension that would change my life. It was what some folks would call a spiritual awakening, and it would transcend the Christian faith teachings I had pursued throughout my life. The most powerful thing I have learned in my journey is that every person, place, thing, or situation is an amazing master teacher if we allow ourselves to see those wonderful messages presented in each moment. Writing this book has brought me together with spirit in extraordinary and miraculous ways. It has taught me how to turn to the

Uncovering Your Personal Animal Totem

Divine, God, the source, the universe, or whatever you call that invisible "all that is" being in a much grander way than I had ever thought possible. Interestingly enough, the connectedness and magic of it all becomes increasingly enchanted and expanded if you give yourself permission to continually navigate these wonderful guiding realms.

Within the pages of this book is an extraordinary journey through the hidden realms of your inner world that will uncover aspects of your beautiful true nature with the help of a remarkable group of wonderful wildlife creatures. These critters will guide your journey toward embracing your true nature in the most delightful ways, for you are the chosen one. Keep in mind that you do not choose your animal totems; your animal totems choose you, which is the amazing part. You become the object of choice, for their mission and purpose is to support, guide, help, protect, heal, and keep you connected to the forces and guidance from the grand invisible realms.

This book is organized to assist you through each step of the process of uncovering your personal animal totems. An animal guide for each of your energy centers, known as chakras, will introduce itself to you in the most magical and enchanting ways. Don't worry if you're not familiar with chakras; this book will easily guide you in understanding what they are and where and how they exist in your body. Each month you will learn a tad about each chakra center, the current state of each chakra, and how each one of your animal totem guides will assist you with opening, clearing, and balancing each one of them. The most spectacular part of the journey is that you will enhance your abilities to interact with and navigate through the subtle energies and powerful universal forces of Divine guidance. In other words, open up your intuitive channels with a new sense of awareness. This book is divided into three parts that will guide newbie's, journeymen, and even chakra gurus. If you're a novice, part I will guide you through the buzz and jargon of the ethereal world and suit you up for a journey through the chakras. For those familiar with chakras, you can start the journey immediately at part II. If you already work with chakras and have identified your totem guides, you will find part III a nice way to rekindle the relationships with your totems and helpful for flexing those paranormal muscles that might need a little workout. Moreover, part III will enhance your day-to-day connection with your totems and give you some insights as to how they can all work together more effectively.

There are voluminous amounts of information available on chakras. Chakras can be traced back thousands of years to ancient cultures and spiritual traditions and to a myriad of metaphysical philosophies and alternative modalities. Each group offers a different perspective of how these subtle fields of energy influence our life. I too have my own philosophy, based on how these forces of energy have influenced my life. The information about chakras contained in this book is based on my studies in

Introduction

parapsychology, as well as my own research and experience with chakras. Working with chakra energy is increasingly recognized as a valid model for promoting health and conquering illness, especially in the areas of complementary and alternative medicine (CAM). The information outlined in this book should not—let me repeat, *should not*—be used as a means for diagnosing disease or illness. I am neither a doctor, nor do a I claim to be one, although I wouldn't mind playing one on TV, mostly because I like the look of those short, white coats and find scrubs to be really comfortable working attire. While I give you a rudimentary snapshot of each chakra, I encourage you to seek more information on how these powerful energy centers can work for you.

The same can be said for your animal totems. Throughout history totems have been depicted as important aspects of ancient cultures, civilizations, philosophies, and mythology. They are considered sacred models that can take the form of an object, animal, plant, or any other natural phenomenon revered as a symbol of the gods, family, tribe, clan, or society. These symbolic totems depict lineage, protection, healing, and guidance, and each symbol has cultural, tribal, or traditional significance and is usually revered and honored as a sacred entity. Each one of your animal totems will offer the very aspects that can be drawn from these ancient tribal traditions. It is my fervent intent that, once this enchanting portal is opened, your animal totems bring to you the same joy, enthusiasm, and guidance that so many of my students, clients, friends, and family have received and experienced. Before you start your journey to embrace your true nature through nature, I will inspire you with a proverb from one of my favorite authors. Alan Cohen is sometimes heard saying, "'How can I be more like you?' she asked the guru. 'The best way to be more like me is to be more like you,' the guru replied." This journey to uncover your personal animal totem is just the medicine the guru ordered. So let's get started on you! Namaste.

PART I

Preparing to Meet Your Totem Animals

Throughout history, animals have played a significant role in guiding and assisting humankind in societies, cultures, religions, mythology, and science. Our primal connection with animals is unquestionable. As you move into the realms that will allow your totem animals to reveal themselves to you, the truth becomes undeniable. The chapters in part I will introduce you to the realms you will need to navigate through and the practice you will need to do to uncover your animal totems. As each animal is uncovered, you will discover your own rhythm within its nature and unearth a newness about yourself that will truly amaze you.

CHAPTER 1

GETTING STARTED

What's Up with This Chapter

∞ Suiting Up
∞ Getting the Right Vibe
∞ Prospecting
∞ Creating Space
∞ Setting Up Sacred Space
∞ Chakras
∞ Timeline

Before starting any venture, especially a journey of exploration, you want to make absolutely sure you have the right equipment and luggage for your travel. Each of us has our own way of traveling. Some of us travel very light, with just a toothbrush, pillow, and attitude, while others of us are more organized and particular about what we bring along. In the *Seinfeld* episode "The Trip," Jerry, seeing George with a big pile of luggage, says, "It's a three-day trip. Who are you, Diana Ross?" George replies, "I dress based on mood." Mood very much affects what we carry on our journeys in life, especially from an energetic perspective. In your journey to uncover your personal animal totem, you will discover the effects of mood on your energy. The good news about mood is that it can always be changed for the better, and transmuting mood energy is one of the first things you will embark upon as you suit up for this expedition to uncover your animal totems.

Suiting Up

Suiting up in the right outfit is essential on your journey to embracing your true nature and uncovering your personal animal totems. Now, I'm not suggesting you run out and purchase safari gear for your expedition. However, I will share with you something my very wise mother once told me as she glanced at my beach garb. She said, "Darlene, don't be foolish, you don't want to be sitting on a hot beach all day with army fatigues on. You'll be uncomfortable. And, besides, the kids will laugh at you." I don't ever recall any of the kids laughing at me, at least not to my face, but I do remember giving my mom silent credit for being smack dead-on right that day. She also planted that little seed of insight in me to pack for comfort if I want to navigate a particular environment; it puts me in the proper mood. The point I am trying to make here is that mood is very important. But you don't need to get all weighed down with luggage to have a great experience with mood. When you travel into your inner world, you want to be aware of what you are carrying, what mood you're bringing with you. Do keep in mind that you will always want to travel light on your journey within. Be mindful of what mood you want to take along, because that is exactly what you will attract. You will discover more about energy and how mood affects it as you travel deeper into embracing your true nature and begin to uncover each of your animal totems.

Getting the Right Vibe

The dictionary defines *mood* as a conscious state of mind or predominant emotion. When you begin the safari to uncover your personal animal totems, you want your conscious state of mind to be open to wonder and your predominant emotion to be peaceful. It is so important that you get that vibe down before you take even the first step over the starting line. A conscious state of mind open to wonder is the catalyst that supports the vibrations of magic, enchantment, and supernatural events into your frequency. You cannot—I repeat, you cannot—expect to uncover your personal animal totems and embrace your true nature through nature if you are harboring anger, frustration, or aggravation. You must be out of that vibration for the process to work. Not to worry, though. Just remember that mood energy is like magic and can always be changed to a much better and higher vibration. The only thing you really need to do is to be aware of the vibe you're putting out.

Prospecting

Now, don't get me wrong. I'm not saying you can't ever get angry, frustrated, or aggravated. In retrospect, some of my best leg-slapping laughs have come while thinking about things I've done in anger, frustration, and aggravation. But that was in retrospect. When you are prospecting, you can't be in that mood. "Prospecting?" you say. Yes, prospecting. Prospecting is all about searching for gold in dense, muddy sediment. But it's also my way of saying to set an intention. Setting intentions is *big* in the spirit world. Do not—I repeat, do not—start your journey without setting an intention. That would be like putting a mustache on the Mona Lisa—you just don't do it. Sure, it might be considered avant-garde, but you will have essentially desecrated a masterpiece. Setting intentions will not only protect you, it will also preserve the essence of the masterpiece, as you are in its essence. Setting intention essentially keeps you from straying from your destination and adds meaning and direction as you journey to meet your personal animal totem.

Creating Space

Space is boundless, vast, limitless; it seems almost indefinable and unconfinable. It can mean so many things. We know both the positive and negative connotations of the word just by how it is used. We say things like "Great space!" to mean I dig your crib, "outer space" to describe a realm not of this earth or a not-so-grounded person, and "I need space" when we're about to be the dumped or the dumper in a relationship. How about MySpace, the social network for people to share in cyberspace what they're into? The list goes on and on. Now that we have an idea about space, let's talk about creating space. The space you will create can be both boundless and restrictive, vast and small, limitless and limited. It's like creating complete opposites, it's like being a nun and prostitute at the same time. You create your own space, your place, your little nook, your altar, your mojo, a place you will go that can be anywhere. It can be a room in your home, the broom closet, a corner in the basement or attic, your car, or a park bench. It really doesn't matter where. It will be your own personal place that suits you up, changes your vibe, puts you in the mood, and prepares you for pioneering, prospecting, and travel. Just the mere thought of going to your space should evoke a sense of peace and tranquility, especially so when your mood is not so great. You will grow to honor this place very quickly because it is your sacred space, where all your worries are left behind. And your sacred space will open you up to the boundless, vast, limitlessness journey to Totemville, where you will meet all your animal totems and embrace your true nature. Your space will put you in the driver's seat and help get you in a conscious state of mind to perceive the journey within.

One way of looking at how sacred space works is to imagine having to venture out to the store during a winter snowstorm. You put on your hat, boots, gloves, and coat and jump into the car. You're sitting there in front of the steering wheel, staring at a snow-covered windshield, waiting for the first swipe of the windshield wiper to clear the window so you can see the road and travel to your destination. That's exactly what your sacred space will do for you. It essentially creates an environment conducive to launching your boundless journey. Your sacred space is your small space that brings you to unlimited space.

Setting Up Sacred Space

Once you have located your space, you'll want to furnish it with pleasing things that will set the mood for your travel. It can be as simple as a towel on the floor next to a nightlight on the wall or as elaborate as a stone altar with a beautiful, ornate candelabra full of candles. This is your space, and no one but you can define it or create it. It's important to create a space that will not overwhelm you with all its bits and pieces or that you will visit with a heavy heart. Remember, we are working with the energies of mood. You want your sacred space to be something that will entice you to visit often and make you feel good just at the sight of it. Your sacred space will always lift your vibration if that is your intention. Your sacred space doesn't have to be etched in stone either. I am constantly changing my altar depending on where I am in my life's journey. Sometimes it's just a candle, some incense, and my prayer book on a snack tray. Sometimes I add little joy trinkets or cartoon characters, sometimes flowers or a gift from the universe found on one of my nature walks. The most important thing to understand is that your sacred space is the place where you will make contact with your guides and all the Divine assistance available to help you connect with your animal totems. It's essential to know that if you're not serious about making the connection with your animal totems, your animal totems won't put any effort into it either. This is called free will. Guidance is always there for us, but we must ask for it, allow it, and work with it. It's our free will to make that choice of use it or lose it.

Chakras

When I was a teenager, I went to a class I found advertised on a flyer pinned up in a local smoke shop billboard headlined LEARN HOW TO BE PSYCHIC. I couldn't wait for that class. My imagination had conjured up wonderful things I would be doing with my new psychic abilities. I would get lost in visions of the endless possibilities that were surely coming my way. The day finally arrived; the class was jam-packed with all kinds of psychic wannabes, myself included. Boy, what a motley crew we all made! The instructor began the class by asking if any of us knew what chakras were and then proceeded to explain how important it was to keep them clear, open, and balanced. She continued to talk about these chakra things for what seemed a lifetime. As she continued on and on in what I perceived as a glum drone into eternity, I remembered impatiently thinking, When is she going to get to the hocus pocus stuff, and why is she going on an on about this chakra stuff? I couldn't even spell the word, let alone say it. I just wanted her to cast her spell and give me my psychic powers so I could be on my way. I figured that listening to her spiel was just par for the course.

Needless to say, I left class that day feeling quite disappointed. Any intuition or expanded awareness I'd had going into the class had been sucked right out of me at its end with all the chakra talk. Worst of all, my best friend, whom I was going to give my first reading to fresh out of the class, was eagerly walking toward me. She could tell by the look on my face that it hadn't been good. She probed me with questions like "What happened?" "What did she say?" "What are they called again?" and "She didn't cast any spells?"

I'd never heard of the word chakra before that day, and any attempt I made to learn more about them only confused me and created a greater mystery for me. There were no local new age centers; the Internet didn't exist. Can you imagine no Google, YouTube, or Wikipedia? Little did I know then that years later I would be sitting in front of my computer tapping out instructions on how to uncover an animal totem for each of your chakras. Divine humor, indeed. To be true to your spirit, you really do teach what you need to learn. The good news is that it's not that complicated. In fact, when you have the animal totems helping you with each one of your chakras, you get some powerful examples of what energy and the chakras are all about. Your animals will help you to keep your chakras clear, open, and balanced, which is the way I like things—nice and simple. So all you really need to know is that the chakra system is the conduit by which Divine energy passes through you. Think of the chakras as the river that spirit navigates through. You will learn more about the details of how each one performs in your inner world as we move though the animal totem journey.

What Are Chakras?

Chakra is not a common word that everyone knows. It would seem that if you are going to uncover your personal animal totem within the chakra system, you should probably know what a chakra is before the animal can be unveiled. Now, going back to my little story about the psychic class, I didn't readily grasp what chakras were either. In fact, it's not really a common word used around the house every day, unless, of course, you have new age parents who practice clearing their chakras daily. If you do, you've probably heard things like "Honey, I'm running late. Can you drop little Zuma off at school while I clear my chakras?" Just to get a feel for what I'm try to convey here, try saying either of these at the dinner table tonight and notice the response: "I had this awesome experience while I was balancing my chakras today" or "I was going to ask for a raise today, but I think I'm having issues with my third chakra." Once you get past the idea that your newfound vernacular is going to be Greek to most people, you won't really care whether they know what a chakra is, you'll just feel really cool that you do. Know that it will be one of those things they will learn when they need to learn it. Kind of like a sump pump—you'll know what one is when you need it. You can trust me on that one.

So, what is a chakra? For starters, it's a word, and it's a word that translates to *wheel*. If you are thinking, "I never heard a wheel referred to as a chakra," you are right. The English language doesn't refer to the wheel as a chakra. If it did, we would hear things like "Grandma's having a tough time getting around, she might need a chakra chair" or "I think I'll just kick back on the couch with a beer and watch *Chakra of Fortune*." See what I mean?

So what language does chakra come from? The answer is Sanskrit. Sanskrit is the ancient language of India, although it is now used only for religious purposes. Chakras are energy centers within our body. You can think of them as little shopping centers that offer different paraphernalia. These little energy centers allow energies to flow in and out of us. The human body has seven major chakras, and these correlate with the colors of the rainbow: red, orange, yellow, green, blue, indigo, and violet. That's why, when you do a search for *chakra* on the Internet, you see depictions of the human body with color dots vertically aligned through it. Each chakra, color, or energy center transmits various expressions of energy in the body. You will learn more about how each one expresses as we start working on unveiling the animal associated with each chakra. Again, I just want to reiterate that chakras are the conduit through which Divine energy passes through you. Say it aloud: "Chakras are the conduit through which Divine energy passes through me." This phrase will be used a lot during this journey to keep you focused on energy.

Timeline

Now that you have a little insight into the essential components of your totem-finding expedition, the only other aspect of the journey to explain is the timeline. You certainly will gain more wisdom and a deeper understanding of all the chakras as you become more familiar with the Divine process of meeting your totems. The uncovering of your complete personal animal totem will take approximately nine months. Interestingly enough, this correlates perfectly with the gestation period of the human child. Equally important, you will actually be discovering wonderful aspects about yourself that have been hidden as part of the human developmental experience. Spiritualists and new age groups term this the "unconscious self." Your animal totems will unearth this wonderful stuff for you. Each month an animal totem will present itself to you. As you journey to uncover your personal animal totems, it is essential to know that your totem animals will come to meet you and will introduce themselves to you in various ways. I recommend that you record your totem journey in a journal. Many of the events of this journey will be quite synchronistic or unfold by what seems to be total coincidence. Having written evidence of these incidences and aspects will not only assure you of their true occurrences but will also give you faith and confidence in the Divine process that is always at play in your life.

Now that you understand the timeline, the only other aspect you need to be concerned with is when to start. When I uncovered my personal totem, I began in the fall and at the beginning of the month. To me, fall seemed like the natural place to start. In New England fall ushers in the harvest, the trees have spectacular color, the days get shorter, and we begin the process of going dormant for the winter—all of which seems to call for a journey within. Some people will use their birthday as a milestone opportunity to journey on a new adventure, while others will start in January, the turning of the new year and the hanging of the new year's calendar. Still others will start the day they read this book. When people ask me when they should start, I invariably answer, "Whenever you decide to launch the journey, know that it will always be the right time. It will always coincide with your personal rhythm and cycle." In essence, the journey is all about you.

CHAPTER 2

SIGNS ALONG THE WAY

What's Up with This Chapter

∞ What I Am Is What I Am
∞ It's All in Your Head
∞ It Is What It Is
∞ Sign, Sign, Everywhere a Sign

Your totems will be very powerful guides. As I mentioned in the Getting Started section, you will not be choosing your animal totems, your animal totems will be coming to meet you. They will choose you, for they hold a very powerful medicine that only you can utilize. Medicine is known as a form of energy that not only deepens our connection to the Divine but also gives us a dose of personal power, healing, insight, assistance or whatever essence is needed at that place and time. Think of it as going to the doctor to get a diagnosis for a particular ailment. You wouldn't say, "I'm going to choose radiation therapy for this blister on my foot because I know it is a very effective, direct, and powerful treatment." Your doctor might simply observe that you are wearing a poorly tuned new pair of shoes and suggest that some flip-flops and a smiley face Band-Aid may serve you better for that blister than radiation therapy. In other words, we sometimes make conditions more difficult than they really need to be. While we might think we know what is best for us according to our learned earthly survival skills, we don't. The animals that come to you do, and they will have the right medicine. The universe and its Divine guidance can be considered your doctor, and it will always make sure you are pointed to the best possible solutions to any obstacles, challenges, or burdens that come your way. You need only be open to its guidance and support. As you begin to trust these powerful forces that are always at play, you will have confidence in the flow of it, and these signs along the way will become more welcome, abundant, and fulfilling. You will soon learn as you begin to uncover your totems that following the signs and road markers that are always available from the Divine source will lead you to a more joyful and lighthearted passage, even if that doesn't seem apparent at that moment.

What I Am Is What I Am

One of the most challenging parts of uncovering your personal animal totem will be trusting in the Divine course that will be presented. It is important that you understand you are embarking on a sacred act that will bring many aspects of your life into the light, and abundant gifts will unfold because of this newfound light. The human mind, in conjunction with our learned earthly survival skills, will want to take immediate control of the ground rules for executing how it all happens. As we are spirit beings functioning in a human body, we sometimes forget that one of the most basic facets of life here on the earthly plane is free will.

Whether it is defined from a philosophical, theological, or scientific perspective, free will is the ability of a human to make his/her own decisions and control the direction of his/her life. So we all have free will and with that comes the choice to follow guidance or not. This is where the challenging part comes in. It's nice to think we can ride the fence, but sooner or later you will become a true fan of the totem process and will need to choose between National Football League or American Football League, the basic meaning being whether to follow spirit guidance or not to follow the guidance. The decision will be yours, but do keep in mind which choice you make when you do. This is where your journal will become your BFF (best friend forever). As you begin to journal about your totem experiences in the theater of your life, you will see the true you emerging, and your totem animals will start playing a significant part in that world.

It's All in Your Head

As you venture into the world of animal totems, you will be learning techniques that will align and open you to receiving visits from your totems. The key to success is to stay out of your head and view things as if you are watching television or a movie. In other words, just sit back and enjoy it. When your totem animals begin presenting themselves to you, it is totally normal for the human mind to become skeptical, questioning, and even find itself being a downright doubting Thomas. We are all very different creatures, and we all have our own ways of seeing things. This, in a sense, is dominated by our conditioning, which is then executed in the area of the brain we spend the majority of our time in. Some of us function more in the left side of the brain, while others find the right side of the brain the place they hang out more often.

Roger Sperry, a Nobel prizewinner for his work with split-brain research, initiated a study of the relationship between the brain's right and left hemispheres. Sperry found that the left half of the brain tends to function by processing information in an analytical, rational, logical, sequential way. The right half of the brain tends to function by recognizing relationships, integrating and synthesizing information, and arriving at intuitive insights. In other words, the left side of your brain deals with a problem or situation by collecting data, making analyses, and using a rational thinking process to reach a logical conclusion. The right side of your brain approaches the same problem or situation by making intuitive leaps to answers based on insights and perceptions. The left brain tends to break information apart for analysis, while the right brain tends to put information together to synthesize a whole picture. If you pride yourself on being the whole-brain type, just be aware of both sides and enjoy the flip-flopping.

This information will be very helpful for you whether you are a left- or right-brained individual. When your animals start showing up, if you tend to work in the left side of the brain more often, you're going to need lots of evidence (data) and rational thinking to reach logical conclusions about your animal. I find that some of my students who are solidly left-brain-dominant tend to dismiss some of the sightings of their animals, at least initially, because the sightings don't make logical sense to them. This will be one of the advantages of writing in your journal; you will have objective evidence of all your animal sightings, no matter what form they take, and you will be building a database that will appease the left brain.

On the other hand, my right-brain-dominant students tend to have such great imaginations and mind's-eye views of things they have a tendency to not play in the physical world or utilize the physical evidence to validate their animals. They prefer to rely on the meditations to confirm sightings of their animal totems. For you folks, I would just add that we are here to experience the physical plane, and the animals that come to you are of service, to help you as part of that assignment. To ensure a sighting is not an illusion and is indeed a reality, I recommend right-brain-dominant individuals really push for evidence of your animal on the physical plane. Trust that it will come and be quite abundant. I will elaborate more on this in the meditation section of the ground rules in chapter 7.

It is essential to know that you are working with the Divine and sacred realm, and you should feel duty-bound to always honor and acknowledge your totems efforts to connect with you, whether it's from a physical point of view or nonphysical, as in your meditations or dreams. "Gratitude gratitude, gratitude" is always my mantra regarding their assistance. Also, remember that you are uncovering your personal animal totem through the chakra system. Balance is the most fundamental part of this process. I would stress being mindful about balance; try to get confirmations through both meditation and sightings in the physical world. When you embark on this journey, the best advice I can give from my personal, spiritual, and professional perspective is to please try to make as many connections as you possibly can with your animal totem in the timeline allotted for each one, and be grateful for every connection, no matter how it presents itself. The more connections you make with your totem animals, the more powerful your Divine connection will be with the spirit realm and your animal totems. You are essentially retraining your spirit self to be open to the subtle awareness that, for the most part, has been forgotten through your habit-forming conditioning. As a child, you were totally attuned to the universal forces. As you evolved, these aspects were slowly made dormant by our human conditioning.

It Is What It Is

"It is what it is" is a cliché popular within circles of coaches and business executives and is better described as a statement of acceptance of a situation that is less than perfect. NASCAR driver Jimmie Johnson, after finishing second in the Nextel Cup championship, said, "We showed up and gave one hundred percent, and it is what it is."

One of the scenarios that sometimes comes up with my students is what I call the "red herring," which is basically a misleading clue or something used to divert attention from the real issue or situation. How this unfolds is that your animal totem is popping up and appearing in all kinds of locations all around you. However, you might have seen a roaring bear or a stealthy panther at one point and liked the idea of that animal as your totem. We sometimes become so fixated on the animal we desire that we cannot see the real totem. I hear students say things like "I saw my animal once, and I haven't seen it again. I have been meditating and looking for it everywhere, but it just won't show itself again." It can be very frustrating. But remember, your totems will be as persistent as you are. However, if we are unconscious to their overtures, they are, in effect, canceled out, even if their appearances are in bloom everywhere around us. To prevent this, allow yourself to be open-minded about the animal that is trying to contact you, even if you prefer another one. There is a reason you are drawn to the animal you want, and your animal totem will help you understand that connection.

This is where it is important to point out that all creatures are under the totem umbrella. That includes water creatures; insects and reptiles, also known as the creepy-crawlies; and birds; as well as all land mammals. All creatures manifest great powers, no matter how insignificant you might think they are in your world. Even if you fear an animal or do not like it, there is a reason for that. In fact, some of the creatures we might consider the simplest and most unworthy have intricate, complex, and amazing capacities and abilities to help you and give you exactly what you need in the form of energy. Did you know that the drag-line silk spiders produce to make the spokes of their webs is one of the strongest substances known to man? It is tougher then Kevlar, stretches better than nylon, and, ounce per ounce, is five times stronger than steel. It is believed that a cord of silk just a few centimeters across could lift a jumbo jet off the ground. While spiders might look fragile and delicate I'd say pretty powerful medicine from a creepy-crawly that usually ends up smashed like a pancake on the bottom of your shoe if you come across it in your home. The point I am trying to make here is that no matter what animal appears for you, it will never be more nor less powerful than any other animal, especially from a spirit-messenger perspective. All you will need to do is notice that animal and be open to letting it appear no matter what that creature may be. It will always be the best animal for your journey. The only thing to remember when it does pop up: It is what it is.

Sign, Sign, Everywhere a Sign

When I was growing up, one of my favorite songs was from a rock group called Five Man Electrical Band. The song was called "Signs." If you haven't heard it, it's about a destitute man who is somewhat annoyed about all the signs around town prohibiting him from being part of an inner community based on his own conditioning. For some reason that song resonated with me and elicited my watchful awareness of all the signs pinned up around my town. As a kid, I delivered newspapers and hiked through many streets and dead-end passageways. Growing up in Cambridge, Massachusetts, nothing on a sign was considered bizarre. There were so many idiosyncratic signs that just intrigued me. To this day signs seem to jump out at me; whether they are displayed as a paper storefront, nailed to a tree, or painted on a flag, I can point them out in the most obscure places. Even on an airplane at thirty thousand feet, I looked out the window, and above the clouds, there on the wing, was a sign that said DO NOT WALK OUTSIDE THIS AREA. I laughed to myself as I pondered the person who needed to know that information and wondered if he or she would even notice that sign as I did thirty thousand feet up. Sign, sign, everywhere a sign. On your journey to uncover your personal animal totems, you will be encountering signs everywhere, both inside— as part of meditations and dreams—and out, as in your home or anywhere in your external world. Your animals will start popping up on the television; you will see them in commercials or nestled in the programs you watch. You will start saying things like "Did you see the deer on the wall when she [the TV character] went into the bedroom?" In the kitchen you'll see your animals on cereal boxes, and they will pop out to you on containers when you open the refrigerator. You will start to ask affirming questions to make sure you are seeing them, like "Is that a frog on that box of Sugar Smacks?" As you venture out into the world and deeper into Totemville, everything becomes fair

Uncovering Your Personal Animal Totem

game for your totem visits. Vehicles large and small will sport your animals on emblems, bumper stickers, dashboards, and more. You'll see them in magazines, art, clothing, graffiti, storefronts—the list is endless. At some point, your meetings with your animal totems will become so abundantly evident that there will be no denying them. Even people who have rolled their eyes at your encounters will start pointing them out to you. As you begin to align and allow yourself to be open to these wonderful connections, like me you will assume a watchful awareness and perhaps start to utter, "Sign, sign, everywhere a sign." And that will, in itself, make you happy and grateful and ready for the next encounters.

CHAPTER 3

A PICTURE IS WORTH A THOUSAND WORDS

What's Up with This Chapter

∞ Grasping Archet.ypes
∞ Finding Your Waldo
∞ Looks Can Be Deceiving
∞ On Your Mark, Get Set, Go

Where, exactly, the phrase "A picture is worth a thousand words" originated is unclear. Some attribute it to Napoleon, who said, "Un bon croquis vaut mieux qu'un long discours," meaning "A good sketch is better than a long speech." Others believe it's a Chinese proverb. Whatever its origin and meaning, direct or hidden, this phrase will somehow be delineated when your totem animals start showing up out of the blue. All of a sudden, the pictures you see will have whole new meanings for you.

Grasping Archetypes

Archetypes are said to be pictures hidden in our subconscious. The subconscious exists in our mind but is not immediately available to our consciousness. It is here that we store all our memories, experiences, and beliefs. We can very efficiently recall frequently used thought patterns and behavioral patterns without even being conscious of them. The truth is that they can rear their ugly heads without our even knowing about it. An example of this would be when your spouse says you are being a complete jerk to someone, while you think you are being playful and witty and don't see that the person is annoyed with you. I can't even begin to scratch the surface with the topic of the subconscious and archetypes, as there are literally thousands of books on the subject from all sorts of viewpoints, just like there are thousands of books on tarot and astrology. Each has its own angle, aspects, and ways to interpret their subjects. I will, however, try to keep this as simple as possible, and if you find the subject of archetypes tickling your fancy, allow yourself to explore it more deeply. As you begin to build a meaningful relationship with your animal totems, certain archetypes will suddenly take shape for you, allowing you to shine a big, fat light on your archetypal patterns and possibly prompting you to dig deeper in your exploration of you.

Archetypes fall into two categories, personal and collective. Archetypes send Morse-code messages to your conscious and subconscious mind, which elicit varying responses or reactions. Let's try exploring the archetype of mother-in-law. Now, that might bring a certain type of response from you, perhaps images, thoughts, and feelings that can be negative or positive depending on your personal association with your mother-in-law, or your parents-in-law, for that matter. But there is also a collective association, or universal view, which is a collection of memories of all human experience from the beginning of time. Collective consciousness would be the mass-media view of mother-in-law. Collective consciousness works kind of like Facebook, where messages are exchanged that can inspire, influence, manipulate, and even piss off, and effectively stimulate a sea of reactions or responses from a collection of people if we choose to tap into it. All you really need to know is that you essentially have two sets of consciousness reverberating through you based on the archetype of a mother-in-law. That can either be good news or bad news for you and your mother in law—that is, if you have one.

As you uncover your totem animals, there will be times when your animal will be obviously close to you but you don't see it for whatever reason, whether subconscious or conscious. That's when the proverbial totem phase "If it was a snake, it would bite you" becomes appropriate. Make a note when these events happen, as they will be called out to you. Once you start engaging with your animals, all your friends and family members will chime in with comments like "Isn't that your wildebeest?" As you uncover your totem animals and dig deeper into understanding your relationship with an individual animal, grasping archetypes will also help you understand why that particular animal totem came to you. In the beginning stages of the process, you only need remember that your animal "is what it is" for all the right reasons, regardless of whether it represents a personal or collective archetype.

Finding Your Waldo

As your animals start to present themselves to you, they will show up in various ways that might defy logic. For instance, you might meet some lady named Marylou Ann with an energetic new puppy bouncing on the end of a leash that is just dying to give you a great big lick. You might think, "Hey, this puppy presented itself to me, it must be my totem." Meanwhile, Marylou Ann is sporting a sweatsuit riddled with the Puma logo—your first encounter with your cougar or mountain lion totem animal.

Distinguishing your totem animal in the sea of unconscious daily living will be like trying to find Waldo. If you are not familiar with Waldo, he is a cartoon character with a distinctive red-and-white-striped pom-pom hat and big round glasses that make him easy to find in a crowd. However, he is put in a variety of amusing environments that involve deceptive use of red-and-white-striped distractions that make it difficult to find him. Your totem animal will come to be your Waldo while you are performing your unconscious routines. Nonetheless, this is a Divine tactic to get you conditioned into being watchful. At the same time, it allows you to be in the moment, which is where spirit guidance will always be found.

Looks Can Be Deceiving

Before you can start unearthing your Waldo, you must first find out what exactly your Waldo can be. This will be quite exciting when your animal starts to pop up all around you. To find the first piece of your fabulous totem puzzle, it is important that you be open to curiosity, magic, and inquisitiveness. Your animals will not present themselves in Waldo's red-and-white-striped hat and big round glasses. In fact, you won't have any idea what outfit your animal will be sporting. Here is where I will give you a few clues to successfully navigate through the Looks Can Be Deceiving passageway.

Let's say you are driving your car and one of nature's critters is standing on the road, just taking its sweet time getting out of the way, almost as if it is daring you to swerve around it or plow over it. It's as if a little mental jousting match between you and nature is unfolding, to the point where you need to make a quick decision: swerve or put on the brakes so you don't slam into the little critter. This animal can be a pigeon, chipmunk, deer, or any one of nature's many creatures. Let's say it's a squirrel. The point here is to take note. This may be the first encounter with your animal totem. Remember that when you first start to awaken to your spirit animals, their contact with you will seem out of the ordinary. Once that happens, the so-called coincidences with your totem animal will unfold and soon begin to multiply, so much so that you will not be able to sum it up as accidental or chance. It will seem almost like you have entered into the bizzaro world. When I teach my animal totem classes, even the most bashful and introverted types are so excited about these bizarre encounters that they want to be the first to share their very often hilarious stories.

Uncovering Your Personal Animal Totem

Let's take this a step further. With the squirrel on the road, you might drive a little farther and find that you're caught in a traffic jam. Still wondering about your squirrel encounter, you see that the pickup truck in front of you has a tailgate held together with bumper stickers. You see one that says GUNS DON'T KILL PEOPLE. DRIVERS WITH CELL PHONES DO. Still another says AS LONG AS I HAVE A RIFLE, I HAVE A VOTE. As you look around the tailgate, sort of summing this driver up with perhaps some judgment, you see I'D RATHER BE HUNTING. And right under that, your eyes are drawn to the little squirrel-crossing-the-road bumper sticker that says SQUIRRELS, NATURE'S SPEED BUMPS. Now, is that a coincidence, another squirrel reference? No, it is not! It is an affirmation from your animal totem, and another dot to connect that you're on the right track. This is essentially your ticket to pay attention and be aware that more sightings will occur, and in some of the most spectacular and undeniable episodes. It's the universe's way of saying, "Stay in the moment, we are here to guide." Notice!

It's important to know that your animal totems can come to you as live and physical animals, as well as images or symbols. Whether they are on a bumper sticker, road sign, license plate, advertisements on tractor-trailer trucks, or even logos on vehicles, you name it, it can be an affirmation from your totem. And it doesn't just happen in your car. They can appear at work or home—things that you have passed hundreds of times or more can suddenly hold your totem. They can appear in your office or cubicle, even pop-ups on your computer screen. Your totem animals can be hidden anywhere and will pop out to you at any time. Even your coworkers will potentially have your totems in their space. Check it out—remember, you are on an expedition and everything now is up for exploration. Anything, anyone, or any moment can offer a totem visit. Each visit will help you change how you look at your landscapes and the people within them. Even that type-A, pencil-thin, sycophant coworker will seem different to you when you notice she is wearing your totem as a butterfly beret, making you smile because it's bigger than her waistline and it's your totem. You might see that your grumpy auto mechanic has a tattoo of the lion that was also on the cover of a magazine at the doctor's office that morning. You strike up a conversation with him and find he's really not grumpy at all, and he charges you less than he initially quoted you. All of a sudden, the world becomes delightfully different. Everything seems to be connected in a weird sort of way.

Each totem sighting will demonstrate to you how interconnected you are with both the spirit realm and everyone else on this planet. Moreover, it will demonstrate how nature, animals, and those things around you that once seemed glossed over have gone from faintly subtle to delightfully alive. You'll find yourself smiling more and nodding with approval as you notice each instance of totem magic. Each totem affirmation will bring you joy. Even a state trooper pulling you over can hold a totem message, for in your aggravation you might notice your eagle affirmation on his badge.

Now, you may be thinking that some of these things seem really far-fetched. At first it will seem a little odd, but as your animals pop up you will engage with more confidence. The spirit world, universe, Divine forces, or whatever you call the energetic realm has a language of its own and does not at all follow our conventional patterns of communication. Being open to everything at all times is so important to your success in uncovering your personal animal totem. Even things overheard at the checkout counter at the supermarket can herald a totem visit. For instance, "I have a coupon for those chicken nuggets" may be a clever way your animal will make its appearance. Later that day you might see a commercial for Chicken McNuggets. Hopefully, these examples demonstrate just how elusive the initial stages of uncovering your totem can be. If you find yourself becoming frustrated by a lack of totem contacts, remember that looks can be deceiving.

On Your Mark, Get Set, Go

One of my students' most frequently encountered scenarios is their forgetting that this is a *journey* to uncover your personal animal totems, not a race. Now that you have an idea of the myriad ways your animal totems can present themselves, it's important I remind you that you are ready to begin the wonderful journey that goes within, not the pedal-to-the-metal road race of the external world. As I mentioned earlier in the Timeline section, your entire personal animal totem will consist of eight animals; each totem animal you uncover will be associated with one of your energy centers, called chakras. Each month you will sequentially move up the chakra system, unveiling the animal associated with the next chakra. I encourage you to spend the whole month working with each chakra and the animal or animals that unveil themselves, even if you are certain of your totem within the first few days of the journey. Your totem will have lots of messages and teachings for you throughout the month, and one of the teachings just might be to dispel assumptions of what animal it truly might be by presenting other animals.

This is part of the process of your soul's awakening. Every encounter you have with nature will have profound meaning if you are open to it. I implore you to please do not rush it and really journey through, at the very least, the twenty-eight-day moon cycle. Think of each new month like visiting a new country. Not taking full advantage of what the month has to offer would be like heading off to Italy, eating a bowl of pasta, taking a snapshot of a vineyard, and returning home. While you would have gone to Italy, you would have experienced it from a very shallow and narrow viewpoint. The uncovering of each animal totem will bring with it excitement, joy, and the tendency to hurry the process to find the next animal in your totem. This will sometimes be very tempting, so please be patient. Allow yourself to experience each month's entire journey rather than focusing on the ultimate destination of discovering your total personal totem. The more you engage with your totems, the more they will come. By journey's end you will be happy that you took the time to enjoy the insights that unfolded for you. Try to remember that it is not the destination but the journey that will bring you the most joy and satisfaction. Follow the guidance of Mr. Turtle—slow and steady wins the race.

CHAPTER 4

TAKING YOUR WHEELS FOR A SPIN

What's Up with This Chapter

∞ Test-Driving Your Wheels
∞ Going Round and Round
∞ Embracing the Road
∞ Care and Maintenance of Your Wheels

If you are a chakra aficionado, chances are you have already taken your chakras for a spin and can readily tune into which are out of balance and make a conscious effort daily to get them back into alignment. For the majority of folks living what I would call an average, everyday life, however, that idea will seem foreign, mostly because a big portion of our society is very much acclimated to the drama, chaos, and turmoil of everyday living. These are the folks with no idea that you can take your chakras for a spin and help reduce the stress of it all. But once you understand the fundamentals of each chakra, your journey will become much less riddled with drama, chaos, and some of the negativities associated with everyday life. In other words, working with your chakras will help you change what appear to be everyday curses into everyday blessings. It only depends on how devoted you are to the process. Putting conscious effort into setting up your sacred space will be evidence enough that you mean business when it comes to exploring your inner world. However, a sustained discipline to show up and try every day will be the key to your success.

As I stated earlier in the Getting Started section, chakras are the conduit through which Divine energy passes through you. Say it aloud: "Chakras are the conduit through which Divine energy passes through me." Like all polar opposites in life—up/down, feminine/masculine, light/dark, yin/yang, Red Sox/Yankees—chakras function at extremes—open or closed, balanced or unbalanced, overactive or underactive. These terms are utilized plentifully in new age and metaphysical centers. Just try tossing them around any old way when you're in one of these stores and the sales clerk will have a number of suggestions to get things back into alignment for you. For example, if you said, "I was going to buy this book on *chakras* yesterday but my checking account was *unbalanced* and the bank was *closed,* but once it was *open,* I was able to *balance* my account, and I can now buy the book," you would probably get a response like, "Wonderful, we are having twenty percent off on all colonic cleansing merchandise, and for every one hundred dollars you spend on crystals, you'll get a house clearing to help create wealth and abundance in your life. If you're interested, we do have monthly fire-burning rituals; you only need bring your intentions." The truth is, your newfound jargon is going to lead you deeper into the bizarro world, so just hold onto your knickers and know that this is the universe's expression of teaching you adaptation, getting you to become more open-minded about going with the flow. But let's really be honest here. You are on a journey to uncover your personal animal totems, and that in itself will get some raised eyebrows.

Learning how to take your chakras for a spin will open you up to a whole new world of what might appear to be uncanny guidance. As you journey through each month's chakra, you will become aware of the amazing energetic forces of the chakras and the role you play in whether your life is in or out of balance. The totem animals that come to you will possess the very medicine you need, which will come in the form of support, assistance, and guidance. The only thing you really need to do is notice your totem animals, as they will be sure to wheel you in the right direction.

Test-Driving Your Wheels

In the journey to uncover your animal totems each month, you will have an opportunity to travel to a mysterious, Divine rendezvous to encounter your animal. Now, keep in mind your journey will be part of your routine, everyday travels, but the landscape of your journey will swiftly turn into a mystifying voyage. As you travel through each chakra center, you will not only uncover your animal totems but amazing nuances about yourself to help you understand those imprints and patterns that are not necessarily yours. Much like test-driving a new car, you want to get the feel of the wheel. Automobile salespeople have a saying: "The feel of the wheel seals the deal." This means if they can get you to test-drive the car and feel the steering wheel, they have a much better chance at a sale. The cool thing about test-driving your chakras is you don't have to worry about making sure you choose one that fits your budget and serves your needs for the coming years. The sky is the limit when it comes to options when test-driving your chakras. You will be in total charge of what you want and don't want, and you will have ample opportunities to make choices about what you like and dislike about your wheels. The only thing you will need to do is feel the wheel and seal your deal.

Going Round and Round

As I mentioned earlier, *chakra* is the Sanskrit word for wheel, and like wheels, they go around and around. Chakras can spin either clockwise or counterclockwise. As with the wheels on a vehicle, it is so much easier to get to where you want to go if your wheels are spinning in a forward direction. Sure, reverse comes in handy when you need to back out of the mudhole you got yourself into trying to save time with shortcuts, but forward is optimal. To get an idea of the forward direction of a chakra, imagine your face is a wall. Now mount a clock to your nose. I said imagine, don't actually do it. People looking at that clock mounted on your face would see the second hand moving from the number twelve and traveling toward the right. This is considered clockwise and what some holistic healers can see when they observe the direction your chakras are spinning. You, looking out from the clock, would see it differently. If this is confusing, just put the hand of the arm you wear your wristwatch on over your chest; the way the second hand is moving is the direction chakras in optimal condition should be spinning. As you open, clear, and balance your chakras, you too will be able to feel the direction of their spin. However, this can take lots of practice and devotion. The only thing you really need to know here is that, like the wheels on the car, you don't need to check which direction your wheels are spinning unless, of course, you're stuck in a snowbank in Boston. Trust me, it's hard to determine which way your wheels are spinning when that happens.

Embracing the Road

Let's repeat our mantra: "Chakras are the conduit through which Divine energy passes through me." Now, if you truly want this Divine energy to pass through you, it's important that you make a conscious effort to be open to that energy passing through you. In other words, embrace the road. Chances are, if your chakras are all closed down, you probably won't be able to get your vehicle out of the garage to embrace the road. Not to worry, even grandpa's rusty old Studebaker taking up space in the garage can be resurrected and made roadworthy with intention, prayer, forgiveness, gratitude, and a good master auto mechanic. The same is true with your chakras, although you might want to forgo the auto mechanic and see a doctor if you're wasting away in a garage like grandpa's old Studebaker. It's important to know that there isn't a chakra that can't be opened. The key is to pay attention to yourself, not others. According to ancient Chinese philosopher Lao Tzu, "Knowing others is wisdom, knowing yourself is enlightenment." Moving toward having all your chakras open is to begin the journey to enlightenment and more or less ignoring what's up with others. Your animal totems will be your new others. Think of your animal totems as your escorts on your chakra journey, regardless of whether your chakras are open, closed, or blinking open and closed like an eyeball with a lash in it. Once you determine just how roadworthy your vehicle is, you will quickly learn which chakras are out of balance and the direction you need to take to move them into alignment. Your totem animals will be there with the help you need to tune up and realign with the road considered the best traveled. Being willing to begin, engage, and discover new things about your inner world is the key to embracing this new road ahead.

Care and Maintenance of Your Wheels

Pretty much everything in life needs some kind of maintenance. Whether it's the plug on a vacuum that's been yanked out of the outlet by the cord too many times, squeaky door hinges, or your drama-queen girlfriend reacting to a bad mascara joke after two cosmopolitans on an empty stomach, everything will—sooner or later; person, place, or thing—need some kind of maintenance. Needless to say, your chakras need maintenance too. However, the good thing about maintaining your chakras is that the conscious act of balancing them will promptly move you into a more subtle and peaceful state of being, even if there is a monsoon of drama going on around you. The journeys you take into your interior world will help you detach and realign with sacred guidance, and that will most often result in Divine humor once you get the knack of how it works. As you learn to pull yourself away from dissonant situations and move toward nurturing and self-care, you will undeniably cultivate open and balanced chakras. The best part about having your totem animals around is that they will tip you off way before the low-fuel sensor chimes on your gas tank—which is great if you don't own a gas can. Preventative maintenance rather than corrective maintenance will certainly save a lot of wear and tear on your vehicle, both figuratively and literally.

CHAPTER 5

SOMEWHERE OVER THE RAINBOW

What's Up with this Chapter

∞ Brown—Foot Chakra
∞ Red—Root Chakra
∞ Orange—Sacral Chakra
∞ Yellow—Solar Plexus Chakra
∞ Green—Heart Chakra
∞ Blue—Throat Chakra
∞ Indigo—Third Eye Chakra
∞ Purple—Crown Chakra

In this section I will give you a brief overview of the location of and color associated with each chakra. When you begin the journey to uncover your animal totem for each chakra, or energy center, I will go into greater detail about that chakra's specific functions. As you spend time each month on an individual chakra, you will become attuned to how the colors play an important role in the frequency and vibration of each chakra. This information will also help you understand why a particular animal guide comes to assist you.

In the movie *The Wizard of Oz*, Dorothy has a run-in with the nasty spinster Miss Gulch, and Aunt Em so patiently (not really) tells Dorothy to "find yourself a place where you won't get into any trouble." This prompts Dorothy to ponder such a place. She muses to her dog, Toto, "Someplace where there isn't any trouble. Do you suppose there is such a place, Toto? There must be. It's not a place you can get to by a boat or a train. It's far, far away. Behind the moon, beyond the rain..." Then she starts crooning "Over the Rainbow." Like Dorothy, you're about to travel somewhere over the rainbow and experience some of the most extraordinary and enchanting happenings in your ordinary, everyday life. As you travel through each color of the rainbow, your totem animals will introduce themselves. While all that is happening, you will develop a new understanding about your true nature, which is essentially the real you. For real! So tap your heels together and repeat three times "There's no place like home." And don't forget your mantra either! Say it: "Chakras are the conduit through which Divine energy passes through me." Enjoy the ride!

Brown—Foot Chakra

For the most part, people are not familiar with the foot chakra. In fact, when I teach my totem classes, I sometimes get raised eyebrows from the so-called more experienced students when I mention that the first chakra we will be working with is the foot chakra. What the hey, even I at some point needed to come to terms with the No Santa Claus theory. But just so you know, there really are foot chakras. However, they are not considered major chakras like the rest of the brightly colored wheels, they're called minor chakras. Foot chakras are more like the smaller ATV (all-terrain vehicle) wheels and resonate to a dirty, muddy, wet-earth color of brown that you usually see on active ATV tires. I want to reiterate, the foot chakras resonate to the color brown. What'd you expect, pretty hot pink? Come on, get a clue. Besides, I'm saving the pink debate for the heart chakra.

Unlike the major chakras, which are singular by their very nature, the foot chakras come in a pair, just like shoes. Yes, there are two, one for each foot. They are located on the "souls" of your feet, a play on words I use to keep things in the new age, metaphysical vernacular. If your foot chakra could talk, it would say, "Every step you take, I'll be watching you," to paraphrase the popular English musician, singer-songwriter, activist, actor, and philanthropist we know as Sting. Unfortunately, foot chakras can't talk, which is sad because I think they would have a lot to say. They do however, talk to your body. For now, the only thing you need to know is that the foot chakras are located on the bottom of your feet and talk to your body with every step you take—but only if you want to listen to your body. Which, by the way, will be what your totem animals are going to help you do, and it won't be just to bring your attention to your feet, but also to listen to your body.

Red—Root Chakra

The root chakra is known as the foundation of the chakra system and is sometimes referred to as the base chakra. I will use *root* and *base* interchangeably, just to keep you on your toes and perhaps to annoy you. The location of this chakra is in the area of the genitals and the base of the spine, also known as the coccyx or tailbone. Suburban home landscapes often offer a good example of the location of the root chakra with lawn ornaments of a fat lady bending over, assuming the gardening position. Yes, that would exactly pinpoint the location of the base chakra and emphasize how when you stand up, it disappears. Now, the color associated with the root chakra is red. I like to use the story of the Three Little Pigs to describe the root chakra, because it hits on your foundation, which can sometimes be a house of straw, sticks, or a bomb shelter of mortar and bricks. As you know, the Big Bad Wolf couldn't huff and puff and blow down the bomb-shelter home of mortar and bricks because its foundation of beautifully layered, red brick masonry was so strong. Boy, you've got to give that one little pig credit. I see you rolling those eyes, but I bet you'll remember the root chakra color and location based on my little-pig-and-brick yarn and fat-lady garden ornament.

Orange—Sacral Chakra

I like to use Britney Spears, Madonna, Beyonce, and Janet Jackson as examples for the sacral chakra. You might think this is because they are creative, talented, and famous recording artists or because of the emotional aspects of being captured unflatteringly in supermarket tabloids. Nope, nope, and nope. While all that might be true, that's not where I was going. What they all have in common is a belly-piercing in the approximate location of the sacral chakra. Actually, it's slightly below the belly button, but I won't go there, especially with those gals. You get the picture of the location.

Like the root or base chakra, which has two names, the sacral chakra can also be called the spleen chakra. I won't annoy you by using their names interchangeably. I think it's annoying enough that the sacral chakra is nowhere even close to or readily associated with the spleen. We can thank C.W. Leadbeater for that reference. His theory was that the function of the spleen chakra resembled that of the spleen from Chinese medicine, and that the chakra belonged to the spleen meridian. Imagine taking a road map of the United States and wrapping it around your body. The spleen meridian would start off in Key West, Florida, and travel all the way up to Albany, New York, then back down to Kentucky. Can you see how annoying that would be, especially if you were a guy and pulled into a gas station to ask for directions to the spleen chakra and told the attendant it runs off the highway of the spleen meridian? Please note that this is just an example, and both the scenarios of the guy asking for directions and using the meridians in Chinese medicine to navigate are highly unlikely. Anyway, just know that the second major chakra can and sometimes will be referred to as the spleen chakra, although you didn't it hear from me.

The color associated with the sacral chakra is orange. Some say it's a fiery red-orange, some say it's the color of the big, juicy oranges from the Sunshine State. Whatever or however the color orange comes up for you will be fine. There are no hard and fast rules to the color orange, as there are literally hundreds of shades and tones. Just check out the orange paint swatches on display at the store with the big orange logo, Home Depot, and you'll really drive yourself crazy. Now, orange you glad I didn't go through the whole list of oranges?

Yellow—Solar Plexus Chakra

As we move up the chakra system, the next chakra we come to is the solar plexus. I like to use SpongeBob SquarePants as an example for the solar plexus location and color association. Metaphorically, SpongeBob hits the nail right on the head in many ways when it comes to understanding this chakra. For starters, he is yellow, and he pretty much resembles the square sponge we use at the kitchen sink, even though he is a sea sponge. This is a good example of imprinting, and I will get to that later when we learn the nitty-gritty of chakra functioning. Now, if you were to look in the direction of where Bob's square pants meet his inordinately large yellow head, that would be just about where the solar plexus chakra resides. Did you know that in the show, SpongeBob lives in a sea squirt, which is another name for the edible sea pineapple, which is depicted as a regular pineapple—illusions, we'll get to that too. Anyway, it's the kind of pineapple you would see the legendary Hawaiian crooner Don Ho surrounded with while he sang "Tiny Bubbles" and played his little ukulele. I'm just telling you this because pineapples are yellow inside, much like the color associated with the solar plexus chakra, and the position that Don Ho would strum his ukulele in is another example of the exact place where you'd find your solar plexus. See how nicely it all ties together?

Green—Heart Chakra

As we move up the chakra system, we finally get to the heart of the matter, the bridge between the lower chakras and the upper chakras. Now, everyone pretty much knows where the heart is located, so I won't bore you with those details, although I once had a client who was convinced that her husband's heart was in another place. Now, that information would not bore you. In fact, as someone who likes to ponder things, I was quite astounded to find that someone's heart could be in that place. All I will say about that situation is that resentment, bitterness, and lack of empathy are all shadow sides of the heart chakra that indicate a need for healing. We will learn about that fun stuff later. It's important to know that none of us is exempt from the need for some kind of healing. That's what I will call our birthright and is basically what we have all come here to learn.

There are two colors associated with the heart chakra. One is the traditional green, and the other—well, I'm not really sure what the logical or illogical reasons are for the second color, pink. Yes, pink. Green makes logical sense, as it transitions very nicely with the rainbow color scheme of red, orange, yellow, green. But pink? Hmmm. So far, everything I've come up with in my studies has me scratching my head. If I had to give my analysis of why the color pink is the middle of the chakra system, I'd say it's because the root chakra is red and the light of the portal to the heavens is white, and when you mix red and white you get pink, right in the middle where your heart is located. You will learn about the science of color a bit later, and that might help clarify this a little better. But, ultimately, the way I see it is you like *potato* and I like *potahto*, you like *tomato* and I like *tomahto*. Pink or green, the bottom line is, whatever color speaks to your heart will work best for you. Be a rebel!

Blue—Throat Chakra

If you're going to be a rebel, you will need to be true and blue to your throat chakra. Your throat chakra is all about your voice and how you speak. In my experience rebels are quite vocal and provide solid evidence of the existence of an energy center in the throat, especially when I think back on some of the rebels I've known. This chakra is all about speaking your truth, giving voice to what you believe in. The throat chakra, like the heart chakra, sports a name that describes the exact location of the chakra itself. Personally, I think chakras would be easier to grasp if they all followed that same convention. The throat chakra is represented by the color blue. I like to say sky blue, as if it were a beautiful, bright, clear day without any clouds in the sky. Some folks will say royal blue and might even try to correct you in kind of a Queen's English fashion, like, "I beg your pardon, but I dooooo believe you have erroneously specified the coloration of the throat's energy center." I say the sky is the limit when it comes to the color blue, and talk is cheap. When you uncover the animal totem for this center, you will learn a lot about your talk, and you won't be as concerned about the color blue as you will about being true blue to your voice.

Indigo—Third Eye Chakra

After you have put a lot of effort into your throat chakra and talked until you're blue in the face, it's only natural that you'd want to see that. The third eye, brow, Cave of Brahma, and ajna are all names for the sixth chakra, where you will uncover your new vision. I like to call the sixth chakra the third eye because it seems logical that you would need a third eye to see what new age, metaphysical people call inner vision. It also seems natural to me that a third eye, from both an exterior design and feng shui perspective of the human face, would probably fit quite nicely in the middle of the forehead, right between the two regular eyes—which, by the way, is where it is located. But then we get into the color debate again. Indigo. What exactly is indigo, and how do you describe it? Okay, here we go, but I just want to warn you that this might be one of those answers where, by the time you finish reading, you may not know any more than you do now about the exact color of indigo. When it comes to the reality of the third eye, it's all about illusions, so keep that in mind as we go along here.

Inidgo dying can be traced back thousands of years. India is believed to be the oldest hub of indigo dyeing, and in some regions of the country the same process is still used today. Isn't it fascinating that in some places some things never change? The color indigo is derived from the plant—big-word warning—*Indigofera tinctoria*, which, for people like me who have trouble pronouncing big words and like to keep it on the pea-brain level, means pea. For the crunchy granola types who like to keep everything on a natural and organic level, it means legume plant. Now, get this, it can blossom into cute little purple and pink flowers. Yes, the color pink again. If you ever have time, take a look on YouTube at the indigo fermentation and dyeing process. You will have a new respect for the price of your indigo blue jeans, and it will also validate that I'm not pulling your leg about some of this stuff I come up with here.

Anyway, back to indigo, so everything was going fine and dandy in the life of indigo, and it became very popular throughout history and traveled through many centuries and countries. It was in the 1660s when a man by the name of Isaac Newton—yes, the guy with the goofy hairdo who was sitting under a tree when an apple fell and beaned him on the head and, *bang!*, he made history. Well, before that, he introduced indigo to the color spectrum with his fancy-pants prism experiment, which was historic, as well. So everyone was pretty happy with the rainbow having seven colors, and indigo fell right between blue and violet quite nicely. India continued to make indigo dye cakes and the leprechauns continued spending all their time busily making shoes so they could add coins to the pot of gold at the end of the rainbow, which Dorothy would eventually croon about somewhere in Kansas.

Here is where you might want to make a gin and tonic or start tapping your foot to move things along. So all was well, as they say in Rainbowland, until these killjoy scientists rained dooky on the indigo color theory. As someone who spent close to thirty years working in the biotech field, I can tell you with great confidence that the killjoy scientist is a widespread archetype in corporate America. Anyway, this group of scientists created another type of science called colorimetry, the science of color, and these dudes came in with their fancy-pants big honka devices with names like spectrophotometer, spectrocolorimeter, and spectroradiometer that measure things like spectral power distribution, tristimulus values, and chromaticity coordinates—all in an effort to poo-poo poor Isaac's hard work. After all was said and done, the long and short of the color indigo is that it's a distinction between four major tones of indigo, meaning good old Isaac was basically right. The only reason I'm telling you all this is because it is one of the those FAQs (frequently asked questions) I get when I utter the word *indigo*. What color is indigo? The answer falls into the category of "be careful what you ask for, you just might get it." For those who think you might carry the killjoy scientist archetype, I've added the four major indigo tones below. The rest of you can come out of that deep state of meditation and move on to the crown chakra. But before you do… *

Pick an indigo:

1. Electric indigo—Spectral indigo is closely approximated by the color electric indigo, which fits nicely between spectrum blue and spectrum violet.
2. Deep indigo—A color intermediate in brightness between electric indigo and pigment indigo.
3. Pigment indigo or web color indigo—Can be obtained by mixing 55 percent pigment cyan with about 45 percent pigment magenta.
4. Dye indigo—The color of indigo dye is different than either spectrum indigo or pigment indigo. This is the actual color of the dye from the indigo plant when swatched onto raw fabric. A vat full of this dye is a darker color, approximating the web color midnight blue.

*The third eye is all about removing yourself from the illusions of the physical world and moving into a quiet place within where infinite possibilities that do not at all come from the intellectual mind beckon. Pat yourself on the back if you did veg out and fall into a coma with all the yada yada yada of indigo.

Purple—Crown Chakra

When I was a kid, there was something about the nursery rhyme "Jack and Jill" that always puzzled me. The part where Jack fell down and broke his crown threw me for a loop. When I asked my mom what a crown was, she said, "His head! And don't bother me when I'm on the phone!" That added another layer of complexity to the rhyme. What does it mean when you break your head? I just needed to understand what a crown was, and everyone seemed to have their own take on it. I remember looking at the pictures in the nursery rhyme books of Jack and Jill going up the hill; Jack wasn't wearing a crown. Perhaps my mom was right. Whether it meant that he just bumped his head or did more serious damage is still open for interpretation in my mind. However, there is a theory that Jack represented Louis XVI of France, who was beheaded in 1793, therefore losing his crown, and that Jill represented his queen, Marie Antoinette, whose head came tumbling after. This theory was made even more perplexing by the fact that the earliest printing of the rhyme predated those events. Actually, it now makes perfect sense to me, considering the portal through the crown chakra is where there is no space and time, and the past, present, and future are all up for grabs.

As you might imagine, the crown is located on the very top of your head. Like a cherry on a hot fudge sundae or an angel on the top of the Christmas tree, it is the defining ingredient that gives way to the enlightenment of the whole. The color frequency associated with the crown chakra is violet, and, in some cases, the purists like to say white. If you remember my spiel about indigo, scientists also believed that white was the fundamental color of light before my buddy Isaac came along with his fancy-pants quartz crystal.

The long and short of all the colors represented in the chakra system is that they are the building blocks that allow you to connect to your energy centers in a multitude of ways. These colored beacons will help guide and direct you—behind the moon, beyond the rain, and somewhere over the rainbow.

CHAPTER 6

YOUR TRAVEL ITINERARY

What's Up with This Chapter

∞ Planning Tips
∞ What to Take Along
∞ Where to Travel
∞ Traveling Alone and with Others
∞ Capturing Your Travel

Congratulations! You are finally ready to start your expedition over the rainbow terrain. You have become familiar with all the colorful locations you will be visiting each month. In each of these expansive sites, these colorful locations, you will be introduced to an animal totem guide. This guide will become a powerful element in supporting your journey through life. So give yourself a little pinch and get psyched for the astounding and magical travel adventure to your interior world.

Planning Tips

The good news about this journey is that you won't be annoyed by the standard protocol you encounter when planning a vacation trip. You don't have to worry about all the hubbub of picking and timing airline flights, airport security, over- or underpacking, weather conditions, who and who not to bring along, securing child or pet sitters, and the big one, how much cash to bring along. Just that right there should bring a level of tranquility and serenity to the whole uncovering-your-animal-totem travel experience. However, there is one minor detail. Let's just pedal backward to a small section of the first sentence in this paragraph, the part that says "you won't be annoyed by the standard protocol." Basically, the standard protocol is you. If you're the type of person who gets annoyed easily or habitually gets up on the wrong side of the bed, this journey will have just that feel, with or without the hubbub of travel arrangements. There is an old saying of my mother's, "Don't be so fixed in your ways." This nine-month cruise is the perfect opportunity to change your fixed ways. Being open to all the great opportunities that will present themselves will help you to both recognize and change those fixed ways or habits.

What to Take Along

As I mentioned in chapter 1 in the Getting Started section, you will want to both travel light and breezy and with open curiosity, as if you are seeing everything for the first time with new eyes. Exposing yourself to these elements allows you to be aware of the indicators your guides will use to get your attention, and it is essential to linking your connections with your totem animals. Your sacred space should be considered your dashboard, as well as your lodging. Utilizing other types of sacred applications can also enhance the effectiveness of making Divine contact. There are a number of holistic modalities—such as reiki, aromatherapy, incense, crystals, and candles—that can evoke and heighten the forces of Divine intervention by your animal totems. I will give some examples of these as we go through each chakra. Also, chapter 7 will give you some ideas about how you can accessorize your journey. Remember that this is your journey, and no one but you can choose what to bring along. The point to remember is, the lighter you travel, the easier it is to make your connections. It's the same theory that holds true when you're trying to catch that connecting flight at the airport.

Where to Travel

Each month you will travel to and disembark at a new, colorful location within the chakra system. At each chakra portal you visit, you will want to get the best bang for your buck. This means that it is essential to get the most of what you can while visiting each chakra center. This will also help you build on and strengthen your intuitive senses. While I will give you some basic information about each port of call, as an avid traveler you will want to know as much as you possibly can about each chakra you are venturing into. I encourage you to read and learn as much about each energy center supplemental to information I provide in this book. The animal totem that presents itself to you at each chakra center will become your tour guide and knows the terrain that will best serve you in balancing, clearing, and healing each center. Trust that where and when your animal guide presents itself, it will have remarkable significance and will aid you in unfurling a path of tremendous transformation. Feel confident and trust that your totem animal will lead and guide you as together you make life a fantastic journey and develop an unquestionable Divine partnership.

Traveling Alone and with Others

As you venture into your interior world, the exterior world will take on a whole new meaning. You will also find that the people in your exterior world will suddenly take on new meaning for you and your personal growth. Any time we venture on a soul's journey in life we find that our true growth is intensified when it is experienced alone. Sure, we all grow in very small ways, and sometimes in very significant ways, when we are with family, friends, and others. But these interactions are familiar, everyday experiences that really don't allow for true explorations of our personality or discovery of who we really are on a soul level. When your animal guides start to pop up in the most extraordinary ways, you are going to want to share these exhilarating experiences with those near and dear to you. This will bring on its own set of joys and challenges. Many of my students, and I too, find that once your animals start introducing themselves and become a part of your personal walk, people that you have shared your encounters with will suddenly want to be part of your caravan and will start pointing them out for you. This can be like having someone yell out when you're opening a gift, "Surprise, it's an iPad!" It's important that you remind yourself that you are uncovering your personal animal totem and it will have to be experienced by you personally, not hijacked by others. If you find that you suddenly have travel companions on your journey and they are indeed stealing a lot your thunder, be aware that it is an opportunity for you to start setting personal boundaries. Allow your totem animal to help you with this, as this is the energy or medicine that your totems will be giving or teaching you to use. Allow yourself to be able to share your experiences, but also allow yourself the experience of the interaction with your animal without an announcer calling the shots. This will not only liberate you but allow you the freedom to discover parts of yourself that may otherwise be inhibited by others.

Capturing Your Travel

You've probably heard the urban catchphrase "Get a life," usually intended as a taunt, which, by the way, is what I am going to use here, a taunt with a little modification: "Get a journal." A journal will help you keep track of all the bizarre and extraordinary events during the expedition of uncovering your personal animal totem. I can't tell you how many of my students regret that they didn't write more about their amazing encounters in the midst of their journeys. I can always tell by their smiles that the delight of the journey remains, even though the details of the extravaganza are vague and a little foggy at best, which they regret. So please heed the advice to get a journal. Another benefit of your journal is that your dedication to writing about your experiences will help shift your frequency, so you'll be aligned with the good vibrations that allow energetic clearing, healing, and guidance to take place more readily. As you travel through each energy center, you will deliberately acknowledge and invite all types of energies to play an important vibratory role in your life. This means you will come in contact with both positive and negative vibrations. This can be analogous to having a lousy dining experience at a restaurant that everyone has absolutely raved about. You will want to be conscious of both the positive and negative aspects of your travel. You will also want to permit yourself to discriminate against traveling with anything that does not bring enjoyment or pleasure. Your journal will help you figure that out and will also be a conduit to spark notable guidance to good vibrations. What you will discover by writing down your experiences is that your guides will be there to help you release those things that do not serve you, as well as bring your awareness to the very things that will bring joy to your journey.

Many of my students will come to class with photographs they've taken on cell phones and cameras, pictures ripped out of magazines, and all kinds of thingamajigs they have encountered as objective evidence of the presence of their animal guides. The silly antics people will go through to capture the magical nuances of their newfound passion makes for lots of fun and laughter. You will always get out of the journey the effort you put into the voyage. Your journal will not only serve as a log of your wonderful adventures, but it will help you unlock your inner wisdom, connect with the magic of the journey, build creative insights, develop your imagination, and tap into higher levels of consciousness. Most of all, it will connect you with the Divine forces of the universe.

Here is my last pitch with the "Get a journal" mantra. Your journal can be as simple as a spiral notebook or a bunch of Post-it notes or as fancy as a beautifully embroidered, leather-bound diary. It can be decorative, whimsical, or just plain-Jane—there is no end to how elaborate or simple it needs to be. You are in charge of how you want to capture your journey. I had one student who would bring a large expanding pocket file for each month of the journey and toss just about anything into it. By the end of the course, a few other students who couldn't bring themselves to commit to a journal had adopted the same technique, were grateful for it, and later incorporated their journey into a scrapbook. How you do it really doesn't matter. Journaling is a great practice for overall stress reduction, as well as self-knowledge and emotional healing, which will dovetail nicely with your animal totem guidance. So get a journal.

CHAPTER 7

SETTING THE GROUND RULES

What's Up with This Chapter

∞ The Five Ground Rules
∞ How to Accessorize Your Journey
∞ Meeting the Inhabitants

When I teach my animal totem course, I always set five basic ground rules. Throughout the nine-month journey, I will start each class reiterating these five rules. If, at the very least, you can adopt these five rules in your journey, they will serve you immensely, no matter where or to what your path leads you.

The Five Ground Rules

1. **Show up and be on time.** While this might encourage students to not be cavalier about promptness and actually show up for class in general, I find that it also encourages courtesy to both the teacher and other students who do show up to class on time. However, this ground rule runs deeper than just the classroom. It's more about allowing yourself to show up and be on time for your own journey, meaning to be present in the experience and uncover all your totems have to offer. This, in turn, will allow you to show up when your totems call. Each call from your totem will be a message from the inhabitants of your spiritual playground and will offer guidance to you. As your totems show up, you should too. This means to be on time and ready for their messages. In order to do that, you must be present, not absently lost in thought. Your animal guides will bring you messages and opportunities to awaken new energies, heal and new insights into issues, balance, creativity, abundance, warnings, and protection. If you are present and ready to receive these messages and opportunites, the benefits will be infinite.

The second half of the rule is to be on time. Again, students will invariably think it means to respect the start time of the class and not be tardy. But it actually runs deeper than the classroom scenario too. When your animal totems start popping up all around you, will you be on time to embrace and accept their guidance? Or will you dismiss or ponder it after the fact and miss the opportunity of the moment altogether? Many times our guides pop up out of the blue; you will see them but not even give the observation a second thought. When they show up, this is your opportunity to connect and be present for the guidance. There will be many times when your totem guides will show up to affirm an approach or direction for you. If you quickly dismiss their help without pondering it, you may find out later that it was clear guidance that could have assisted you had you not been so quick to discount it. The good news is that you will always be given another opportunity to follow guidance. So don't beat yourself up for overlooking it. Just understand it's part of the teachings to help you become more present and aware. Remember that you can't paint a new color on the wall with just one brush stroke; it requires quite a few strokes of the brush to see the new color. With patience, devotion, and a dedicated effort to stay present, you will have spectacular results. Remember, you are grooming yourself to not get caught up in the cycle of "should have, could have," and to look "forward ever, backward never." So show up, and be on time!

2. Always be conscious of your breath. Before you can even begin to connect to your guidance, it's important that you first connect to yourself. Our thoughts are so often consumed with the events and business of other people, places, and things that we forget we are in a physical body here on our own journey and need to turn inward to assess how we are doing and where we are going. Your physical body will never lie to you. It is always giving you important information on how you are doing. When we are so involved in the external world, we essentially disregard the sensations of our internal world, which are the messages our body gives us. When we ignore or overlook these messages, we create blocks in our energy flow. Trust me, we all have blocks. These repeated offenses to our being become routine and, in a sense, numb and obscure our ability to comprehend what our body is trying to tell us and hinder the aspects of our energy flow. Being mindful of your breath as much as humanly possible will always bring you back to you, and will also bring you back to the present, away from the thought process you were consumed by. Training yourself to constantly be attuned to your breath will allow you to be in tune to what your body is trying to tell you. The wonderful thing about your body is that once you begin to pay attention to it, you can begin the process of clearing stagnant energy that has built up. As you become more efficient at this, you really do become more open to the guidance trying to connect with you, and your overall energy, health, and wellbeing increases.

Setting The Ground Rules

The benefits of breath work are astounding. Regardless of the fact that we need it to survive, breathing is something we so often take for granted and rarely think about. Though many people suffer from stress, anxiety, depression, and other physical disorders that can be effectively relieved and reduced by simple breath work, it is something we will generally reject or even fail to look at as an option, even though it can be performed anywhere, with anyone, at any time. Go figure.

I would like you to do a few cycles of breath work before moving on to the next ground rule. Let me explain the different breathing styles so you are aware of which will benefit you and which won't. We typically breathe in two ways. One is chest or thoracic breathing, the other is called abdominal or diaphragmatic breathing. I will give you an example of chest breathing and how you can identify it in yourself and in others. Hopefully, you will use this example to explore breathing patterns in those around you but also as a gauge to be aware of your own breathing patterns.

This is something I witnessed years ago and is what I call a "black-humor drama cocktail," but it really helps give a flavor of how the same breathing pattern works on multiple levels. Even though it happened years ago, I can still see it as if it were yesterday. I was invited to a Fourth of July barbecue party. As the afternoon progressed, the couple hosting the party seemed to be in a tiff about one of the husband's friends, who was a bad choice of party guest, according to the host's wife. This guy's intoxicated antics were somewhat entertaining but became more annoying to the host's wife and many of the guests as the hours went on. The final straw was when he tried to light his cigarette with one of those Fourth of July sparklers, which seemed to malfunction and caused quite a fireworks display on the curly, tangled pile of hair atop his head. I still remember thinking how he looked like an animated version of the Olympic torch as he ran to the nearest hose spigot, trashing everything in his path before ultimately submerging his head in the dog's water bowl. At the conclusion of this fiasco, three people were in the midst of thoracic breathing: the sparkler goofball, who now resembled a chemical experiment gone bad and the true essence of a bad hair day; the host's wife, in a fury of embarrassment and appalled by the whole chain of events that had just unfolded; and, of course, the husband, whose imminent response to the incident was to send his party pal to the nearest exit. The most astounding thing to me was that as I watched the sparkler dude being escorted out, he still managed to have that cigarette in his mouth.

Chest breathing is often linked to stress, anxiety, tension, headaches, and, in this example, drama, and is easily identified by shallow, irregular breathing that essentially stays upstairs in your chest and doesn't get downstairs to support the organs in the abdomen. In fact, the upper 10 percent of the lungs transports less than 6 mLs of oxygen per minute. In thoracic breathing, we are only utilizing the top 10 percent of our lungs. On the other hand, abdominal breathing allows you to take in air to the lower 10 percent, which can transport 40 mLs per minute. This type of breathing is performed when we inhale air deep into the lungs; our abdomen expands outward, giving our diaphragm room to inflate downward. This is the natural breathing pattern of newborn babies and adults in sound sleep. Abdominal breathing is slower and deeper than chest breathing. Abdominal breathing allows our respiratory system to do its job of producing energy from oxygen and, in turn, removes waste products from our system. Chest or thoracic breathing will have a taxing effect on our system, while abdominal or diaphragmatic breathing will:

- help you relax and release tension
- reduce and even eliminate the symptoms of stress
- increase your awareness of your inner experience
- help you to be aware of how your body speaks to you

Let's try a few cycles of abdominal breathing. Bring your attention to your breath and notice how you are breathing right now. Is it chest or abdominal or a combination of the two? Concentrate on your next breath and allow yourself to take a big breath in through your nose. At the same time, bring your awareness to your abdominal cavity expanding with this wonderful dose of oxygen. Try to think of your breath as an ocean wave coming to shore. As you exhale completely, also through your nose, imagine your breath as the wave receding back to meet the next wave, your next inhalation, coming in again. Your inhalation and exhalation become a gentle rhythmic wave. Just a few minutes of breath work will enable you to feel the benefits of relaxation almost immediately.

Observing people's breathing is one of the quickest ways to determine if they are at ease or not. Try doing some people watching in restaurants, departments of motor vehicles, supermarket checkouts, when you're stuck in traffic, even observe your coworkers. You will be surprised at all the chest breathers around you. Not only will this little experiment bring you into the present moment, it will also help you breathe and relax. So take a deep breath!

3. **Pay attention to subtle energies.** Our creator gave us five amazing senses that we can readily use to determine what is happening around and beyond us at all times. These are our senses of seeing, hearing, feeling, tasting, and smelling. Unfortunately, our evolution into adulthood pretty much inhibits the sensitivity of all these, especially if we have been unconscious to keeping them calibrated and tuned up. Fortunately, you can always enhance and sharpen their sensitivity. Working with this ground

rule throughout your journey to uncover your personal animal totems will help you recover and/or enhance any senses that have been compromised in the course of your life. As you travel up the chakra system, each chakra location will give you an opportunity to both become aware of the work needed to engage a particular sense and enhance the sensitivity of those particular senses that have been diminished during your walk through life. By becoming aware of your conscious perceptions of your five senses, you will open the vibrational portal to your own personal awareness and intuitive guidance and also to that of those around you.

4. **Meditate.** Meditation is the most important part of the journey. Many people are not interested in meditation. In fact, some of my students start getting fidgety in their seats when I mention that meditation is going to be part of the totem journey. I have found that my students fall into two extreme scenarios when it comes to meditation: those who meditate readily and easily and those who don't and say they can't and won't. Each of these extremes has its own drawbacks when uncovering your animal totems. If you see yourself as one of the extremes, these guiding principles will help you with uncovering your animal totems in their truest form.

Let's get a clear understanding about these two extremes. If you can readily and easily fall into a meditative state, meaning that just merely mentioning the word meditation will send you into the cosmos and away from what is happening around you, I say more power to you. However, it can be challenging for you to keep your head out of the clouds while important things are going on around you and in my class. This is mostly because the group classes tend to vibrate at a higher frequency, and the energy is conducive to meditative states. I almost feel a need to grab these students by the feet to pull them back down into the classroom. While these students seem to almost immediately make contact with their totems in the meditative state, it is important for them to rely on the physical affirmations of their totems more than the meditative connection. I find that some students who are very intuitive will sometimes get so caught up in the wonderful and enchanting world of tuning out meditatively with their new animal friends that they overlook what one would call the elephant in the room, the clear physical verifications of their totems. The unfortunate aspect of this is that they can really miss out on the Divine guidance in the physical world, which is one of the most magical and astounding parts of the journey.

One of the great joys and part of the magic of following spirit guidance is how the other dimensions play out in our three-dimensional world. Our animal totems are at the very core of making these encounters obvious. If we can't affirm them physically, then we can very easily be directed by what is called illusion. In a spirituality sense, illusions block our ability to see truly or clearly. By challenging yourself to go beyond your habitual way of interpreting what is true, you not only open the door to a new way of seeing but also toward balancing the tendency to be on the extreme end of the spectrum. One of your animal totems' many gifts will be to help you steadily move toward balance. However, not being in denial about where you are on that scale is important.

The same analogy is true for those who find it difficult to meditate. I find that my students on this end of the spectrum will depend so much on the affirmation in the physical world that they convince themselves they don't need to meditate to make the connections. What I find is that they can fall into a trap of micromanaging their totem occurrences with logic that the affirmations they receive in real-life situations are essentially banished by the left-brain's data. The students then become frustrated that they are not getting totem encounters. If you feel that you fall into this category, allow yourself to notice your resistance to utilizing the right side of your brain— the home of your imagination and the place where you allow guidance to come through—and move toward enhancing its capacity. The best way to do this is through meditation. Even if you start with two to five minutes of complete quiet and simply notice where your mind goes, you will begin to slowly take control of what is called the monkey mind. Once you allow yourself to conquer your mind's drive to allow those thoughts to overrun your quiet time, you can release any thought, go back to no thought, and you will soon notice a shift that enhances your intuitive perceptions. This will also encourage you to trust the totem sightings you receive in the physical world, as they will be precursors to your meditations.

The guiding principles above are suggested to aid and enhance the journey of uncovering your personal animal totems. It's a profound expedition that is all about you. Meditation is one of the tools that aids you in this journey of self-discovery. There is no right or wrong way to a journey of self-discovery; it is you who chooses and you who discovers.

5. **Drink plenty of water.** Never underestimate the power of hydration. It helps rid our body of toxins, keeps our vital systems happy and working efficiently, and it refreshes and energizes us. For me, this is one of my most challenging ground rules, mostly because I am very active, and I certainly don't always eat or drink the elements that augment hydration. I can tell you that when I do put in the extra effort to not just consciously be aware of my hydration but to actually put the effort into being hydrated, the benefits are amazing. While every now and again I do find myself relapsing into decreased water intake patterns, I am aware of it much more quickly than in the past, and the awareness really helps. This is one of the areas where guilt becomes a benefit and will aid you in staying hydrated. I will cover water and guilt further when we get to

the section where you uncover the totem of your sacral chakra. Until then, I will give you the same spiel I give my students.

The activities you are about to embark on will bring you new insights, flush things out, heighten your psychic sensitivities, and prompt change and hopefully growth in your conscious awareness. This is what the new age, metaphysical, and spiritual people call deep soul work. Soul work clears the mind, body, and spirit very effectively and successfully. It breaks up stagnant and blocked avenues in our being and stirs them up to be released. Just like a mulcher quickly and efficiently clears a new pathway from nature's remnants of leaves, shrubs, and overgrown areas to bring forth new growth and beauty, you will want the tainted impurities that get stirred up in you to be removed from your beautiful being. The best way for that to happen is to stay hydrated, which will allow the poop to be removed quickly but also will allow you to stay functioning at a new and improved higher vibration. So grab your mug and have a drink on me—the journey is about to begin.

How to Accessorize Your Journey

The most significant aspects of the journey to uncover your personal animal totems will be your identification of and navigation through very subtle energy realms. As you attempt to tune in and become familiar with these vibrations, there are many tools that you can use to help invoke these subtle realms. I call them accessories. In the fashion world, accessories are the wonderful frills of studded belts, dangling earrings, and feathered fedoras that make your dancing jumpsuit want to get up and boogie, even if you don't. Basically, the outfit says it all. Accessories in the metaphysical world are categorized into what I call the five elements: earth, fire, air, water, and ether. I utilize accessories constantly in my daily activities but also in my classes to help students identify and connect to the subtle realms.

Specifically, the accessories come in the form of candles, incense, crystals, essential oils, sounds, or any of the number of trinkets and modalities available to aid you in the process of tuning into the subtle realms. For each chakra in your journey, I will give you examples of the candles, incense, crystals, and essential oils I use in my classes. Again, these are the accessories that make my jumpsuit want to get up and boogie, even when I don't. I encourage you to explore your own accessory avenues and identify what elements will help you keep boogieing throughout your journey, especially when you don't feel up to it. Sometimes just the sight of them on your altar can summon you to visit. Below are some examples of how each accessory may serve you. Go ahead, accessorize your world.

Candles

Candles come in a variety of shapes, sizes, colors, and fragrances. Each season and holiday offers some spectacular aromas for your environment. Candles help to set the mood, and their evocative fragrances can invite your animals to connect with you. Candles welcome the energies of purification and inspiration into your realm as they open the doors to other realms. I make it a habit to go candle shopping before the start of each new season to usher the upcoming season's magical energies into my home. Candles also help connect you to the strongest expression of the element fire, especially if you do not have a fireplace. The fire element connects us with our passion and is said to be the wings of our courage, compassion, and devotion. Each month I will give candle ideas you might want to incorporate into your journey as you uncover a new animal totem and work with a new chakra.

Incense

Incense has been used throughout the ages to aid in meditation, purification and clearing rituals, aromatherapy, and to cover up unwanted odors like marijuana (but you didn't hear that from me). Incense helps to invoke the element of air while keeping the fire element at a nice glowing ember. Air helps us to connect with the higher realms and tap into our intuition. Incense is sold as sticks, cones, ropes, and smudge bundles or smudge sticks. There are a ton of different types of holders, as well. There are literally hundreds of incense scents that can come in various combinations, even within the same stick. Incense is great for clearing all kinds of energies. Use it before moving into a new home, after a conflict or an illness, to enhance meditation or relaxation, or just to make your home smell nice. Each month you will get new examples of different types of incense.

Crystals

I bought my first crystal as a kid. It was one of those little fake gold rings with your birthstone the size of a BB pellet secured with tiny metal prongs. I purchased it at Woolworth's, the five-and-dime store up the street. My stone was peridot, a crappy, dull, pale green stone that I couldn't even pronounce, never mind spell. I remember looking at that tiny stone and thinking if I had been born ten days later, I could have had a pretty, dark blue stone. When I became serious enough to learn about crystals and their energy properties, I found that what I didn't know then was the energies of peridot were just what I needed, and it wasn't such a crappy stone at all. It also turned out that green is one of my favorite colors. Each month you will get new examples of different types of crystals to be used in conjunction with the chakras.

Crystals are another modality you can incorporate into your journey. They too come in a variety of colors, shapes, and sizes and offer energies that aid in healing, clearing, protecting, and blocking just about everything you can think of. Unlike incense and candles, you can readily carry them around in your pocket, sport them as jewelry, display them on your altar or in your home, or just keep them securely tucked in a velvet pouch to call upon when needed. Crystals are a great way to connect with the element of earth, as each one is a manifestation of the Earth's very core. When we connect to earth, we are able to act on our passions and intuition and create our own wonderful expression. There are a number of crystals available that vibrate to the frequency of each one of the chakras. I encourage you to find which ones appeal to you. Shopping for crystals is a wonderful way to help you activate your intuitive sensitivities. It opens a door for you to tap into the subtle energies of each stone you touch. Even though you might feel like you can't sense a perceptible energy transfer, it is happening on a subtle level. By allowing yourself to tap into these energies, you will start to experience noticeable results.

Essential Oils

Essential oils can be beneficial in a number of ways, although I must caution you on their usage as they are very concentrated and flammable, and both of these characteristics can have unfortunate results. Not that playing with candles and incense doesn't have its hazards. However, as long as you are aware of and adhere to the safety precautions when using oils, their therapeutic benefits are innumerable. One of the best known uses of essential oils is through inhalation. For example, a few drops of eucalyptus oil on a tissue or added to a pot of boiling water can provide analgesic, antiseptic, antiviral, and decongestant healing relief. This is because eucalyptus oil is toxic to the bacteria that cause colds and sinus conditions. By adding your favorite essential oil to water, you can not only invoke the water element, which will help in calming, clearing, and healing dark emotions, but also accelerate relaxation and revitalization. Essential oils can be added to your baths, Jacuzzis, saunas, vaporizers, and diffusers to really enhance your water connections.

The list goes on and on when it comes to the uses of essential oils. I suggest that when you are shopping for essential oils you use what I call the "wave method." It's what I learned the hard way in chemistry—uncap the solution about a foot away from you, then fan the opening toward your nose. This will reduce the pungent, overpowering smells of the oils that can sometimes make the essences of your favorite aromas seem dreadful. Each month you will get new examples of different types of essential oils that can aid you on your journey.

Be aware that as you move deeper into the journey of uncovering personal animal totems, your senses will become more attuned and sensitive to certain types of stimulation, both positive and negative. As they do, it's up to you to determine which accessories will allow you to slip back to the sanctuary of higher vibrations. Your accessories will promote the healthy harmonious frequencies that keep you in alignment and open to your animal totem calling card. As you become more conscious of the different vibrations, you will begin to notice how each element plays a key role in your personal vibration. You will be very surprised at how they all work together and how you can be the magician and alchemist who tames them.

When I teach my animal totem classes, I push my students to exercise their intuitive muscles by helping them become aware of the subtle energies in and around them. I use sound therapy, as well as all of the items outlined in the chakra totem accessory charts each month. It's important that you make a conscious effort to experience and engage with the elements stimulating your senses. Over the years of our so-called growth, these senses have been numbed and desensitized. Unless you are constantly working them, they can become dormant. This journey over the next nine months will reawaken them. I encourage you to use these items to stimulate your *clairs,* French for "clear." These are your seeing, hearing, smelling, tasting, and feeling abilities, also known as clairvoyance, clairaudience, clairalience, clairgustance, and clairsentience. Building on all of these senses will help you to trust your claircognizance (knowing). It will clearly be a wonderful experience.

Meeting the Inhabitants

Anytime you encounter something foreign or unfamiliar in life, it doesn't take long to realize that your standard method of practice isn't going to work and you will undoubtedly need to pay attention and possibly adopt some new ways to deal with the situation. As you begin to uncover your personal animal totems, you will find that the spirit world and its infinite guidance do not operate in the logical manner you have been primed to grasp and understand. In other words, when you meet these new inhabitants, they are not going to speak your language or interact with you in the way you are accustomed. So you will need to adopt some new methods to help you blend together the two worlds if you are going to be open to your totems' guidance. In the initial phases of uncovering your personal animal totems, your animals will come through very subtly and will be awfully easy to overlook. Your logical mind will want to dismiss the appearances with skepticism, and your ego will want to downplay them with doubt and cynicism. So it will be extremely important for you to be aware of the role your logical and ego mind are playing in the initial stages of the journey. Remember, your goal is to travel light—that is, without the energies of overanalysis and reason—and be open to a childlike curiosity by letting your imagination take over. Following these concepts right out of the gate will help you build a strong Divine foundation and transport you into the energetic flow you will need to welcome your animal totems quickly and clearly. Remember, you cannot control the Divine forces or process of guidance—you must allow it. This means you must allow yourself to be open to the way guidance is at work in your life. Think of it as visiting an ancient tribal ritual. You wouldn't take over the event and say things like "Hey, that fire is much too high, and that constant banging on the drum thing is really starting to grate on my nerves!" Your animal totem guides will contact you through their own rituals and meet you at a juncture that will lead you to profound insights. You must not only be present to receive them, but you must also be open to and aware of the way they are communicating.

Your animal totem guides are inhabitants of the spirit world, and they will communicate magically and subtly. Their mission is to give you quick affirmations that put you in direct contact with messages and guidance from them, as well as from your intuitive support system, which includes angels, spirit guides, ancestors, and even loved ones who have crossed over to the spirit world. Your animal totem guides will help you remain in constant contact with some very powerful guidance. For the next nine months, getting to know them is going to be a tremendous opportunity for great growth and development of your intuitive gifts and will also offer you a renewed sense of wonder, trust, and sometimes inexplicable delight. So fasten your seatbelt and enjoy the ride, and remember these words from writer Henry Miller: "One's destination is never a place, but a new way of seeing things." Bon voyage, my friend!

PART II

Making Friends with Your Animal Totems

This section provides you with the outline of what to expect on your journey and how to navigate through the chakra of the month. Know that each one of your chakras is functioning just as it should for where you are in your journey in life. In fact, it is no mistake that you are taking this journey. The Divine plan is always present in our walk in life. Whether your current circumstances are positively or negatively charged, it is important that you honor your current situation. This will allow for great clearing, healing, and abundant manifestations to take place on your totem journey. For each chakra center you visit, you will need to honor the energies that are apparent and learn which energies are not serving you and will need to be surrendered. The animal totem that unveils itself will hold the medicine that will assist you in aligning with the frequencies needed to clear, balance, and harmonize each energy center. As you notice excessive or deficient chakra imbalances, you will have a better understanding of the purpose of your animal totem. Remember, your totem picks you. The standard format for each month will be to get an overall understanding about the chakra, honor your current situation, release the chakra's negatively charged energies, learn its optimal balance state, and move toward shifting your energy in that direction. Last, but not least, the ritual to welcome in your totem animal is just as important as the one used to uncover it. As you make friends with your animal totems, your relationships with them will become more powerful as the months progress. So buckle up—the journey begins. Enjoy!

CHAPTER 8

THE FOOT CHAKRA TOTEM

What's Up with This Chapter

∞ Uncovering Your Foot Chakra Totem Animal
∞ What Is a Foot Chakra?
∞ Let's Get Physical
∞ Honoring Your Feet
∞ The Foot Chakra Totem
∞ Connecting with Your Foot Totem
∞ Welcoming Your Foot Totem Animal

Uncovering Your Foot Chakra Totem

So you're finally ready to meet your totems. If you have followed all the instructions to this point, you're basically suited up and in the right vibe, you've engaged in some prospecting to set your intention to meet your new companion, and you are sitting peacefully in your newly created sacred space, ready to begin the initial steps to uncover your first animal totem. Each month will begin by learning a little about the chakra your totem animal is going to help you open, clear, and balance. At first, you must honor the current state of that chakra, whether you feel it is good or bad, or you just don't know the state. This will help you understand the wisdom and intuitive awareness your animal totem will bring you regarding that chakra. You will start each month by performing a guided meditation, which can be found at the end of the book. This will initiate your connection with your totem animal and allow the amazing and enchanting visits of your animal to pop up all over the place, especially when you least expect it. Feel free to modify the meditation to work for you.

What Is a Foot Chakra?

In chapter 5 you became familiar with the foot chakra's color and location. I will now take that a few steps further so you can get a real feel for how the foot chakra energy centers operate. The foot chakras are considered minor chakras. Much like the seven major chakras, the minor chakras play key roles in vital body functions. The foot chakra will be the only minor chakra you will work with while uncovering your personal animal totem. Feel free to explore the other minor chakras if you so desire, as they have great energetic significance. The foot chakras are our anchor to Mother Earth. It is so vitally important for our spirit to connect with her on our walk in life. This is one reason why I believe the foot chakra should be included not only as part of your personal totem but also as part of the major chakra system. Your feet have been your true witnesses to your walk thus far in life, so it seems fitting to include them as part of your personal totem, although I know I'm going to have a tough time changing ancient traditional views on my campaign to make them a major chakra.

The foot chakra, as you can guess, is associated with your feet. Once you learn more about the foot chakra and its purpose, you may find yourself paying more attention to how your feet serve you greatly in life and how you might have been taking them for granted. Your foot chakra totem animal will guide and assist you in many ways, but one of its most valuable gifts will be to lead you to opportunities. These opportunities will manifest both in your inner world and your outer world.

Our feet facilitate us in walking our talk, which figuratively means that we do what we say; in essence, you take action (your walk) on what you say (your talk). Plenty of opportunities will be revealed to you in your walk to allow you to make this happen. I will refer to some of these opportunities as your shadows. Your shadow is that side of you that you don't see, or want to see, for that matter. The universe will always help us see that dark shadow of ours by shining a big light on it. However, we are always in charge of making the choice of seeing the light. You will find as you proceed through the journey of the chakras that they are all interconnected, and there is always a subtle dance taking place with each one of them. You will see this play out in what I call sticking one's foot in one's mouth, also known as foot-in-mouth disease or foot-in-mouth syndrome, which basically means having a tendency to make remarks that are inappropriate or embarrassing at the worst time. If this is an issue for you, your foot chakra totem can assist you in this area of your life, as well. It's most important that you don't take any of this stuff personally. We have all suffered from foot-in-mouth syndrome a minimum of once or twice in our lifetime.

The Foot Chakra Totem

I remember once going out for drinks with a few coworkers and one of them wanted us to meet his new female companion. As she proceeded to chug-a-lug several glasses of beer very quickly from the pitcher, I was a little taken aback. When she advanced to fill yet another glass, I commented, "Wow, what, do you have a wooden leg?" As she proceeded to fill the glass again, she looked me straight in the eye and said, "As a matter of fact, I do." To which her companion added, "She really does." Needless to say, I was mortified by what had just flew out of my mouth and apologized profusely. Regrettably, there was not a thing I could say or do to change those uttered words. She was a total sport, had a great sense of humor about the whole thing, and actually went quite out of her way to try to make me feel better, which made it even worse for me. Interestingly enough, my foot chakra totem is a blue jay. Blue jays are known for their loud, noisy, and sometimes raucous calls. They can be both possessive bullies and great protectors of their territory. My jay totem has revealed to me tremendous insights and opportunities for growth, especially when it comes to my big mouth. The wonderful part about this journey is that you will find that the animal associated with each of your chakras will help you with many aspects of your life, and they all will actually work together to some extent. Your totems will help you recognize patterns that have long been hidden and will very humorously point them out. They will allow you to see, understand, and liberate those patterns through the wonderful universal energies that will guide you to great conscious expansion. Remember that mantra about chakras we learned earlier? Say it: "Chakras are the conduit through which Divine energy passes through me." Wonderful! The foot chakra is where it's all going to begin for you.

Let's Get Physical

Physically, the foot chakras are located on the soles of the feet, or, as I like to say, "souls" of your feet. Metaphorically, our soul's journey is carried out by our feet and our mouth, our "walk" and our "talk." which open, clear, and balance our heart, which is our true purpose in life. We will learn more about walking our talk as we get deeper into the journey. The foot chakras are considered to be two split centers; however, they essentially function as one whole center. Let me try to make sense of that. If you put your two feet together, the two chakras would magically combine to make one whole center. Yet it doesn't matter if the feet are physically next to each other; these two split centers are always linked and always complete. That's one of the many cool things about energy. I tell my students to imagine they are putting both feet into a huge elastic band and then envision themselves walking around. As the elastic band expands and contracts, it mimics how the two chakras stay linked as a whole. Even though it might appear they are split and independent when the feet are apart, they are actually still functioning as a whole. So as you are be-bopping through life, your foot chakras are expanding and contracting and moving energy in and out of you through one whole unit. I find that fascinating.

Think of your foot chakra as a door in your house. Whatever you bring into the house to sustain your wellbeing will sooner or later need to be taken out. What I'm talking about here is your trash, your garbage, or just plain old junk that doesn't serve you any longer. Yes, even your chakras have a trash responsibility that needs to be looked after. However, that duty is cleverly camouflaged with the word *grounding*. So the next time someone is annoying or aggravating you with their petty patterns, arrogance, or irritations and just being plain unconscious of others, suggest they get grounded. It's a nice way of saying, "You reek and it's time to take out your trash."

Now, here is a very interesting piece of information about the foot chakra. The mainstream buzz in chakra philosophy is that the root or base chakra, the next chakra above the foot, is the grounding point, or where you get rid of your trash and bring in the Divine universal energy. However, the root chakra is an energy transformation point. This is where energy is slowed down so it can pass into Mother Earth quickly and effortlessly. While the root chakra converts the energy, it does not pass the energy to Mother Earth. The foot chakras actually do that work. It's kind of like the game of football, where every play starts with a snap, the action where the offense's center gives the ball to the quarterback. It's the quarterback who actually gets rid of the ball. Unless, of course, the quarterback's blocked, which can also happen with chakras. We'll address that later. The most important thing you need to know now is your mantra: "Chakras are the conduit through which Divine energy passes through me." Say it three times. Awesome! You are really getting it! As you are saying this mantra, there is a wonderful, crystal-clear stream of Mother Earth energy flowing up into your being by way of your foot chakras. Pat yourself on the back; you have just had your first experience working with energy. See how simple it is?

Honoring Your Feet

Now that you have had an introduction to the foot chakra and understand a little about this minor chakra's important task, you can get a real feel for your feet and the major function they play in carrying you around town. They are a team, the foot chakras and your feet, and you will need to honor that team before you can even begin to call on a totem to join them. So the best place to start honoring is at the beginning. To do this, you will take a journey with your feet. As you read the following exercise and think about your relationship with your feet and the service they have provided you, I'm sure you will recognize areas where they have truly been taken for granted. Take inventory of the here-and-now condition of your feet. For example, check for corns and calluses, examine your toenails, consider the shoes and socks you put on your feet. The little foot-journey poem below honors the important role your feet have played in your walk of life up to now. During this exercise take the opportunity to write in your journal both positive and negative aspects that might come up. Also, write down your thoughts on the current condition of your feet and what you can do to honor them even more. If things come up that have nothing to do with your feet, write them down, even if they don't make logical sense. This will help clear the chakra and also any stagnant energies that may have accumulated over time. These stagnant energies can cause what the new agers and metaphysical gurus call blocks in the chakra.

Bring your attention to your breath and take three deep, cleansing breaths. Make sure both feet are touching the floor. Barefoot works best.

The Journey of Your Feet

Travel all the way back to being an infant just after birth,
Your feet gently waiting for their first connection to Mother Earth.
As you grow to be somewhat older,
They finally touch ground and you're suddenly bolder,
Learning to walk and learning to run,
Learning to skip, jump, and have lots of fun.
They helped you to play; they helped you to grow,
They helped you to learn the things you did not know.
As you grew,
They grew too.
They brought you to school
To learn some new tools,
They walked you through childhood,
Your adolescence, and now adulthood.
This amazing odyssey of your feet
Is the vehicle where you and the world meet.
So think of how your feet serve you today
And how they support you in every way.
Your feet are your support, they allow you to stand upright.
They transport you everywhere, all day and even at night.
They are a symbol of your stability and lots of your strength.
It's time to acknowledge this, and really at length.
It's important that you honor them for all they are worth,
For they are your key to staying grounded and connected to wonderful
Mother Earth.

Take a moment to write any thoughts that came up while you were reading.

Ways to Honor Your Feet

Pedicure
Foot bath
Cozy socks
Reflexology
Fluffy slippers
Buy new shoes
Warm your feet by the fire
Walk on the beach barefoot

The Foot Chakra Totem

Now that you have learned a little about the foot chakra and how it functions and have also spent some time reflecting and honoring your feet and the tireless role they have played in your life, we will take a look at how your foot chakra totem will benefit you. Our physical walk in life throws us all kinds of curve balls, obstacles, chaos, and illnesses. Some of these can have negative effects on our being and create patterns such as procrastination, better known as dragging our feet, or instability or unsteadiness that causes us to waver or hesitate on an energetic level. As we encounter these obstacles, hurdles, and roadblocks, our hope is that they very quickly turn into stepping stones from which we grow and improve our way of life. But sometimes we get stuck in some of these not-so-desirable places for a bit. Your foot chakra totem will provide you with the medicine you need to facilitate the change and the help you need to break the patterns that keep you stuck in the muck. Animal totems are amazingly powerful at guiding you to resolution around roadblocks in life. Your foot totem animal and its essence can be regarded as your anchor to the physical world. This animal will help you become grounded and connected to Mother Earth but will also connect you to the intuitive guidance from the higher realms. Because it is the first animal you will uncover, it will play an intimate role with you and your guidance. Just as your feet carry you to opportunities in life, the totem animal for your feet will guide you toward opportunities and around those obstacles that limit opportunities. When you allow your feet to act on the Divine guidance being communicated to you, all is well. As your relationship grows with your foot totem animal, you will notice that its appearance signals an opportunity to stay tuned to helpful guidance there to assist you. The first step in your journey is to simply notice your totem; the successive steps will require that you follow the guidance.

Meditation

Now you turn your eyes from an outward view to an inward view. By performing the guided meditation at the back of the book, you will call forth the frequencies needed for your first encounter. Those who engage in a regular meditation practice will find this step acceptable, pleasurable, and satisfying, or you may even want to use your own practice. Those who don't have a meditative base or who have never meditated might find it a little trying to get into the flow of it. My advice is that you at least give it a try and push yourself a little further each time. While there are some parts of the meditation that seem a little far-fetched, allow your imagination to stay tuned to the guided aspects. Remember that meditation is a gift to your mind, body, and spirit and will always have great benefits. Even if you don't think it is working, it is. Just like starting a new exercise program, you must build up your meditative muscles, just as you would build up your leg and arm muscles while training for an athletic event. If you find you are still having difficulty, I suggest you track where your thought process is going and write down whatever comes up in your journal. This will help remove the thoughts so you can meditate and help you become aware of the blocks or obstacles inhibiting your capacity to stay connected to the guided meditation. Our monkey mind will always want to be in charge and control the meditation process. Journaling the interferences will allow your monkey mind to simmer down and put you in charge of where you want your mind to go. Your mind has been running the whole show; now it's time to take back that control. You can always go back to your journal later and address those thoughts with a more lucid approach, although you might find that they really weren't that important anyway. As your animals start popping up, you will grow to look forward to the meditative process.

Refer to the guided meditation at the back of the book to evoke and initiate your first encounter with your animal totem. Choose a meditation that works best for you whether it is your own or the one at the back of the book. You can even create your own. I suggest that you repeat the meditation for three consecutive days. Again, feel free to modify the meditation so it is workable for you. You can make meditations more powerful by recording your voice reading the meditation. There is also a Guided Animal Totem Meditation mp3 that can be downloaded from my website. During the meditation, your animal quite possibly will come to you or you might get a very quick glimpse of some distinctive characteristic of your animal. Again, write anything down, even if it seems odd. Also, watch how the synchronicities or so-called coincidences begin to unfold. If you do not see any evidence of your animal during the meditation, that is okay too. Remember, even though you don't think anything is happening, it is—be patient because the best is yet to come.

Uncovering Your Personal Animal Totem

Over the next few days, allow yourself to be more attuned to nature. Again, nature vibrates to unconditional love and is a true connection to spirit. Exposing yourself to these frequencies and energies will always be helpful to your personal vibration. Even just looking out the window can align you with such energies. For the next twenty-eight to thirty-one days, you will be discovering and working with an animal that will play a significant role in your life. This animal will be your teacher, guide, kindred companion, and more. Your foot totem animal will lead you to opportunities and messages and anchor you in the most intimate way. It will assist you in connecting to source, great spirit, the universe, or whatever you call the God force or Divine power of all that is. Your foot totem animal will assist you in staying grounded and aware in your journey. The more you honor your feet, the more you allow your foot totem animal into your world. Below is a list of accessories that can be used to encourage and enhance your expedition with your foot totem.

FOOT CHAKRA TOTEM ACCESSORIES	
CANDLES	Use candles in your sacred space or anywhere you travel. They are a wonderful way to invoke a connection with your animal totem and create a relaxing ambience wherever you are holding space. Select candles with brown or dark, earthy tones. Scents such as cedar, sandalwood, musk, and pine can create a warm, cozy, inviting feeling for you and your foot totem animal. Candles connect you to the fire element.
INCENSE	Use incense for clearing any space and calling upon your foot animal totem. Incense adds a wonderful tone to your clearing rituals. Scents such as cedar, sandalwood, a variety of musks, and pine add a nice touch to your meditation or relaxation sessions. Incense helps connect you to the element of air with its wispy trail of smoke. It can also soften the fire element with its glowing ember. The aroma and smoke trail can help invoke and align you with your foot totem.
CRYSTALS	Use crystals for their color and energy qualities. There is literally a crystal for every emotion, body part, or circumstance. Several crystals benefit the feet. Brecciated jasper, which is jasper veined with hematite, will help keep your feet on the ground, especially if you have any airy tendencies. Onyx is beneficial for foot disorders. Pietersite promotes walking your truth. Green apophyllite helps those undertaking fire walking, as it facilitates a meditative state and cools the feet after the walk. Smoky quartz is one of the most efficient grounding and anchoring stones and raises vibrations during meditation. It is a protective stone with a strong connection to earth and the base chakra. Crystals help connect you to the earth element and can very easily be carried on your person.

AROMA-THERAPY	Essential oils can be used for healing, relaxing, invoking, clearing—you name it. They are a perfect way to enhance your home spa while utilizing the water element. Their therapeutic properties can boost diffusers, vaporizers, humidifiers, bathtubs, and fountains to create a botanical utopia in all of your environments. Remember that essential oils are very highly concentrated, volatile, aromatic essences of plants. I suggest buying them from all-natural stores and vendors, as experienced personnel can guide you in their proper use. For footbaths, I use a few drops of lavender. In my ultrasonic aroma diffuser, I will use either pine or atlas cedarwood when working with the foot chakra.

Connecting with Your Foot Totem

When an animal first appears, whether it's real or symbolic, thank it. Talk to it. Don't be afraid to ask it questions. This animal can be a messenger for your totem or your actual totem. The way the animals come to you will have great significance, and you should take note of how it unfolds. Mostly, try to determine where your thought process was when the animal appeared or what environment you were in. These are important aspects of the awakening of your intuitive gifts. As your animal begins to make repeated visits, it will become undeniable that it is your totem. I have had skeptical students say things like "How could you not see a bunny around Easter and springtime? They are everywhere!" only to find their skepticism diminish when they are introduced to a woman named Ruth who says, "You can call me Bunny." This is what I call Divine humor, and it's quite amusing once you awaken to it all. When your true animal appears, the affirmations and confirmation will be humorous and astounding and will sometimes knock your limited thinking right out of the water.

Once you have determined your animal, learn as much as you can about it. Does it fly? Is it big or small? Slow or fast? Does it like cold weather or warm? What does it eat? Where does it sleep? How does it communicate? These questions all have significance in how this animal will assist you in life, as well as in balancing the unknown blocks and imbalances of your foot chakra. Remember these are your shadows. In Jungian psychology, the shadow or shadow aspect is a part of the unconscious mind, consisting of repressed weaknesses, shortcomings, and instincts. These are the parts of ourselves that we tend not to see—or tend to not want to see, for that matter. Your totem animal will very compassionately and gracefully help you out with the shadow thing, as I like to call it. You will find that it is not only mind-blowing but also humorous how your animal assists you with your shadow side. The shadow sides of ourselves limit us from reaching our true potential and can cause a tremendous amount of turmoil in our life until we come to become aware of them.

Another key element in learning more about your animal is to look at the traditions, myths, cultures, religions, and folklore about your totem. I particularly like fairy tales. Type your animal's name followed by the word *totem* into a Google search, and you will get a tremendous amount of information on the medicines your animal will hold for you, along with other paths for understanding how it will assist you in life. I always encourage my students to find a small replica or picture of their totem and keep it with them throughout the month. This helps you to stay focused on your connection with your animal. I had one student tell me that just seeing the figurine of her animal totem on her desk during a stressful deadline period at work brought a level of comfort she had never experienced before. Never underestimate the power of your animal totems; they carry sacred Divine forces, and once harnessed, they will serve you immensely.

If you feel like you are not making contact with your animal, don't panic! This is not any reflection on your ability to work with subtle energies. It's just a matter of devotion and enjoyment. Devotion is a dedicated and earnest effort toward making something happen. Enjoyment is the act or condition of receiving pleasure. These two elements are a necessary part of the journey. It is not a race, nor is it essential that your totem pop up in a day, week, or month. It's your personal journey with the Divine. Remember that when you are working with Divine forces, there is no space and time, only infinite possibilities. Space and time are part of the three-dimensional world and can trigger narrow thinking and limited promise. Everything will happen according to Divine timing. Meanwhile, if you are having problems connecting, review the Tips, Tricks, and Divine Wisdom section at the back of the book.

Welcoming Your Totem Animal

Once you have unveiled your foot totem animal and spent some time throughout the month kindling a friendship by learning the traits and qualities of your new companion, it's important that you honor that connection by welcoming this powerful animal into your being. Some of my students journal about their totem's appearances throughout the month and the experiences they shared with their totem. Others print the animal totem information from the Internet, and some bring in beautiful pictures or replicas of their animal. Just as you performed the sacred ritual to unveil your animal totem at the beginning of the month, it is important that you perform an honoring ritual to welcome it into your being. This will assist you in embodying the medicine the animal has to offer you and will also support the energy center you are awakening. Being mindful about assembling and disassembling energies is very important when you are playing in the playground of subtle energies. Opening and closing rituals allow only the purest, highest, and best to come through. Unwanted or lower-vibrating frequencies love to try to infiltrate or permeate the higher vibrations. If you keep your rituals open-ended, it will create ideal conditions for harboring lower entities. The Internet service AOL used to offer a great example of an opening and closing ritual. When you signed on, you would hear a cheerful voice say, "Welcome, you've got mail!" At the end of the session, you'd hear "Good-bye." Years ago when I subscribed to AOL, the closing "Good-bye" always prompted my dog to jump up out of a sound sleep, as it meant we were going for a walk. Remember, you are the commander of the energies you carry, and if you don't care, you will welcome squatters that do.

One of my favorite parts of teaching my totems course is the session in which students welcome their totems into their being. The students have shared their monthly expedition, they are full of laughter, joy, and enchantment, the vibration is very high, and the atmosphere is alive with the frequencies and aromas set by the foot totem accessories. This sacred circle holds the perfect ambiance to welcome your animal totem into your being. Once you have honored the introduction of your animal into your sacred place, it is nice to recite a prayer of intention and gratitude and welcome it into your being.

Below is a prayer I use to welcome the foot totem animal. One of the most significant aspects of growth I have encountered, cherished, and honored in the writing of this book is the power of prayer. There have been many times in my life, and I'm sure in yours, that prayer has been that last resort or resource when all looks bleak. Whether it's an emergency illness with a family member, danger suddenly lurking, unexpected trouble, even death, prayer suddenly becomes our outreach or saving grace in the dark. However, prayer does not have to be something that is called on only in times of trouble. Prayer is also about honoring, thanking, and just connecting with the Divine. The prayer to welcome your animal totem is more than just a welcoming token. It is a ritual to bring closure to the foot chakra journey and honor the gift of the experience, and a conscious allowing of your totem into your being. This ceremony also opens the door to the next chakra, the root chakra animal totem journey. Moreover, it also plays a significant role in helping you to connect to Mother Earth through this anchor of your foot chakra. Prayer is one of the most important instruments in the orchestra of your journey, and the results of its practice is extraordinary. Enjoy!

FOOT TOTEM ANIMAL PRAYER

I now reflect on the journey with my foot totem animal. I recall the moment its essence first arrived. I honor that this animal has unveiled itself to me in so many magical and wonderfully Divine ways. My foot totem animal will help anchor the essence of my true nature to Mother Earth. This animal will help me be aware of all the glorious gifts, lavish abundance, and great opportunities that await me. My foot totem animal will guide, assist, and encourage me to become aware, understand, and know that the forces of Divine guidance are present each and every moment of my journey. I only need notice and my foot totem animal will lead me to the opportunities that will align me to the highest and best potential for my soul's voyage in this life. I trust in this Divine guidance, and I give my foot totem animal permission to support me on my journey. I now welcome my foot totem animal to become a part of my walk.

AMEN.

CHAPTER 9

THE ROOT CHAKRA TOTEM

What's Up with This Chapter

∞ Uncovering Your Root Chakra Totem Animal
∞ What Is a Root Chakra?
∞ Let's Get Physical
∞ Honoring Your Roots
∞ The Root Chakra Totem
∞ Connecting with Your Root Totem
∞ Welcoming Your Root Totem Animal

Uncovering Your Root Chakra Totem

Congratulations! You have just completed the first leg of the journey in uncovering your personal animal totem. You and your new companion foot totem animal are now ready to get down to the root of things, so to speak. After your first month's travel, you should now feel fairly comfortable with the process of allowing yourself to receive subtle information from the world. As you continue your excursion through each chakra, you will become even more attuned and accustomed to the swing of things in the subtle areas, also called being in the flow, and you'll find you just can't wait to safari to the next chakra. Now we are laying the foundation, doing the groundwork to make all that happen. So grab your foot totem by the hoof, paw, wing, fin, or whatever root, pun intended, of travel your foot totem uses to get around, and let's travel to the first major chakra in your journey.

What Is a Root Chakra?

Back in chapter 5, you became familiar with the location and color of the root chakra. You will find that both examples I used in that chapter— the bent-over fat-lady lawn ornament for the root chakra's location and the little pig's bright red bricks for the chakra's color— hold great metaphorical significance as you learn the essentials of keeping this chakra balanced and cleared.

Much like the foot chakra is associated with your feet, the root or base chakra is associated with your roots or the base of your personal foundation. If you look up the word *base* in the dictionary, it is defined as the bottom support of anything or the lowest supporting part or layer of something. This pretty much sums up the first chakra. It is the lowest supporting part of the major chakra system, but it has the greatest significance in supporting proper alignment and balance of the other chakras. In fact, it's the foundation of the chakra system. Interestingly enough, it is associated with the earth element. The Earth is a solid, physical entity and is the very core and source from which everything we utilize in this world today has been created. When you harness the Earth's energy, it is mind-boggling what can be created. Our foot chakra anchors our connection to Mother Earth, and our root chakra represents how we interface with that connection on the physical plane. The state of our root chakra indicates how easy or how difficult it is for us to manifest or create in the physical realm. The answer to just how effective you are at this can be found in your roots.

Now, let me explain this a little further. You might want to grab a gin and tonic and put your feet up for this one. In the many years I worked in what some folks call faceless corporate America, Murphy's Law, which states, "Anything that can go wrong, will go wrong," was ubiquitous, as was the red tape to fix anything that went wrong. Of course, the biotechnology field had fancy corporate terminology for these errors. They were called deviations, nonconformances, or some term that included the word *discrepancy*. People who knew the least about what went wrong were put together in multipurpose task teams to perform analyses to determine the root causes of the things they deemed discrepant. Lots of time, effort, and energy went into solving what sometimes seemed the most obvious problem. The root causes were invariably concluded with heaps of paperwork and then officially signed off. Usually the bottom-line conclusion of the whole fiasco was that the operator had inadvertently turned the wrong valve, inadvertently touched the wrong thing, or inadvertently pushed the incorrect button. The root-cause analysis initiated what was called a corrective action process to make sure that the error never, ever happened again. This was then termed a preventative action, which sequentially added another level of paperwork and complexity to the

The Root Chakra Totem

process and kept the multipurpose task team quite productive. Anyway, enough about corporate life.

So now I bet you're ready for another gin and tonic and wondering where on earth I'm going with this whole corporate multipurpose task team stuff. The long and short of what I learned about the corporate discrepancy experience is that it's all about awareness, and we all go through life somewhat inadvertently unaware. Notice the key word *inadvertently* again. It is our purpose in life to become aware of whom we are, and it all begins with a root-cause analysis. Just like corporate America, you have a multipurpose task team to help you with that task. It's your family, your spouse, your friends, your coworkers, service people— you name it. Everyone you encounter is part of your root-cause analysis team, and you are inadvertently unaware of it. Believe it not, your animal totem guides, in conjunction with your multipurpose task team, are going to help you with your life's purpose by helping you become advertently aware. Notice that it is *advertently* aware, not *inadvertently* aware. The good news is that your animal totem guide will be helping you without all the drama, imprints, conditioning, or patterns associated with your multipurpose task team, and you will soon learn that your totem support team's is the best guidance to follow.

Now let's take this a step further. But first, take a breath and repeat your mantra: "Chakras are the conduit through which Divine energy passes through me." It's important to remind yourself that you are working with energy—and Divine energy, at that. If you recall, back in chapter 1, we learned that each chakra or energy center transmits various expressions of energy in the body. The root chakra expresses an energy associated with survival. Our basic survival needs are shelter, food, clothing, safety, and for some folks, cable TV. Yoga teachings link the seven major chakras to a seven-year cycle. It all starts at the root chakra when the umbilical cord is cut and we take our first breath, then moves up a chakra every seven years. So for the first seven years of your life, you experienced your overall influences for survival from your multipurpose task team. Yeah, that team—Grandma, Grandpa, Ma, Dad, your sibs, Auntie Aggie, friends, teachers, and even creepy Larry down the street. The point here is that hopefully you really didn't need to worry about your survival needs. When you were wet, you were changed. When you were hungry, you were fed. When you were cold, you were warmed. When you needed comfort, you were cuddled. However, keep in mind that this was only as effective as the adeptness of your multipurpose task team. Like the folks in my example from corporate America, they too were pretty much inadvertently unaware. So you really can't blame them for any lack or compulsiveness in your nurturing. They were only doing what they too learned in their first seven years of survival. Can you now see how rooted our root is and why the root chakra is called what it is? It's also easier to understand why there are a lot of so-called slackers in corporate America. But you didn't hear that from me.

So your job is to look at how you are coping with your basic survival needs, which are based on the energies that influenced you during the first seven years of your life, whether good, bad, or indifferent. The good news is that you can achieve anything you want in life regardless of your multipurpose task team, and your root totem animal is going to do an amazing job of supporting and assisting you with your survival necessities, ensuring you can achieve whatever you want in this life. Just as you began the process to uncover your foot totem animal by honoring the current state of your foot chakra, whether it was good, bad, or you just didn't know, you must perform the same task for your root chakra. If you reflect for a moment on your multipurpose task team, I'm sure you have a pretty good idea of your root chakra's current state. It's okay if you don't; this next exercise will help you understand some of the wisdom and help your animal totem will bring regarding your root chakra. You may also be surprised at how inadvertently you navigate through life.

I will also repeat what I mentioned in chapter 4, as the root chakra is where it is imperative that you be most honest with yourself. Remember that saying of automobile salespeople, "The feel of the wheel seals the deal," meaning if they can get you to test-drive the car and feel the steering wheel, they have a much better chance at a sale. The opposite side of that coin is also true; you can buy into a vehicle that really doesn't suit you. I'm sure you have seen many a hairdo, interior décor, and fashion that brings to mind one question: What in the name of H-E-double hockey sticks were they thinking? This is the chakra where a true self-assessment is in order. No worries, though, if you neglect or choose not to see it. Wherever you fail to glimpse at your true self, it will certainly be uncovered in the higher chakras. As you travel through each chakra center, you will constantly be brought back down to the foundation, the earth element, of your house, which will effect your plumbing, the water element; your electricity, the fire element; your H&V (heating and ventilation), the air element; and your space, the ether element. Earth, water, fire, air, and ether are the universal elements that allow everything on Mother Earth to grow and develop. But only when these elements are in optimum balance do they work best for you. You will learn more about identifying and working with these elements as we step through each of the chakras. But first, you are going to take a little test-drive around your earth to determine the nature of your soil. Don't be surprised if you run into some of your multipurpose task team members along the way. I encourage you to just drive by and wave; don't take them onboard, for they will only interfere with a true assessment of your root chakra.

The Root Chakra Totem

When I teach my totem class, for this exercise I use the sound effect of a car starting up and backing out of the driveway, as well as all the items outlined in the Root Totem Accessories Chart below to stimulate the vibrations and frequencies of the root chakra. If you go back to chapter 2, It's All In Your Head, this exercise encourages right-brain stimulation, which will help build your clairvoyance and other *clairs* as you awaken your imagination and intuitive self. I tell my students to imagine whatever vehicle they wish they owned as part of this exercise. I also pass out what I call a "steering wheel," divided into quadrants. You can use a paper plate divided into four sections, like four nice big pieces of pie. Imagine it's apple pie to stay with the red theme. Label each section with the following: Home, Work, Money, Me. We will keep score on our little ride. You will be asked three questions in each section, and each question will be answered with a number between one and five. Write the number on the paper plate that best reflects each scenario. Please note that this is not a pass/fail test and there are no right or wrong numbers. This is where you begin to unearth your true nature, so being honest with yourself is essential. Record your perceptions using the numbers below. Don't worry, for each question, I'll give you answers that are not as sterile as these:

    1—Totally deficient
    2—Slightly deficient
    3—Neutral, right in the middle
    4—Slightly excessive
    5—Totally excessive

This exercise is designed to give you a closer look at your root and your imprints, conditioning, and adopted patterns to determine whether those elements I mentioned are in the right proportion to meet your optimal survival needs. So sit yourself in front of your sacred space with your journal and a red pen. A red outfit is optional and will definitely raise the fun factor and curiosity of those at home wondering what you're doing. Then get ready to capture your foundation ride.

Begin by first taking a breath and repeating your mantra a few times: "Chakras are the conduit through which Divine energy passes through me." Now imagine yourself sitting in a way-cool car. Position your paper-plate steering wheel so the Home quadrant is at the top. I want you to bring your attention to your home. If there are others living in your home—whether family, roommates, or squatters—I want you to think of how *you* respond to your home, not what the others do in your home. This is about how your home reflects you.

Imagine you have just pulled up in front of your home. Take a ride around the exterior, just checking it out. Notice what you like and what you don't like about the exterior of your home. You are now moving toward the front door and entering your home. What's the first room that comes to mind when you come through the door? Why are you drawn to it? Remember, good, bad, or indifferent, it doesn't matter. Look around—does your home support your needs, or is it geared more for someone else's needs? If the latter, what is missing, how could your home better meet your needs?. Write down in your journal anything that stirs your thoughts. Now let's look at how functional your home is for you. Are you constantly looking for or losing things in your home? Is it so organized you know exactly where everything is and could put your finger on anything right now if you were asked? How would you rate the functionality of your home on the following scale?

1—So deficient you can't even move without knocking something over, and you're always looking for something.
2—The place is not a total disaster, but it could use some help.
3—Right in the middle; its disorder and order are addressed in a balanced way.
4—You tend to be a bit anal about the way things are around the home. Here, let's grab a coaster for that glass.
5—You can only focus on seeing everything in its right place, and you must constantly touch or manipulate things in some fashion to meet your liking. Here, let me fluff that up before you sit there.

Write your number on the paper plate in the Home section, and continue to look at your home in your mind's eye. Remember, we are utilizing the right side of the brain here to help stay detached so imagine yourself driving around in your way-cool car, observing all the rooms in your home—your living room, dining room, if you have one, bedrooms, the bathroom—just imagining each one. Are the carpets in need of a vacuuming, the floors a mopping? Can you see out your windows? Are there dishes in your sink? If you were to give the paths through your home an overall highway inspection, how would they rate?

1—So deficient that one would need a shovel and dumpster to clean them. Lots of detour signs, and some paths are actually closed.
2—The paths get somewhat out of hand before the street sweeper comes through.
3—Right in the middle. I exercise the right amount of effort to keep the paths clean in a balanced, reasonable way—not overly excessive, but not negligent.
4—I am somewhat excessive about cleanliness, and there is a need to tidy up before any relaxing can take place.
5—My place is so clean I'm afraid to actually live in it, and it is obvious. It's immaculate, spick-and-span, and I'm proud of it. Just look at the place. Please don't touch that!

Again, focus on your response to your space, not blaming others in your environment. It's all about you and how you feel about it. Write your number in the Home section; you should now have two numbers here. Then get back behind the wheel.

The Root Chakra Totem

Now let's look at how welcoming your home is to visitors. Imagine visitors pulling up in your way-cool car.

1—My home is not inviting at all, and I do not invite others in. The shades are down. Make a U-turn, friends, no one's home.
2—My home is somewhat welcoming, although I'm sometimes self-conscious about letting others visit.
3—My home is welcoming, and I feel very comfortable with and find great enjoyment in having visitors.
4—My home is very welcoming, and I go a bit out of my way to prove it when I have visitors. Would you like me to supersize that drink?
5—My home is the nines, totally a palace, and I will go out of my way to show you just what a mansion I live in. And, yes, the purple-heart trim around the doors did actually come from the Amazon rain forest.

Write your number in the Home section; you should now have three numbers here. Now add your three numbers and circle that number.

It's time to drive to a new location, so turn your paper-plate steering wheel so that Work is at the top. If you do not have a place of employment or do not work, lucky you. But do look at the source of your support and choose a number that best fits your situation. Those of you who do have a place of employment, you probably know that the majority of your time is spent there. This place is crucial to meeting your survival needs. Now, in your way-cool car, drive around your place of employment. Does your job provide the right source of revenue for you?

1—My money-grubbing, scumbag employer underpays me, and I bust my butt for every digit on my paycheck. I'd never say that, though. In fact, I can't believe it just came out of my mouth.
2—I am underpaid for my performance, but, hey, that's life. I have a job and times are tough. I dare not blow my own horn or point out all I do.
3—I feel my salary compensates me based on my skill set. It's a fair salary for what I do.
4—My salary is greater than my work efforts, and I should probably try a little harder. But I don't.
5—My salary is more than adequate for the work I do. In fact, I'm even thinking about asking for more.

Write your number in the Work section, and continue to drive around your place of employment. Do you really dig this job?

1—This job sucks, and if I didn't need the paycheck, I would tell them where to go.
2—It's not the greatest job, but with the economy, I'll just play it safe.
3—My job satisfaction is balanced, with some challenges and some flexibility. Overall, I feel valued, and I kind of like it.
4—I've got a pretty good gig going with some real nice perks, and I like telling people what I do.
5—I'm in total charge, no one questions my ethics or integrity, and no one dares to challenge me. I love this job.

Uncovering Your Personal Animal Totem

Write your number in the Work section; you should now have two numbers here. Continue to drive around your place of employment. What's the atmosphere like at your workplace?

1—This rat-infested company wouldn't be so bad if it weren't for my slave-driving taskmaster boss and my cutthroat coworkers.
2—The environment is workable, and my boss is only somewhat disagreeable. There is a clique to deal with now and again. All in all, it's not that bad.
3—My work environment and business associates are very inclusive, and I feel a great sense of recognition from the team.
4—The atmosphere is created mostly by me, and I influence a lot of the business decisions, good and bad.
5—I take full responsibility for both the environment and my boss, and no one will challenge that practice. I am in charge, and everyone knows it and submits.

Write your number in the Work section; you should now have three numbers here. Add them up and circle the number for that section.

Now let's take a ride around the money department. Turn your steering wheel so that Money is at the top. We all have our own ways of managing money. Now see yourself still driving around in your way-cool car. You're stopped at a traffic light. I come up to the window, hand you five hundred bucks, and tell you to have a ball with it, do as you please, it's all yours, no strings attached. What would you do with it?

1—Whatever I have, I spend, and even if I don't have it, I spend it. Consider this spent!
2—I will sometimes spend outside of my means and then worry about it later. I wonder what I can buy with this?
3—I am pretty good at balancing my cash flow. I don't spend in excess, and I'm not stingy or greedy. I'll spend some on me, some on others, and put some away.
4—I'm sometimes reluctant to spend cash, and I will put some real thought into it before I slap my cash down on the counter. I'll just tuck this away for now.
5—My savings comes first, and my cash flow is carefully managed. I'm already writing the deposit slip in my mind's eye.

Write your number in the Money section, and continue to drive around in your way-cool car, experiencing money management. Why, look up there on the sidewalk! It's Mr. Letter Carrier, and he looks like he has just recognized you and your way-cool car. He's waving a letter at you to stop. As you slow down to say hi, he tosses a pile of bills on the passenger seat and shouts, "Have a nice day!" How do you feel about the pile of bills?

1—If I didn't have debt, I would have nothing to think about. I came into life with no money; I'll go out of life with no money.
2—I tend to get a little behind in my payments, but I do manage to keep on paying them.

3—I can balance surplus and debt without a whole lot of fuss.
4—I tend to have the bill paid in my mind before I even purchase something.
5—Not only do I have a purchase paid for before the bill comes, I look for cost-saving perks to make the purchase even more worthwhile.

Write your number in the Money section; you should now have two numbers here. Continue to drive around in your way-cool car, managing money. Now let's go back to that five hundred bucks I gave you. How are you doing at keeping track of that cash?

1—What five hundred bucks? I couldn't tell you what cash I had or where it went.
2—I have a little bit to show after spending, but it takes me a while to figure out how much.
3—I keep pretty good records of where all my money goes, both saved and spent.
4—I keep receipts from all my expenses and can readily hand them over. Do you want last week's, last month's, last year's?
5—I know where every dime has gone since my umbilical cord was cut. In fact, I still have that first dime.

I think you have had enough of managing money, so write your number down in the Money section. You should now have three numbers here. Add them up and circle your total.

By now, you must be tired of driving around. Let's turn your wheel to the final stretch and focus your attention on your way-cool body and how it's feeling after this ride. Write down any feelings you might be experiencing at this moment. Your body is your real vehicle in life, so let's look at how you treat it. What are those things you eat, drink, or slap on? Do you do things in moderation? What kind of fuel do you put into your way-cool body?

1—I don't care what I expose my body to. In fact, I sometimes challenge my body to see how much it can take.
2—I will generally say, "What the heck?" then overindulge and regret it later.
3—I try to balance the types of things I expose my body to and am careful not to overindulge.
4—I will generally say no and deprive myself, then feel a little awkward as everyone enjoys.
5—I run a tight ship when it comes to what I expose my body to and will grimace when I look at what others are doing to theirs. In fact, I don't care about anything except my body, my body, my body. Boy, do I look good.

Write your number in the Me section. Just like a dog needs to go out for walks or to chase cats or tennis balls, we too need to maintain some level of activity to keep us trim and fit. Do you honor your vehicle with regular rides around the block?

1—I exercise my fingers every time I pick up the remote.
2—I engage in some physical activity but rarely stick with it.
3—I try to expose my body to a balanced level of rest and activity.

Uncovering Your Personal Animal Totem

4—I generally don't allow a day to go by without executing my exercise regimen.
5—I am constantly trying to break my personal exercise record. I'd love to talk, but I gotta run. Literally, I gotta run!

Write your number in the Me section; you should now have two numbers here. Just as every vehicle should have a scheduled maintenance plan of tire rotations and oil changes, so should your body. Do you pay attention to your body's medical needs?

1—I haven't seen a doctor since my polio immunization.
2—I see doctors now and again but rarely listen to what they have to say.
3—I see my physician once a year to check on my body's overall wellbeing.
4—I tend to make frequent visits to the doctor. I mean doctors—foot doctor; skin doctor; ear, nose, and throat doctor.
5—I have my doctor on speed dial and check in weekly, even if nothing is wrong. I double-check every little twitch or pain.

Write your final number in the Me section. You know the gig—add the numbers and circle the total.

If you stayed awake for the whole ride, you should have three numbers in each section that have been totaled so that there are four circled numbers. Now I want you to put a big cross through any circle that holds a seven or less and any circle that holds eleven or greater. Totals of seven or less represent a deficiency, and the bar will need to raised a bit to bring that section of survival into alignment. If any of your totals were eleven or more, you need to simmer down; you don't need to raise any bars, you need to go to some bars. These numbers indicate excessive imprints or learned behavior in that section of your survival. Many times my students are very surprised by the results of their little joyride around foundation. In fact, some find that just the opposite is true of what they'd thought about these areas. The big "Aha!" is discovering your multipurpose task team's influence and power in your life and knowing that there are amazing spiritual forces waiting to help you transcend them.

The good news is that simply bringing those areas with deficient or excessive tendencies to your attention will launch a heightened awareness about your foundation. The most extraordinary part of this awareness is that your root totem animal guide will pop up to support you, offering guidance to help you advertently place a bright red brick in those areas of your foundation that need work or repointing. Repointing is a term I learned from the little masonry pig. Over time, weathering and stress can cause voids in the joints between foundation bricks, allowing undesirable entrance of all kinds of stuff. This stuff can and will eventually effect your wellbeing. In repointing, these joints are cleaned and cleared and fresh mortar is added, bringing a bright new luster, integrity, and solidity to your foundation. Which is exactly what your root totem animal is going to help you achieve.

Let's Get Physical

Let's now take a look at that lawn ornament—you know, the fat lady bending over, assuming the gardening position—for the location of the root chakra. For starters, the caboose, which is what I call our rear end, plays an important role on a train's journey. Did you know that the caboose was designed for the shelter, safety, and basic survival needs of the train crew? It had a bed, woodstove, an amazing, ever-changing countryside view—all the comforts of home for those long journeys down the tracks. While your root chakra isn't shaped like a caboose, it is located at the end of your train, so to speak, and it does vibrate to your basic survival needs. However, don't forget that the caboose is a follower and is essentially fashioned to support the needs of the engine, which, in a sense, is the leader. As we travel up the tracks to each chakra, your root totem animal will assist you in transforming your little following caboose into a commanding engine leader.

As we physiologically travel our chakras, you will find that each one of the seven major chakras is essentially associated with a gland of the endocrine system and its related organs. For those not familiar with the endocrine system, it is an information-signaling network somewhat like our nervous system, although it functions quite differently. I won't bore you with the long laundry list of hormones produced by the endocrine system, but I will tell you that their names begin with *testo-*, *cort-*, and *andro-*, and end with *-rone*, *-tonin*, and *-roid*. To get a feel for what I'm talking about, take any prefix and suffix, add your favorite draft beer, and you will have a created a hormone. Try it—*testobudlightrone*. See!

Anyway, the root chakra is associated with the adrenal glands. Our adrenal glands allow us to have superhuman strength in the event of a perceived emergency that threatens our survival, like your mother in-law driving over your golf clubs in the driveway or the gorilla that suddenly scales its zoo enclosure after you have been annoying it for awhile. This is called the fight-or-flight reaction, which produces a biological stress hormone response. This hormonal response can sometimes be overly exaggerated, a false alarm, or right on target, so get the H-E-double hockey sticks out of Dodge. The adrenals are also responsible for our metabolism, which includes regulating water and salt levels in our bodies.

So, what's all this have to do with the root chakra anyway? Well, if you remember anything about the root chakra, it is fundamentally a warehouse of all your survival instincts, patterning, and conditioning. Your adrenal glands, in conjunction with your root chakra conditioning, can stir up some pretty interesting fight-or-flight responses, especially on a subconscious level, where energy is constantly and invisibly at work. The good news is that your root totem animal is not only going to wake you up to this conjugal quagmire between your adrenals and root chakra, but it's also going to help you set some new boundaries around that armory you have constructed because of those influences. However, this will require that you, with the help of your root totem animal guide, dismantle every fear rocket they can launch at you. Fear causes that fight-or-flight substance to hang around and pretty much block up your root chakra. Once you become adept at recognizing where the fear is coming from, you and your animal totem guide will find great sport in taking on these fear factors. Before you know it, you and your root totem animal will be dancing to Gloria Gaynor's famous disco song "I Will Survive." You know, "At first I was afraid, I was petrified…kept thinking I could never live without you…la de da…"

Okay, before you and your animal totem start getting physical on the dance floor, it's important that you clear that dance floor. This means removing any stagnant debris squatting in your root chakra so you won't stumble while performing your ball-change, do-si-do, grapevine, or whatever moves you perform on the dance floor. In your way-cool car ride around your foundation, you got a glimpse of some deficient and excessive areas in your root chakra that can be responsible for triggering both unapparent and/or obvious fears in those four survival sections of your steering wheel. These fears can be those little things that jump out while you're driving on your road of life, causing you to put on the brakes, swerve, or just plain slam into something. To get a better perspective of what this means, let's go back to the elements. As I mentioned earlier, the element for the root chakra is earth. In order for you to cultivate a plant from a seed to the harvest stage of flower, herb, or veggie, the earth or soil you use must have the right nutrients, drainage, and texture, the proper conditions. It's similar to when you're driving; you don't want to be hitting potholes or swerving to avoid huge puddles or boulders. You want your road to be nice and smooth and easily accessible to drive-thru nutrients. Determining the state of your earth will require some tillage. Tillage is the agricultural preparation of the soil performed by very big and powerful machines with lots of masculine energy behind every turn of the wheel. They clear out the rocks, weeds, and extraneous stuff so the soil is fit for the growing season.

If you were taking my class, this is where I would hand you a small plastic bag of soil I borrowed from my neighbor's yard (wink) and an envelope with a few seeds and ask you to find your own potting vessel. I'd send you on your way to till the soil, plant, and grow your little seed and return to the next class with a report of how it is going. Student results range from cell phone photos of little green, growing vegetation to sob stories of how the seeds must have been duds, the student didn't water, the student overwatered, the student totally forgot about it, blah, blah, blah. Some students can be so melodramatic. Anyway, the long and short of this exercise, whether you perform it or not, is that no matter how you approach the task, in order to grow your little seed to its best budding potential you need all the elements—your earth, water, air, fire, and ether—in the proper proportions. The animal totem guide that comes to you will offer the assistance and support you need to make your own earth—your root chakra—the most fertile soil money can buy. It will also show you the right amounts of each element to grow your most bountiful harvest.

I encourage you to buy a pack of seeds—flower, herb, vegetable, whatever appeals you. Grab some dirt from your yard, local park, or even your neighbor; it takes less than a cup of earth to grow a few seeds. Till it, clear out all the twigs and pebble debris, and plant a few of your seeds. Nurture them for the four weeks you are uncovering your root totem and write down your results in your journal. You will be very surprised how the results mimic the current state of your root chakra—metaphorically, of course.

Honoring Your Roots

By performing the two exercises above, you allow yourself to observe and honor the current state of your root chakra. Yes, even growing a little seed is a way to honor your root chakra, as it nurtures the seeds of divinity that rest within you. While for some of you such a practice might seem a little vague, childish, and impractical, you will find as we move forward through each of the chakra centers that these exercises will all have great meaning and align with what your totem animal guides will be teaching you. Just as the foundation supports the structure of every abode, the root system supports the growth, development, and continued existence of the plant's structure. Your base or root chakra is essential to fortifying your wellbeing with life force energy, and you want it to be as balanced and clear-flowing as possible. Let yourself really take a look at how your roots function to your highest and best potential and support your buds as they flower. But also take note of those twigs, pebbles, and materials in your earth that will need some elemental adjustments. In the days to come, your animal totem guide will appear. This animal will show you some of the most delightful ways to heal, clear, and balance the most stubborn boulders in your terrain. You can honor your root chakra by connecting to the earth in a number of ways. Allow yourself to experience the world of nature around you.

Ways to Honor Your Root

Go on a hike
Go horseback riding
Have a picnic at the zoo
Walk or sit on the beach
Work in the yard or garden
Sit on a park bench and watch nature
Visit an arboretum or botanical garden

The Root Chakra Totem

So now you have learned a bit about your root chakra and have a better picture of how the bricks have been laid in your foundation. Additionally, you understand that the condition of your earth is instrumental in achieving your greatest potential, which, by the way, is the first step in embracing your true nature through nature. With that said, you may have better insights of the help your root animal totem guide will provide for you. Keep in mind that it is not unusual for your foot chakra animal totem guide to help forge the connection with your root chakra totem. Remember, your foot totem animal guide will lead you to opportunities and help anchor you to scenarios that will connect you to the universal forces of the Divine. When your foot totem animal guide appears, be open to the prospect of opportunities it may bring. Consider it your catalyst to connect to the subtle energies at play around you. Many of my students convey that just before their root animal appeared, they had witnessed their foot totem. It was almost as if the foot totem was pointing the root totem out to them. Others complain that they just keep seeing their foot totem and nothing else. Any appearance of an animal totem is Divine guidance at play, and it is up to you to take note, pay attention, and muse on its message.

Your root totem animal guide will assist you with your basic survival needs and will teach you how to proceed forward in your ventures in life without fear. When you traveled around your foundation in the earlier exercise, you made some observations of your home, work, physical body, and views on abundance and perhaps discovered things you might not have been aware of. Your root totem animal guide will help you stay true to regarding these areas more pragmatically. Your animal guide will work on both your interior and exterior worlds. The groundwork that goes into your landscape outside is integral to what happens inside your world, and vice versa. It is important to notice as many characteristics as possible about the creature that comes, no matter what that creature may be. This creature holds the keys to the elements you need in both your inner and outer worlds. Notice what element best describes this animal.

Does it hold a strong earth connection, with four feet, to help you get more grounded to earth? Is there a water connection to help you connect with emotions? Does it fly, suggesting an air connection needed for a lighter journey? Is its nature fiery or gentle? The survival aspects of your animal totem guide in its natural world will be noteworthy and a valuable tool if you embrace them physically and energetically. The very essence of this animal will demonstrate the exact proportions of the elements you need as part of the survival aspects or roots of your life. For instance, if you have a very grounded animal, like a deer or a lion, its teachings will suggest connection to the earth and an ability to stay grounded. However, the natures of these two animals conflict, as one is aggressive, the other gentle; one can be considered prey, the other predator. To a shy or apprehensive person, the lion might present itself, as its attributes of courage and fearlessness would be quite valuable to that person. To a person with an overly assertive or pushy temperament, the deer might present itself, as its medicine of gentleness would help balance forceful tendencies.

My root totem animal is a squirrel, and its guidance has helped me harness, heal, and address some of my deepest survival needs and issues. When it first presented itself, it seemed to me to be a little ordinary and too common to be a messenger of extraordinary guidance. However, as my bird pal Mike, owner of the Bird Watchers General Store, once said, "There is no way you can overestimate the cleverness of an Eastern gray squirrel. They can do it all—climb, jump, swim"— bet you didn't know that—"dig, chew, and according to some, spit acid and breathe fire"—you probably knew that. "They have the jumping skills of a kangaroo, the grabbing ability of a spider monkey, and the brain of a chess champion. And it all comes in a twenty-four-ounce package." My root totem's assistance continues to astound and humble me more intensely each day as I continue to evolve in my own levels of consciousness. Never underestimate the power of any creature that comes to you. These guides are what are called *Kalyana Mitra*, Sanskrit for friend of virtue, well-wishing friend, and good counselor. As we travel through life, we encounter and connect with all types of friends that support and guide us. The same will be true of your totem animals, though their connection will be more profoundly apparent and they certain will not carry the drama of any of the multipurpose task team members.

Whatever animal comes to you, take a hard look at its teachings. See how it will help you in the areas of survival in your home, work, physical body, and even your views on abundance. Your first chakra represents your strongest connection to earth and therefore with nature. Don't underestimate the power of the earth.

Now let's touch a little on the fear factor. As I mentioned above about the fight-or-flight reaction, we can sometimes overly exaggerate, fuel a false alarm, or be very much right on target. The same is true about our fears in life; they too can be overly exaggerated, a false alarm, or very much right on target, but they are all based on your perceptions. Your root totem animal guide will help you to see this, bring these perceptions into focus, and assist you in prevailing over them, instead of their prevailing over you. The root chakra is the place to look at and change any of those stamped patterns or imprinted influences that are not a part of who you are from a Divine perspective. By writing these observations down in your journal, you will help remove them from a personal energetic ownership state within your being and allow them to more easily transmute into energetic forms for new approaches.

Meditation

This is the part were you go inward again. Just as you applied the guided meditation to call forth the frequencies needed for your first encounter with your foot totem, you will again take the same route. Carry out the meditation three days in a row. If you haven't become accustomed to a daily practice of meditation, perhaps you might want to use your root totem chakra as an opportunity to build on that practice and begin incorporating some new imprints. Your most basic conditioning has settled into the first chakra; whether you think those imprints are good, bad, or indifferent, you always have an opportunity to change them. As you begin to condition yourself with new imprints, it is just as important that you unlearn and release old ones. I will repeat that meditation is a gift to your mind, body, and spirit and will always have great benefits, even if you don't think it is working. Trust it. It wasn't until I started my daily practice of at least twenty minutes a day that I truly began to see the benefits.

Over the next few days, allow yourself to be more attuned to those sections of your survival steering wheel that you put a cross through as you traveled around your foundation. Those are the areas that need to be brought into balance. Your attunement will also invoke the frequencies connecting you to the root chakra animal totem that will help you with those areas. Connect to nature and the outdoors as much as you can. Remember, nature vibrates to unconditional love and is a true connection to spirit. Exposing yourself to these frequencies and energies will always be helpful in raising your personal vibration. In the next thirty days, you will discover an animal that will help you clear, balance, and connect to your root chakra on a deeper level. This animal will be your teacher, guide, and kindred companion and will be instrumental in connecting you to source, spirit, the universe, or whatever you want to call the Divine forces of guidance that will all be helping you with your root center.

Below is a list of accessories that can be used to both help and enhance your expedition with your root totem.

The Root Chakra Totem

ROOT CHAKRA TOTEM ACCESSORIES	
CANDLES	Using candles to stimulate the root chakra can be a wonderful way to invoke a deeper connection with your animal totem and create a relaxing ambience wherever you are holding space. Select candles with red or dark red, earthy tones. Any of the scents used with the foot chakra can also be used in conjunction with the suggested root chakra scents of cinnamon, sage, patchouli, cedarwood, and myrrh. However, any scent that you feel grounds and centers you is just as appropriate. Some people prefer flower or fruit scents. Choose your own adventure; it is your journey. There are no right or wrong scents, so don't be afraid to try something new. Remember, fire is your passion element.
INCENSE	Use incense for clearing any space and calling upon your root animal totem. Incense adds a wonderful tone to the opening and closing rituals for your root chakra totem. Scents such as cinnamon, sage, patchouli, cedarwood, and myrrh add a nice touch to your meditation or relaxation sessions. Incense can help connect you to the element of air when you follow its wispy trail of smoke. It can also soften the fire element with its glowing ember. The aroma and smoke trail can help to both invoke and align you with your root totem. Allow yourself to experiment with different incense scents that appeal to you, especially on a whim.
CRYSTALS	Use crystals for their color and energy qualities. There is literally a crystal for every emotion, body part, or circumstance. Many crystals can benefit the root chakra. Red jasper is considered a grounding stone and is sometimes referred to as the "supreme nurturer," as its properties have both calming and protective energies. Obsidian is a very powerful stone, bringing out honesty, sincerity, and truth, as its reflective surface reveals its special ability to act as a mirror, helping you see your own shadows honestly, alter your behavior, change harmful patterns, or overcome obsessions. The gemstones ruby and garnet not only possess the brilliant red tones of the root chakra, their healing energies help regenerate the body and blood. Garnet fortifies, activates, and strengthens the survival instincts. Ruby encourages a passion for life, but not in a self-destructive way. Again, smoky quartz is a both a grounding and protective stone with a strong connection to earth and the base chakra. Crystals help connect you to the earth element and can very easily be carried on your person, especially when incorporated into jewelry.

(Continued)

	ROOT CHAKRA TOTEM ACCESSORIES (Continued)
AROMA-THERAPY	Essential oils can be used for healing, relaxing, invoking, clearing—you name it. They are a perfect way to enhance your home spa while utilizing the water element. Their therapeutic properties can boost diffusers, vaporizers, humidifiers, bathtubs, and fountains to create a botanical utopia in all your environments. Remember that essential oils are very highly concentrated, volatile, aromatic essences of plants. I suggest buying them from well-known vendors or all-natural stores, as experienced personnel can guide you in their proper use. The following essential oils support the root chakra and help you connect your physical body to the Earth: frankincense, clary sage, geranium, rose, patchouli, and ylang-ylang. Some vendors also offer combinations of two or more oils in one vial specifically formulated for the root chakra. Many places also offer reference charts for the product line they sell. Don't be afraid to ask!

Connecting with Your Root Totem

You will engage in all the same techniques you used to connect with your foot totem. Keep in mind that when an animal first appears, whether it's real or symbolic, thank it. Talk to it. Don't be afraid to ask it questions. This animal can be a messenger for your totem or your actual totem. This is why it is imperative that you not dismiss any animal, especially if it is unappealing to you. The way the animals come to you will have great significance, and you should take note of how it unfolds. It is essential that you try to determine your thought process and environment when the animal appears. Is the mood upbeat, stressful, peaceful? These are all important aspects of the awakening of your intuitive gifts, and as you travel through this journey, you want to continue building your awareness muscles. As your animal begins to make repeated visits, it will become undeniable that it is your totem. Challenge any skepticism with an inquisitive wonder. This will allow you to align with the affirmations and confirmation; they will be humorous and sometimes so astounding they will knock your limited thinking right out of the water.

As with your foot totem animal, once you have determined your root chakra animal, begin to learn as much as you can about it. What element best describes it? Look for hybrid elements, like water and air, fire and earth. These are the elements that will be apparent in growing your seed and will also likely be those needed in the survival sections of your wheel in the foundation exercise you performed. The more you observe the characteristics of your animal, the more attuned you will become to understanding its medicine for you. Is it big or small? Slow or fast? Does it like cold weather or warm? What does it eat? Where does it sleep? How does it communicate? These questions all hold significance in how this animal will assist you in life and also in correcting the unknown blocks and imbalances in your root chakra. Remember, your totem animal will play a key role in helping you bring to light your shadows and those parts of yourself you can't or don't want to see but others do. Your totem animal will compassionately and gracefully help you to see them. As you work at dismantling the shadow aspects you enable the road to your passions and desires to become a more trouble-free path.

Your root totem animal will also bring to light your fears and actually help you determine whether they are live or Memorex. Look at how your animal responds when it is in a fear state. Is this animal common prey, or is it more commonly known as a predator? Again, look at the traditions, myths, cultures, religions, and folklore about your totem. In fairy tales, even the meekest animals can possess great wisdom and power. Enjoy investigating all possible aspects of what your totem animals can offer you.

Welcoming Your Totem Animal

Now that you have unveiled your root totem animal and spent the month kindling a friendship by learning the traits and qualities of your new companion, it's time to honor that connection by welcoming this powerful animal into your being. Take note of those appearances and encounters you've experienced throughout the month. If you have been recording your interactions and observations, reading through the sequences of events is a wonderful way to honor the connection between you and your totem animal. Any roles that your foot totem animal played during the month should also be honored and recorded. This will help you expand your energetic frequencies and more easily attune to the way your animals all work together, which will be key once you have uncovered your entire personal animal totem. Chapter 16 contains more information on this.

I will continue to emphasize the importance of being mindful about energy. Whether you are taking on energy or removing it, it is important to not only be aware of it but also be well-versed in taking it apart and putting it together, otherwise known as bringing it on and letting go. The opening and closing rituals allow you to set the intentions that move you from one energy to another, giving you the opportunity to practice with only the purest, highest, and best energies. The more fluent you become with these energies, the easier it will be to recognize the lower-vibrating frequencies and stop them before they filter through.

Below is a prayer I use to welcome the root totem animal. Remember that the prayer to welcome your animal totem is more than just a welcoming token. It is a ritual to bring closure to the root chakra journey, honor the gift of the experience, and consciously allow the root chakra animal into your being. This ceremony also opens the door to the next chakra's journey, the sacral chakra. Moreover, the ritual helps you connect to the Divine forces of the universe that are infinitely available to you every moment.

ROOT TOTEM ANIMAL PRAYER

I now reflect on the journey with my root totem animal. I recall the moment its essence first arrived. I honor that this animal has unveiled itself to me in so many wonderful and powerful ways. My root totem animal will connect me to the true essence for my abundant survival and make me aware of my connection to the Divine forces that guide and support me with all my survival needs. When I am fearful, I only need notice that I am, and its guidance will lead me to the opportunities that align me to the highest and best potential for my soul's voyage in this life. My root totem animal will guide me, assist me, and help me to be aware, understand, and know that Divine guidance is ever-present in my journey at every moment, and I have nothing to fear. I trust in this Divine guidance and give it permission to help, assist, lead, and support me on my journey. I now welcome my root totem animal to be a part of my walk in life.

AMEN.

CHAPTER 10

THE SACRAL CHAKRA TOTEM

What's Up with This Chapter

∞ Uncovering Your Sacral Chakra Totem Animal
∞ What Is a Sacral Chakra?
∞ Let's Get Physical
∞ Honoring Your Sacral
∞ The Sacral Chakra Totem
∞ Connecting with Your Sacral Totem
∞ Welcoming Your Sacral Totem Animal

Uncovering Your Sacral Chakra Totem

So, look at you here at the threshold of the sacral chakra! Well done! You have survived the trek through the root chakra and come out on the other side with an additional guide and hopefully a new attitude about your survival techniques, which you will continue to refine throughout your journey. Don't worry if you feel like you still have some work to do in that area; your root chakra animal totem will help you figure out all that stuff. If you were taking my class, the sacral chakra is where I would start harping about the ground rules. Mostly because the students have spent a few months in the trenches being exposed to subtle energies and have shared all kinds of animal encounters and experiences, yet they're still feeling a little awkward and uncertain. This, in part, is because they have arrived at the feeling center. You too may be more receptive to your emotions and feeling a little more sensitive. But let's really state the obvious here. For the last two months, you have been working out in the playground of subtle energies, learning to flex your awareness muscles and beckoning the vibrational forces to come hither with your attention and intention. What'd you expect? So with all this playing, flexing, and bringing it on you're doing in the energetic realm, it's important that you review the ground rules again, as they will help you assess those energies you're taking on. As you continue to open up to the energetic realms, you expose yourself to all energies—positive and negative. The sacral chakra is the feeling center, and it is where you become adept at filtering the high-quality energies from the lower-resonating ones, which, for better or worse, are all part of what I like to call our creation and relations in life. These are the energies I refer to as the pain and pleasure vibrations, and they can have a powerful effect on whether you feel all pumped up or all washed out.

Last month when you were hanging out at your root chakra, you spent some time on a conscious level reviewing the four sections of your survival. The symbol for the root chakra is a four-petaled lotus. The flower's four petals represent those four sections of your survival, and much like the four tires on that way-cool car you drove while you observed your foundation, when one is flat or out of balance, it will affect your ride. Or the four legs of a table; if one is wobbly or unsteady, it's going to impact the stability of the objects on the tabletop. Consider your sacral chakra as energetically connected to all the objects you would put on that table. Another analogy for the sacral is that the root chakra is the foundation of your house and the sacral is the house and everything in it. And I mean everything—all your survival needs, all the physical material furnishings, the big enchilada, the whole kit and caboodle, warts and all, be it pleasures or pains.

The animal totem for your sacral chakra will help you understand just how those pleasures and pains play a big part in your intuitive guidance. This is the chakra where you learn to become much less riddled with drama, chaos, and some of the negativities associated with everyday life. This is where you begin to become conscious of those patterns and move to change what appear to be everyday curses into everyday blessings. Your sacral totem animal will help you become aware of how you feel about all that energy, and it will support you as you change that which is not serving you.

What Is a Sacral Chakra?

The sacral chakra is the second in the chakra system. It is associated with your emotions and how you create and relate in life. This is one of the reasons I call it the feeling center. It encompasses both your emotions and your sensuality. The symbol for the sacral chakra is a six-petaled lotus. Imagine that each petal represents one of your senses—hearing, seeing, smelling, touching, and tasting—and the sixth represents your sixth sense, our energetic perception that works in conjunction with our five senses. The sixth sense is our keen intuition. To help you get a feel for how your intuition and feelings work, let's go back to the root chakra and visit with your multipurpose task team members for a moment. As you recall, your multipurpose task team essentially influenced the imprints and conditioning of your survival for the first seven years of your life. The team's members cared for your needs based on their perceptions and needs. Your five senses of hearing, seeing, smelling, touching, and tasting were at peak performance back then, and you could easily distinguish your likes—those good vibrations—and your dislikes—the negative vibes—with proficient perception. All your senses were fully calibrated, and everything was sensing absolutely perfectly. Over the first seven years of your life, your multipurpose task team inadvertently—there's that word again—began to refine your senses based on, again, their perceptions and needs, which essentially trumped all yours. They sort of numbed your seeing, hearing, smelling, touching, and tasting to their liking, which some people find very sad until they learn the true value of those experiences. Then they become happy for it all.

Anyway, the sacral chakra starts its seven-year blossom between the ages of eight and fourteen. During this time, our world really begins to expand from the root dynamic of family and close caretakers to a more expanded collective dynamic of relationships. Corporate America would call them consultants. This is when we begin to spend more time outside our familiar circle and move to a wider, more diverse audience, be it school, the neighborhood, cultural and social events, or whatever our multipurpose task team deemed appropriate or inappropriate activity outside the confines of the house. This essentially assembled your belief and value systems and/or your feelings and emotions about them. I call it your BS, better known as an acronym for something else, but what I define as your belief system.

Years ago the comedian Kevin Meaney did a great skit on the things his parents said to him when he was growing up. "Hey, mister, where do you think you're going with those tight pants? We're a big pants family; you're not going outside with those tight pants! Who do you think you are going out with in tight pants? You get back up there and put your big pants on. Going out with tight pants. That's not right! We're a big pants family!" Our parents' mantras will always ring in our head. Their belief and value systems affect how you interpret what you see, hear, and feel, and can also inhibit what you desire. In the beginning you might think your belief and value systems are independently yours; however, the moment you prance down the stairs with your tight pants on, so to speak, you will find your beliefs have been crafted by your multipurpose task team. When you come upon a situation that challenges your belief and value systems or something you specifically desire conflicts with your beliefs, you are essentially handed the slippery fish of choosing to abandon your tight-pants style for the multipurpose task team's fashion. If you choose to ditch the team design, you enter the muddy waters of inner turmoil that results in either guilt or resentment, as the multipurpose task team's responsibility is to get you to conform to their belief system, which I will again refer to as BS.

In other words, the shadow side of the sacral chakra is that it is a warehouse of your emotions and sedated senses. It's the place where your wounded inner child wrangles as it seeks some kind of deprived pleasure related to your feelings and emotions based on your belief and value system. Until each of us can independently figure that out, it can sometimes have a haunting effect on our relationships and creative endeavors. No worries, though. Your sacral animal totem guide will guide you as you reawaken each one of those senses back to its perfect state of being. More importantly, your totem animal will help you seek and embrace the pleasures in life instead of resisting or destroying them. In the world of animals, once a creature's survival needs are satisfied, it will naturally turn toward play, pleasure, and a little catnap.

Let's Get Physical

The sacral chakra is located in the lower abdomen, just below the navel. If you remember back in chapter 5, I used some popular female musical artists' navel piercings as an example of where the sacral chakra is located. There is a method to my madness. Those sexually appealing, amazingly talented performing artists have all been able to harness the creative feminine energy forces of the second chakra. In fact, we are all able to harness these wonderful energetic forces, and more, if we so desire. However, it does take devotion, dedication, and a willingness to assess your true feelings and desires. What a co-inky-dinky, you have arrived at the best place to make all that happen: the feeling center.

To understand the sacral chakra on a physiological level, let's take another look at the navel-piercing area of those performing-artist gals again. The sacral chakra relates to the whole area that gyrates during those amazingly supple, choreographed dance moves we see in concerts and videos. For those who don't know those moves, it's basically the abdomen, hips, lower back, and genitals, which I'll refer to as simply the reproductive area. To explain additional areas where the sacral chakra has influence, it's essential to go back to our cosmic elements of earth, water, fire, air, and ether.

The sacral chakra is associated with the element of water. Many modalities associate the element water to our emotions. If you were a good doobie-doobie and stayed hydrated by following ground rule number five and actually carried out the assignment of propagating a little seed in your earth in last month's exercise, you're already quite adept at working with the water element. Although sometimes when I do get a glimpse of my students' seedlings, it's obvious this element needs a little tweaking. I encourage you to really observe the condition of your plant, as it literally and figuratively will help you determine the nature of your own sacral chakra. Even though that may seem a wee bit odd, it will be right on target. While water does help things grow, over- and underwatering can have serious effects on your little buds, as well as on you. The second chakra relates to the water aspects of our body—the kidneys, bladder, and urinary tract. This chakra is also the fear epicenter, where the fear signal is activated by your feelings, consciously or unconsciously, in that fight-or-flight reaction. So, in a sense, you can add the adrenal glands to the list again.

The sacral chakra class is one of my favorites to teach. As I mentioned earlier, the students have spent a few months in the trenches being exposed to subtle energies, they've shared all kinds of animal encounters and experiences, and yet they still feel a little awkward and uncertain. This is because the sacral chakra is the threshold where you reawaken those sleepy, sedated senses. This is the center where you exercise those five senses so they might pop open, grow, and enhance your intuitive awareness. This whole process can feel a little awkward and uneasy at times. This is the center where you give yourself permission to seek, discover, and recover the lost sensual pleasures in life. One of the most basic support and guidance aspects of the animal totem guide that comes to you will be to assist you and remind you to experience pleasure and nurture your creative desires.

All my classes take place in a circle filled with Divine items to stimulate the energies of the particular chakra we're working on. When my students arrive to the sacral chakra class, they are immediately enthralled with all kinds of delicious epicurean delights that bring their attention to their five senses. I love to witness the eyes becoming more focused on the beautiful array of colorful flowers and scrumptious treats. Joyful music bounces with wonderful beats and rhythms to encourage dance. The students' taste buds tingle in anticipation of the mouth-watering flavors about to be sampled, and their noses seem to twitch at all the fantastic aromas of the bountiful display. It's a lot like watching a bunch of children waking up on Christmas morning. At first, the students seem reserved in their choices among red and white wine, truffles, and exotic fruits and vegetables—some familiar, some unusual, all offering some kind of heightened experience for the senses. Before the students can move toward the touch sense to nibble their delights, I challenge them to take the opportunity to confront the energetic patterns of resistance, denial, and guilt. It is a powerful way to become aware and actually listen to what that inner voice is saying about this opportunity for pleasure presented before them. I love to watch what I would call the type A personality actually surrender, taking a chance to break a pattern resisting sensual pleasure. I'll hear things like, "I think I will try that. Oh my God, this is so good!" Give yourself permission to enjoy the sweetness of life this month, and your totem will undoubtedly be present.

Uncovering Your Personal Animal Totem

Reawakening your senses compels you to become conscious of how you sometimes resist pleasures provided so abundantly by the universe. It should also provoke you to ask why you resist those pleasures. I will sometimes allow my senses the freedom to be open to new tastes when grocery shopping, so much so that my grocery basket will have nothing in it that's on the list. When I get home, I will invariably get that look from my spouse. I'll say, "Likes can turn into dislikes and dislikes turn into likes— allow yourself be open to that scenario." There are some folks who eat the same thing every day of their life and never question it or even think of trying something different. The sacral chakra is all about looking at everything in your life with the fresh, open curiosity of a child. This is where you discover that the ordinary things in life can be made extraordinary with just a little different perspective and a stimulated sense. When I was a kid, there was a saying used when your pals became bossy and tried to tell you what to do. It was "Quit acting so big!" When you set out to explore and excavate the lost pleasures in your sacral chakra, you are taking the steps to heal that wounded child within you, and you too will need to stop acting so big to let yourself go there, as this is where your true nature will emerge.

To really help you tap into and awaken your five senses, I suggest you perform this next exercise, called Testing Your Senses, for the entire month. Even if you already know what your sacral totem animal is, it will deepen your connection to it. In order for you to really tune into your intuitive guidance and the guidance your animal guide has for you, the key is to be aware. The best way to ensure you are aware is to be attentive to the subtle traces that each one of your five senses communicates to you. Each one of these senses will need a workout. Think of it as taking them to the gym or yoga class. You will need to do this on a regular basis in order for them to perform at peak performance. The best way to do this is to be mindful about what you expose your senses to, and more importantly, expose yourself to the things that bring you pleasure. Our fast-paced world has conditioned us to harbor the harsh aspects of life without consciously being aware of it. You see crap on TV, while driving your car or shopping, at home, and at work, and it can easily become part of your energetic field. This exercise will help you separate and select which energies you want to take onboard and which energies you want to block. It will help you be aware of the energies around you that are so comfortable jumping aboard your vessel. Regardless of whether they are positive or negative, you must learn to be aware of them.

The more you carry out this exercise, the more you align yourself with the forces of the universe that will continue to bring you pleasure energies. It's imperative that you write down only the things that bring pleasure and joy to your senses in this exercise. While you may think that writing down the things you don't like will bring clarity to your likes and dislikes, it won't put you in the vibration of joy and pleasure. In fact, it cancels it out. This exercise is to help you reawaken your senses, and there are several ways you can perform it. One is to just walk around your home and test each sense with something that brings you joy and pleasure. As you find more and more things within your home, expand it to other sections of your life, like work, friends, and entertainment. The more you perform this exercise, the more you stimulate your senses. I encourage you to record your pleasures and joyful experiences in your journal. Writing your pleasures down will allow the left and right sides of your brain to learn to play nicely.

Uncovering Your Personal Animal Totem

TESTING YOUR FIVE SENSES

Looks Good—Open your eyes to your environment. Record the things you see that bring you pleasure. Really look around and focus on the small things, as even these subtle things hold tremendously high vibrations.

_____

_____

_____

Sounds Good—Listen to sounds in your environment. Write down the sounds you hear that are pleasing to you. Make your own joyful sound, if necessary. Even the ticking of the clock can be a peaceful sound.

_____

_____

_____

Smells Good—What smells are engaging you in your environment? Write down those you like or invite some new smells into your environment. Flowers, candles, or just opening the window can provide a pleasing fragrance.

_____

_____

_____

Tastes Good—Try to really tap into the ingredients of the foods you are eating. Sometimes we miss subtleties because we don't care to notice. Try something new or treat yourself to something you like with a greater awareness of its good taste.

_____

_____

_____

Feels Good—Pay attention to what feels good in your environment. The fabric on your furniture, your clothes, your linens, soaking in a bubble bath. Write down things that you touched or felt that brought a sensation of pleasure to you. Animals are the tops for this one.

_____

_____

_____

Honoring Your Sacral

The sacral chakra is very powerful. It embodies the potent forces of our darkest shadows, as well as the most illuminating light within us. To conquer the hidden jewel of this chakra is to awaken our five senses and identify those dark shadows that separate us from the light that holds our highest potential. Use the seed-growing exercise as a clue about the current state of your sacral chakra. Too much water can flood your earth with too many emotions, too little will deprive or deny your earth of emotions that can connect you to life. Whether your emotions are excessive or deficient doesn't matter; it's a shadow that you will sooner or later need to bring into the light. Our wounded inner child holds on to the shadows that challenge our survival, as that is the place where we learned how to cope. All our hurts, heartaches, sadness, grief, regrets, resentment, and anger stem from this little inner brat; abandoned, wounded, or spoiled child; bully; or whatever you want to call that little one within you in need of self-nurturing. Honoring your sacral chakra and preparing it to welcome your animal totem guide will entail that you look at what pleasures you are depriving yourself of. What desires or passions have you neglected or avoided for whatever reason, known or unknown? Allow that little inner voice to express itself and harness the creative forces available to you. Any effort you make toward pursuing pleasure will promote healing and wholeness and allow your passions and desires to flow to a portal where you will find your true nature. So put on your fancy pants, honor your sacral, and go ahead, let your hair down.

Ways to Honor Your Sacral

Soak in a tub
Play a game with a child
Engage in some form of art
Follow that desire or passion

> Watch baby animals on YouTube
> Pamper yourself with a massage
> Indulge in some kind of sweetness
> Work your five senses with pleasure

The Sacral Chakra Totem

Your sacral animal totem doesn't have to be a water animal to connect you to the water element. No matter what animal comes to you, it will have a symbolic connection to your water that will help you harness that aspect. Your sacral totem will be an important link between your root chakra and your solar plexus chakra, as these three separate chakras perform like the strands in a braid, each equally zigzagging through and overlapping the others. You will learn more about this next month in the solar plexus section and more innately as you move up through all the chakras. One of the greatest gifts that your sacral chakra animal totem will hold will be to help you recognize and transmute guilt, resentment, sorrow, or whatever dark energies prevent you from welcoming pleasure and joy and embracing sustained harmony in your creations and relationships. This totem will help you discover a deeper understanding of your blocked senses and support you in connecting to the wounded child within who needs to be freed from emotions that can trigger negative sensations and reactions. When we are awakened to these energies and move toward looking at them, we will suddenly find ourselves on a mission to heal this part of us in need of nurturing. Moreover, engaging this part of ourselves helps us connect to our true intuitive nature. This is where you connect to that creative reproductive section of your being that flows like a river of Divine infinite knowledge, so fertile and nourishing, uncovering the most treasured desires and passions of your true nature.

Your root totem animal will be instrumental in assisting you with your fears about survival, while your sacral totem animal will assist you in transmuting guilt and resentment into untapped pleasure, joy, and delightful gratification. This is the place where you—much like the popular music artists—harness your creative forces. Your sacral totem animal will guide you to tap into these universal forces that are ready and waiting for you. These will be the wonderful experiences you will discover through your desires, feelings, sensual passions, and vitality. Your animal totem will be there to guide you, support you, and help you heal the aspects of your life that influence your resistance so you can recognize and transform them into new channels that bring joy and pleasure. This animal will hold the key to your setting healthy boundaries that will allow expansion of your self-nurturance and true nature.

The Sacral Chakra Totem

Meditation

As you go inward this month, take the opportunity to recognize those areas in your life where you seem to block joy and pleasure. We all unconsciously block pleasure to some extent. Read through some of the things you wrote in the Testing Your Five Senses exercise, and give yourself permission to expand the list. It's always easier to add to the list when you are in the pleasure zone. Setting intention and being consciously aware of the things that bring you pleasure will not just align you with those facets but will also bring them forth for you. The more you can make this a part of your practice, the more you clear your energetic field and open up to your psychic circuitry. Look for any role that your foot and/or root totem may play in your meditations and write it down in your journal. These visits will have a significant message that will assist you with your sacral chakra. Carry out your meditation three days in a row, as this really primes the energetic forces. Meditation is the means by which you not only connect and stay tuned to energetic forces of the Divine realms but also become receptive and perceptive to them. Use any of the sacral chakra totem accessories to enhance the levels of your meditations.

SACRAL CHAKRA TOTEM ACCESSORIES	
CANDLES	Using candles to stimulate the sacral chakra can be a wonderful way to invoke a connection with your animal totem and create a relaxing ambience for stimulating your sensual essence. Select any candles with bright orange or red-orange tones that are pleasing to the eyes. Really, any colors or scents that allow your senses to engage or your passion to soar will create a stimulating experience. When shopping for candles, allow yourself to experience all of their pleasing aspects: their shapes, number of wicks, colors, scents, even their names. Monikers like Mountain River, Ocean Breeze, Island Springs, and Morning Dew can invoke the water element. Remember, fire is a passion element and when mixed with the water element can create some steamy passions.
INCENSE	Use incense for clearing any space and calling upon your sacral animal totem. Incense adds a wonderful tone to the opening and closing rituals for your sacral chakra totem. Much like the candle-selection process, allow yourself to find pleasure in exploring different types of incense. Incense can help invoke those feelings of pleasure and add a nice touch to your meditation or relaxation sessions. Incense connects you to the element of air when you follow its wispy trail of smoke. Try following the delicate stream to catch a glimpse of your totem hidden in the smoke trail. Scents that can invoke the sacral chakra are patchouli, sandalwood, rose, jasmine, tangerine, and ylang-ylang.

(Continued)

SACRAL CHAKRA TOTEM ACCESSORIES (Continued)	
CRYSTALS	Use crystals for their color and energy qualities. There is literally a crystal for every emotion, body part, or circumstance. Several crystals can be beneficial to the sacral chakra. Carnelian is one of the most common crystals used for this chakra, as it is excellent at restoring vitality and motivation and great for stimulating creativity. Tiger's eye helps heal issues of self-worth, self-criticism, and blocked creativity and helps you tap into your talents and abilities. Tangerine quartz helps balance deficiencies in the sacral chakra and is especially useful for calming after a physical or energetic trauma. Opal is a very delicate stone with a very fine vibration. It can stimulate originality and dynamic creativity and is associated with love, passion, desire, and eroticism.
AROMA-THERAPY	Essential oils can be used for healing, relaxing, attuning, clearing—you name it. They are a perfect way to enhance your home spa while utilizing the water element. Their therapeutic properties can boost diffusers, vaporizers, humidifiers, bathtubs, and fountains to create a botanical utopia in all your environments. Remember that essential oils are very highly concentrated, volatile, aromatic essences of plants. I suggest buying them from well-known vendors or all-natural stores whose experienced personnel can guide you in their proper use. The following essential oils will support the sacral chakra: patchouli, gardenia, sandalwood, rose, jasmine, ylang-ylang, and champaca. Some vendors will also offer combinations of two or more oils in one vial specifically formulated for the sacral chakra. Many places also offer reference charts for the product line they sell. Ask for assistance; you may be pleasantly surprised by a gift from the universe.

Connecting with Your Sacral Totem

As I mentioned earlier, your sacral chakra totem doesn't necessarily have to be a water animal to connect you to the water element. While a camel is not a water animal, it is associated with the desert and environments that lack water. But camels hold powerful medicine in regard to water. A camel can convert water from the fat stored in its humps, and the oval shape of its blood cells allows blood to flow easily through its body when it is dehydrated. So the camel is an animal with very powerful energies connected to water. Symbolically, the camel would hold great medicine for those lacking the water element, especially those needing to find pleasure amidst the inhospitable environments that might have been part of their childhood. Your sacral totem animal's only connection to water may be that it simply needs to drink it to survive. How does your animal go about fulfilling its need for water? Symbolically, that will help you quench your thirst for pleasure in life. What mythical or metaphorical symbolism is associated with your animal? Many of my students discover that when their totem animal shows up, it has a great significance to their childhood, although they do not know it at the time. Sometimes it is a favorite kind of pet or cartoon character that they enjoyed as a child, especially during a time when there was a strong influence by a multitask team member. Your totems are amazingly wonderful at linking your past, present, and future with Divine guidance, weaving them all into a beautiful tapestry of your life.

My sacral animal totem is a gull, an infamous groupie of dumps and landfills with a definite water connection. While the gull is one of the most abundant and common seashore birds, I am always amazed at sightings of them in the most unusual places, especially for such a large bird with a four- to five-foot wingspan. Once while I was sitting in an outdoor theater not far from my home, feeling a little down about something that was going on in my life, I heard this incessant laughing that sounded much like someone's loudmouthed aunt after a few highballs. When I turned to see what the hey was going on, I noticed a laughing gull perched on one of the lampposts, clamoring at me, summoning me to snap out of it. It was such a realistic cackle that I found myself starting to crack up, laughing as my totem completely mocked me. It knocked me right out of my somber mood and back into the flow of spirit connection. This is an example of the many wonderful little graces your animal totems will grant you to get you back into the flow of spirit guidance, especially when you need to be reminded about joy and pleasure.

When my students are so enthusiastically sharing how their animals have appeared, I will start questioning them about the animals' characteristics. The how and where of the animal showing up will be so exhilarating that students can sometimes lose sight of what the animal holds for them in terms of the sacral chakra. Notice what teachings your animal communicates to you about your five senses. Your animal totems mission is to lead you from experiencing the yucky aspects of life to living the yummy side of life. As you continue to excavate your true nature, your relationships with your animal totems will become so much stronger and the teachings will be so intimately reflective of what is going on in your life. This animal is your guide to pleasure, wonder, joy, harmony, and all the powerful energetic forces that will guide you around and through the great chaos of drama, drama, drama. Your animal will direct you inward to your center of peace and remind you that, as Fergie, another amazingly creative artist, put it in the "My Humps" song, "You don't want no drama. No, no drama, no, no, no, no drama." Check it out!

Welcoming Your Sacral Totem Animal

So here you are at the end of another twenty-eight-day cycle of the moon with another new companion. Hopefully, you have spent the month reawakening those sleepy parts of your senses, are enjoying some wonderful new experiences, and are ready to embrace the new sensual opportunities that lie ahead. This is when you reminisce about the month's astonishing interactions and observations as you got to know your sacral chakra and met your new guide. Acknowledge any of the help your foot and root totems may have contributed in the process, for their guidance will be abundant and you will always want to offer gratitude for the chance to dance with them all.

This is the part of the ritual that honors and welcomes the company of your new guide. Now you can review your journal and bask in those sensual vibrations. But this is also a time to look at those not-so-great aspects and allow for the letting-go. Perhaps you recognized some age-old beliefs that really don't serve you anymore. Your journey with Divine guidance will always be there to rally your passions and desires and help remove anything that is not serving you. Below is a prayer that will welcome your sacral totem animal. Light a candle and allow the bright energetic orange of the sacral chakra to seep into your being as you welcome your sacral animal totem guide.

SACRAL TOTEM ANIMAL PRAYER

I now take the time to reflect on my journey this month with my sacral chakra totem animal. I honor how my sacral totem animal has unveiled itself to me in so many sensational ways. My sacral totem animal will connect me to the true essence of my awakening senses. This animal will help me to be aware of all the glorious gifts, bountiful abundance, and generous opportunities that await me through all kinds of wonderful sensual encounters. My sacral totem animal will guide me to be open to opportunities for pleasure and joy. It will help me to be aware of any belief system that limits, prevents, or interrupts my passions and desires. It will help me to be conscious, to embrace all creative energies with freedom and grace and without resistance or constraints. My sacral totem will lead me to the crystal springs that flow within me, where the nurturing and healing love of the Divine forces resides. I have faith in the Divine process, and I allow its guidance to help, lead, and support me on my journey. I now welcome my sacral totem animal into my being to assist me on my walk in life.

CHAPTER 11

THE SOLAR PLEXUS CHAKRA TOTEM

What's Up with This Chapter

∞ Uncovering Your Solar Plexus Chakra Totem Animal
∞ What Is a Solar Plexus Chakra?
∞ Let's Get Physical
∞ Honoring Your Solar Plexus
∞ The Solar Plexus Chakra Totem
∞ Connecting with Your Solar Plexus Totem
∞ Welcoming Your Solar Plexus Totem Animal

Uncovering Your Solar Plexus Chakra Totem

Congratulations! You've opened yourself up to another wonderful new level of guidance and have welcomed a new totem to assist you in this area. Well done! Hopefully you are still savoring some of those experiences of joy and pleasure. Maybe you have even started a bucket list and revived some of those old desires and passions you thought were long gone or out of reach. Watch for appearances of your sacral animal totem, for it will help guide you and keep you aware of those things. The next chakra you visit will be instrumental in helping you set your intentions for those desires and passions and actually carry them out. The solar plexus is where you harness the power that governs your will to put action into those choices, to make it all happen. Your personal power and will are where you exercise your freedom of choice. This is all based on your self-esteem and the strength of your personal power. Learning how to catalyze the power of this center to work for you is to understand the intrinsic forces at play between your intellect and your spirit, which is where you really begin to unfold the true nature of you.

The solar plexus is a powerful center where your ruling ego tries to outshine and overshadow your magnificent spirit. Last month you hopefully got some nice snapshots of things pleasing to your spirit, which were identified and experienced through your sensual faculties. However, allowing yourself to sustain the things pleasing to your spirit requires a bit of tug-of-war between your ego and spirit. But here's the funny part: your spirit doesn't like to play tug-of-war. So your spirit ties its end of the rope to your heart, so your ego is essentially just pulling on your heartstrings. The ego's end of the rope is anchored to the intellect or the monkey mind or whatever you call that inner resisting, bullying, can't-do-it, have-to-do-it, you-know-what that is always telling you what to do or not do. This is the playing field where you will learn by following your spirit's guidance that you can gracefully outmaneuver the ego's tendency to rain dooky on your grand parade of desires.

The animal totem for your solar plexus chakra will assist you in understanding and recognizing the voice of your ego that stomps on the inner voice of your spirit. The solar plexus is where you learn to identify the unbridled forces of the ego and harness them to your intentions so your desires and passions—which are connected to your true nature—can come to fruition through the inner voice of your spirit. Your solar plexus animal will assist you in determining what type of actions are needed to catalyze your personal power. Once you become conscious of the shenanigans your ego and intellect play on your personal power, an interesting concoction will emerge. This new awareness will permit your spirit to merge into your physical vibration. When you choose to partner with your spirit, the guidance, support, and help you need to connect to your desires and passions will become amazingly apparent. The solar plexus chakra is your minilaboratory, where you experiment with the frequencies of your unconscious patterns and purify them into energies that strengthen your personal power. Then you can take the appropriate actions to meet your passions and desires, no matter how big or small they may be. The solar plexus is metaphorically the point where the rubber meets the road. Your solar plexus animal totem guide will offer great guidance for staying true to that road.

What Is a Solar Plexus Chakra?

The solar plexus chakra is the third chakra in the chakra system. It is associated with your intellect, self-esteem, strength of will, and the role you play with responsibility. The symbol for the solar plexus chakra is a ten-petaled lotus flower. Some spiritual practices link each of the ten petals to our spiritual ignorance and the ten ego states we must overcome to jump over the river from our persistent unconscious interest in the physical realm to the awakened compassionate heart that is a conscious cocreator with the higher spiritual realms of the universe.

The Solar Plexus Chakra Totem

The solar plexus starts its seven-year blossom between the ages of fifteen and twenty-one. As you recall, your multipurpose task team essentially influenced your survival imprints for the first seven years and your belief and value systems in the next seven years. When your solar plexus lotus flower began its blossom, you literally took over the controls, allowing you to express your own mojo. Keep in mind that your own mojo during these ages had everything to do with testing the parameters of your multipurpose task team. This is also tied to what I call the know-it-all attitude that manifests in almost all teenagers and can permit them to sidestep and dodge responsibilities. In this phase we expanded ourselves with our own personal rites of passage—our educational drive, learning to drive, awakening to our sex, and all the hip and cool things that were so vital to the social circle that drove our mojo. This is where we had the gall to descend the stairs in our tight pants. The solar plexus is where you exercise your power and control, much of which is based on your first and second chakra imprints, with your own little personal twist of course.

The solar plexus is an amazingly powerful energy center. When its energies are channeled with sincere fortitude, the courage and strength that emerges from this center can move mountains. When the power of this center is blocked by unreleased manipulations of power and control coming from codependency, aggressiveness, or the vain and narcissistic focus of the ego at the expense of others, only harmful results lay in its wake. I call the areas of the solar plexus where these shadow sides lie fault lines. If you are not familiar with fault lines, they are giant gashes on Mother Earth related to fractures below her surface. These fault lines are a constant reminder to us of her incredible power, especially when an earthquake strikes. In fact, you can't have an earthquake without fault lines. Earthquakes are caused by friction, stress, and gravity pushing on these fractures, and when these forces of energy intensify and erupt, great devastation and catastrophe results. We all possess these fault lines, which have the potential to rock our own private Idaho. Just as seismologists monitor the seismic waves of Mother Earth, we too need to monitor our own personal energy vibrations. Last month, while you were in the playground of pleasure and joy, you were actually preparing your senses to be vigilant in monitoring these seismic waves in your being. With every effort you put into experiencing pleasure and joy, you were essentially grooming your senses to be more attuned and sensitive to good vibrational frequencies. This in turn produces a sensitivity to the intrusions of lower dissonant frequencies that have the potential to quake your world.

The energies of the solar plexus allow you to either take action or execute a reaction to those lower dissonant vibrations. To take action is to quickly detach and bring yourself back to a peaceful place that allows you to carry on with your desire. If you choose the reaction route, just know that life's tough and get yourself a helmet. If you find you are frequently visiting the reactive mode, you might want to go back to chapter 4, Care And Maintenance of Your Wheels, where I gave you my spiel on preventative maintenance over corrective maintenance, saving a lot of wear and tear on your vehicle. You might also revisit chapter 9, What Is a Root Chakra?, where you, just like corporate America, can initiate a preventative action, which is really a corrective action based on your root-cause analysis of your little event that ensures it never, ever happens again. This is one of the great things about your solar plexus animal totem guide; it will head you off at the pass, letting you know there is an opportunity to flex your action muscles instead of the brute force reaction ones. When you heed this guidance, you will find that it's always better to prance off with a feather in your cap from having conquered another unconscious pattern than to be licking your wounds with a bee in your bonnet over the same old flare-ups.

Let's Get Physical

The solar plexus chakra is located just above the navel in the upper part of the abdomen. This is where your lumbar and thoracic vertebrae meet, your backbone, so to speak. From this jam-packed cavity of the body radiates a tremendous network of nerves, veins, arteries, organs, muscles, and it quite possibly may be the place where lost socks end up. The solar plexus works much like an engine and pulls your caboose. In fact, you could probably call it a steam engine. Steam engines are fueled by burning combustible materials—coal, wood, oil, or remnants of your ex-partner's possessions, but you didn't hear that from me—to produce steam, which drives the engine. As long as you have water and some kind of fuel, your engine can travel anywhere, and you have total control over its power.

To understand the solar plexus on a physiological level, let's go back to the elements of earth, water, fire, air, and ether. The solar plexus is associated with the element of fire, and, of course, your cavity jam-packed with all kinds of biological stuff is responsible for making that fire. This is mostly because the solar plexus, on an energetic level, is associated with the stomach, gall bladder, liver, pancreas, kidneys, spleen, the nervous system, and pretty much everything in that cavity is linked to fire energy. Each one of these organic sites is fashioned to combust some type of biological material into fuel to allow you to gyrate whatever part of your body you choose as your choreograph dance gig of life.

As you can see, there's a lot of fire going on inside you, and if you mix it with a little bit of knowledge it can be a dangerous thing. A little knowledge and some fire have the potential to pack a lot of punch. This is why the teenage years can be so exhaustively taxing to parents. Learning to manage your fire will be one of your most challenging aspects in life. Here is how the whole fire thing works. Too much fire, even if it's with good intentions, can turn people away; with bad intentions, it's even more disastrous. Too little fire and nothing gets done, and some folks might find you physically, emotionally, and even intellectually cold. Let's take these elements one step further. It's only fair to warn you of a nerd factor here, so do whatever you need to deal with nerd talk—have a shot of tequila, download a new app, eat a donut, look bored while tapping your finger—or be a good doobie-doobie and use this as an opportunity to meditate or even practice your mantra: "Chakras are the conduit through which Divine energy passes through me."

If we use the metaphor of your little plant again, you know that over- and underwatering can seriously affect its growth. Too much or too little sun, a symbol of fire, can also have the same serious results. Likewise, as you add another element to your growing experience, it can quickly affect the whole growing process and each one of your elements will need to be adjusted. For instance, if you have lots of sun, you will need lots of water, and your earth will need to be able to retain lots of water to keep things flourishing. So all your elements— earth, water, and fire—will need to be fine-tuned and balanced to harvest your desired blossoms. The same is true as you move up the chakra system. Each one of your chakra elements will influence your ability to stay in the flow of what you are trying to achieve. It's important to point out that as you move up the chakra system, not only do you add another element to help your true nature grow, but the rate at which each chakra affects the flow also increases. This is because the spinning vortex flow of the solar plexus chakra is faster than the sacral, and the sacral spins faster than the root chakra. This is why getting grounded works so successfully. It allows you to consciously take all the energy from those noisy, unbalanced chakras upstairs and simmer them down so you can muse on where you want that energy working.

Back in chapter 5, I used SpongeBob SquarePants as an example of the color and location of the solar plexus, so I'll just continue using him, like everyone else on his show does. Though it might seem my using SpongeBob to explain the solar plexus is a little redundant, he actually provides a lot of valuable structure, at least symbolically. SpongeBob is energetic, optimistic, and incessantly struggles to do the right thing, all while wrestling with his self-esteem. Moreover, he dwells in the underwater city called the Bikini Bottom with a cast of characters who constantly manipulate, demean, exploit, undermine, and use him in various ways for their own advantage. SpongeBob's life consists of trying to take no offenses and moving beyond those egos he encounters in his daily life, all in an effort to meet his desires. Which, by the way, is exactly what we are meant to do, but creative animations make it look so much more entertaining and unbelievably easy to accomplish. One big reason for this is that we are unconsciously influenced energetically by those around us. It can sometimes seem impossible to make even the slightest change in our interior world because of all that's going on in our exterior world.

When I teach my animal totem classes, during the lecture on the solar plexus I pass around a bunch of photographs of various animals yawning and continue to blather on about power and control and how programmed we all are by the subtlest of things. Meanwhile, I watch the whole class stretching and yawning like a bunch of bears that just came out of hibernation. As they continue to yawn, I ramble on until someone becomes conscious enough to observe what's going on. I'm always flabbergasted by how quickly people take on that energy and, moreover, how long it can take people to make the connection and actually call it out. This is also a good technique to determine if someone is paying attention to you; try it at home during dinner and watch everyone slowly fall into a stupor. I remember testing the theory when I rode public transportation back and forth to work. After paying my fare at the front of the bus, I'd let out a big yawn as I moved toward a seat. Seconds later I'd scan to see who was yawning, and there was always, at the very least, a few, but more often anyone who'd watched me board was yawning. The point I'm making here, of course, is not that I have a latent sadistic tendency to control people. It's to demonstrate how easily we can be entrained by the subtle aspects of everyday life, and most of the time we are not even aware of it. Keeping a steady flow of consciousness in your inner world amid a multitude of things happening around you in your outer world and assessing the impact the outer world has on your inner world takes a certain amount of bandwidth and guts. Bandwidth and guts are the hallmark of the solar plexus.

I remember back in the day, when I was a kid, I would stand on the hump in the middle of the car behind the front seat. I could see the whole world ahead through the windshield, not to mention what was going on in the front seat. This, of course, was way before car seats, seatbelts, safety restraints, and regulations took hold. Back then, kids were allowed to do what every dog does when you roll down the window—stick its head out, blow the fur off its face, and bark and drool at anyone it passes on the ride. I had one aunt who kept every flavor of Wrigley's gum in her glove compartment. I remember standing there on my hump in the backseat, hanging over the front, begging for another piece. When I was asked what had happened to the piece I'd already been given, I responded that I had swallowed it. My mom's alarmed response was "Cripes! You don't swallow gum, it will stick to your guts!" I remember conjuring that very image of gum being stuck to my guts, an image that stuck in my head every time I chewed. Of course, I had no idea what guts looked like. I just imagined this big blob of pink stuff in my stomach with every piece of gum I had ever swallowed stuck to it.

Years later I would learn it takes seven years for gum to digest, another aspect I would ponder, yet another old wives' tale about my innards that would prove to be fiction.

I've learned a lot about my guts over the years, but perhaps one of the most visceral things I've learned is to trust my gut and the feeling that comes from it. As you begin to open up to the energies of the solar plexus, your gut will be your most important indicator. This is because the solar plexus deals with our organs of digestion and it is associated with the pancreas which is both an endocrine gland and organ. The solar plexus is what I call your guts, and it's all about what we can stomach and what we cannot. In its raw form it's all about power and control, how much you have, how much you don't. Your stomach will let you know how you're controlling your power, and your guts will help you to have the power to change the whole thing. Your solar plexus animal totem will possess the power and controls needed to make it feasible for you to stomach everything. But only if you choose to follow the guidance. And if you don't, you'll still feel it in your gut.

Honoring Your Solar Plexus

To honor your solar plexus is to give yourself permission to look at the role that power and control are playing in your life, for this is what drives your engine. The ego will always be challenged by this, especially if it is preoccupied with controlling and overpowering everything with its energies. If you feel like you want to react to or dismiss this statement, that's awesome, honor it. It means that you are aware of the ego's tendency to wield power and control over the elements in your life maybe without your truly seeing the effects. Your solar plexus animal totem will help simmer down your reactions and assist you with insights to quell the frictions, stresses, and gravities that could potentially rock the world you presume you drive. On the opposite side of the coin, if you tend to hand your power and control over to those preoccupied with it, honor that too. This same animal totem will assist you with reclaiming and regaining those aspects of you that don't take action, that allow you to hand over your fire to those with a tendency to use your fuel. Do know that we all, to some extent, play both sides of this coin as we perceive this dynamic energy brings what appears to be great benefits. This stems from fears in the root chakra, and it keeps both parties enslaved in weakness. The good news is your solar plexus animal totem will guide you to see both sides.

We all have areas of power and control with dark sides. They are our own personal fault lines, those fractures below our surface that need healing. Even what we perceive to be our smallest shadows have the potential to mushroom into dark clouds when we least expect it. The seemingly little dark dots and dashes of Morse code that signal our gut, that we so often push down or dismiss, all have the potential to tap a geyser. You can see them mount to the surface in trivial or petty annoyances, like missing a belt loop after you've taken time trying not to, pushing the unlock door button again and again as someone continues pulling the handle at the same time, the candy bar ultimately not dropping after you rubbed the dollar on every part of your body to get the vending machine to take it, being cut off in traffic after you just kindly let someone go, waiting for eons to give your order to the server, empty ice cube trays after you just filled them all, and even overly long examples of things that can annoy when you got the message after the first one. They all send little seismic waves to our core that demonstrate we are not in control. This is the universes way of showing us that things are out of balance and changes will be required.

Ultimately, the universe will eventually turn up the heat to get your attention and encourage you to embrace your true nature. It's called shame, and, boy, do you feel it in your gut. Whether it comes from embarrassment, humiliation, disgrace, or chagrin, it will certainly influence your fire. You'll either use it to run, retreat, and hide like a frightened turtle or to more obsessively assert yourself like an overzealous draft horse. Shame gives you an opportunity to honor your fire, to look through a focused lens at where you are giving or taking control and power. It not only gives you an opening to evaluate where you are putting your actions, but more importantly, what kind of acceptance or recognition you are trying to generate from them. As you honor the current state of your solar plexus, allow yourself the power to surrender the need to control that playground you romp in. This will allow the Divine forces of the universe to illuminate your play spaces with sparks of light that will outshine your shadow and ego tendencies every time.

Ways to Honor Your Solar Plexus

Make a campfire
Have a fire ritual*
Roast marshmallows
Record your gut signals
Eat foods that balance your power**
Wear colors that balance your power**
Go to the beach and enjoy the sunshine
Consciously detach from the little irritants
Practice ground rules, especially breath work

*Fire rituals are a great way to release and let go of those things that are no longer serving you. Write down things you want to let go of—maybe behaviors, relationships, memories, or anything you feel takes up space in your being that you just don't want there anymore. Write each one down on a little slip of paper and fold it as if you are packing it up for a journey out of your world, because that is essentially what you will be doing. Once you have your pile of "no-longers," bring them to your fire source—be it fireplace, woodstove, campfire, or barbecue grill. Be creative, but use safety. Consciously add each folded slip one by one to the fire, watching it transition into a new energy that will bring sparks of joy to your world.

**Colors and foods offer a tremendous amount of fire energy. To tone down fire, wear cool colors like blues and grays. Wear oranges and reds to turn up fire energy. Cool foods, like ice cream and salad, also tame fires, while hot foods can give you fire. Play with colors and foods and observe their effects.

The Solar Plexus Chakra Totem

Learning to be empowered by your fire and empowering others with it will be challenging. Your solar plexus animal totem will play a major role in helping you manage and balance these powerful fire forces. Think of this animal totem as your personal commander in chief. You will use the forces of your animal totem's army and marines to reinforce your earth, energizing your root to excavate your true nature with a fire that helps you transmute your fears into adventure. The forces of your animal totem's navy and coast guard will help liberate your waterways in the sacral areas, which have the tendency to snuff your fire with the emotional triggers of the wounded inner child, hijacking your pleasure and robbing you of the freedom to navigate the open seas. The energies of your animal totem's air force will protect and guide your first three chakras, which are associated with your physical body. But its greatest mission is to help you pilot your air and space with the fire needed to take you into the heart, where kindness, compassion, love, and the infinite possibilities of the Divine universe are ever-present. Your solar plexus military forces will assist you in all aspects of your chakras. I'll explain how this works.

In my personal experience, and as I mentioned earlier, the three chakras below the heart perform like a braid of three separate energy strands, each literally zigzagging and overlapping the next. The ego likes this flat, solid, intertwining three-strand structure, as this tight, narrow interlace has been conditioned with patterns that influence a limited perspective, a pseudosense of strength that controls light, and it is not easily separated. You can feel how this works when adverse external forces hit any strand of the braid. Usually, when you push to execute a change in your life, like break a habit, or, even worse, a startling change is unwontedly executed for you, the chakra that receives the blow—whether it's your survival, emotional, or power and control action center—will have a reverberating effect on all the others. They will all ripple, like a—big-word warning here—coalescence cascade, where one single raindrop in a pond causes a wave action. However, what is invisible to the eye is that the droplet merges with the pond for a millisecond, then pops up into a slightly smaller droplet that causes a ripple by its merge. That happens again and again and again, until the smaller droplets and ripples eventually die down to calmness.

You can feel these ripples waving around in your inner world when something challenges this braid. As your earth gets a shock wave, so do the energetic strands of your water and fire or any combination of the three, until the forces of the ripples simmer down. This is why it's so hard to let things go, especially when someone says to you, "You just gotta let it go!" It's the ego's job to make sure all of your braid's strands stay woven together so you can continue the game of tug-of-war. That gives you a false sense of strength to monitor your border controls, which essentially blocks out your true light and tugs on your heart. One of the great areas of guidance your solar plexus animal totem will have for you will be helping you gain control of the ego's tight enforcement of the braid strands. Your totem will guide you through the maneuvers of untwisting the strands and loosening the grip on the ego's game of tug-of-war.

Your solar plexus totem animal's mission is to help you recognize the tremendous grace and benevolence of power and control when it is not so tightly wound and is instead balanced in the right proportions. Every single one of nature's creatures offers an amazingly unique example of balancing these very forces. Their teachings have nothing to do with a roaring power of dominance, muscle, and brawn or the fierce intensity required for jungle survival. Rather, they show us the warm, gentle, tender care and unfaltering nurturing we see in wildlife as they teach their cute, cuddly offspring how to survive in the natural world. Each of your totem animals will play a significant role and hold amazing pieces of the puzzle that will help you embrace your true nature.

Meditation

As you go inward this month, take this opportunity to reflect on the nature of your fire. Allow yourself to look at your playground and see the places where your ego might singe those who might like to frolic and play. Allow yourself to also see where you might be scorched by those hot flames that show up on the playground. To some extent, we all unconsciously bring fire to the places we play, but we can also be very good at taking that fire away. This month allow yourself to look at the places where your fire can empower someone else's need to grow and glow. But also look at the places where your fire hinders others or tends to dominate them with your blaze. Give yourself an opportunity to play with your fire. Allow yourself the courage to raise the flames in those shadowy places that need more light. But also allow yourself to reduce the heat of your bonfire so others can come closer.

The Solar Plexus Chakra Totem

The solar plexus is where you put your fire into action to make the jump over the river to the wonderful playground of the Divine realms, which will assist you in embracing your true nature. To do this it will require that you play with your fire and examine the effect it is having on the road that takes to the heart center. Last month you set the intention to become consciously aware of things that bring you pleasure, joy, and the wonder of it all. This is the path that clears your energy field and opens you to the psychic circuitry the road offers, but you must put your fire actions into gear to get there. This month is where you blow fire into those intentions, for they will be the ones that blaze the trail over the river and into the heart chakra. The animal that comes to you on this journey will have tremendous teachings for you in the uses of fire.

Continue to carry out your meditation three days in a row. By now, you have likely figured out your own rhythm and cycle for meditating. The more you meditate, the more the puzzle pieces of your totem will emerge. Do take note of any animal parts—like wings, claws, horns, fur—or any subtle descriptions that float into your meditation, as they will have the potential to affirm the landscape in the physical realm. Use any of the solar plexus totem accessories to enhance your meditation experience.

SOLAR PLEXUS CHAKRA TOTEM ACCESSORIES	
CANDLES	Using candles to stimulate the solar plexus chakra can be a wonderful way to invoke the fire element to connect with your animal totem. Select any candles with bright yellow or orange-yellow tones that are pleasing to the eye. Really, any colors or scents that incite your senses to engage or your passion to soar will stimulate a fire experience. When shopping for candles, allow yourself to experience all their pleasing aspects: their shapes, number of wicks, colors, scents, and even the names. Monikers like Early Sunshine, Island Sunset, or Evening Flame can enhance the fire element. Remember, fire is the passion element and will work wonderfully with your meditations.
INCENSE	Use incense for clearing any space and calling upon your solar plexus animal totem. Incense adds a wonderful tone to the opening and closing rituals for your solar plexus chakra totem. Much like the candle-selection process, allow yourself to find pleasure in exploring the different types of available incense. Incense can help invoke those fire energies and add a nice touch to your meditation sessions. Incense can connect you to the element of fire and air when you watch its ember send out a wispy trail of smoke. Try following the delicate stream to catch a glimpse of your totem. Scents that can invoke the solar plexus chakra are mint, rosemary, clary sage, juniper, and ginger.
CRYSTALS	Use crystals for their color and energy qualities. There is literally a crystal for every emotion, body part, or circumstance. Several crystals can be beneficial to the solar plexus chakra. Citrine is one of the most common crystals used for the solar plexus chakra because of its powerful cleansing and energizing properties. I was surprised that my birthstone, peridot, had such wonderful healing properties, especially in relation to the liver, digestion, and detoxification. Although used for calming and stress release, yellow smithsonite helps balance the solar plexus and release old patterns. Amber is one of my favorite stones. Healers use it for the stomach, kidneys, bladder, liver, and gallbladder. I like it because it is said to bring a sunny, carefree disposition. Let yourself experience which crystals you are drawn to, and don't be surprised if you feel it in your gut.
AROMA-THERAPY	Essential oils can be used for healing, relaxing, invoking, clearing—you name it. They are a perfect way to enhance your home spa while utilizing the water element. Their therapeutic properties can boost diffusers, vaporizers, humidifiers, bathtubs, and fountains to create a botanical utopia in all your environments. Remember that essential oils are very highly concentrated, volatile, aromatic essences of plants. I suggest buying them from well-known vendors or all-natural stores whose experienced personnel can guide you in their proper use. The following essential oils will support the solar plexus chakra: rosewood, sandalwood, chamomile, rosemary, lemon, and ginger. Some vendors will offer combinations of two or more oils in one vial specifically formulated for the solar plexus chakra. Many places also offer reference charts for the product line they sell. Don't forget to trust your gut when you're shopping.

Connecting with Your Solar Plexus Totem

When I teach my solar plexus totem class, this is the area where many students really begin to start to question things from the intellect, that logical side of the brain. This is normal, because the third chakra deals with the intellect. You too may be feeling a need to question things or make logical sense of your experiences, more so in this month's journey than the other months'. The most essential tools your solar plexus totem animal holds for you are those of discernment and action. There are a number of legendary, mythical, and astrological creatures associated with the powers of fire and solar symbolism. Try not to get caught up with the logical aspects of the animal that comes to support you with your fire.

I'll add this note to further help you understand my reasoning here. When I was a child, I had a very strong connection to my fire sign, the lion, for I am a Leo. I ferociously read everything I could about it and readily connected with its energetic forces and characteristics. While I was writing this chapter on the solar plexus, the osprey came into my life with such incredible force, both physically and energetically, I was completely astounded by what it had to offer. However, the polar bear is actually my solar plexus totem, and its medicine has been extraordinary in teaching me the powers of trusting the mystical and spiritual aspects among the many other things happening in my life. I did not ever think that the lion was my solar plexus animal when I uncovered my personal totem. Well, maybe I did a little from a logical point of view. But the affirmations I got from my polar bear were completely confirming and verifiably blatant.

The point I'm making here is try not to worry that the animal that comes to you is the right animal. You will most definitely know the right one through the sometimes zany affirmations that unfold, and they will the more you question. This is part of the magic to get you out of the intellect and into trusting guidance. Every animal that comes to you will be a messenger with some essential piece of guidance, and it will supplement, strengthen, or reinforce the connection with your totem and with following guidance in general. If you are getting repeated visits from an animal, trust it. If you are getting visits from a variety of different animals, trust that too. Remember, as you open up to these subtle vibrations, you are essentially asking the Divine sources for help. Do not just assume that the guidance you are receiving is specific for unveiling your totem. You may very well be getting some critical guidance for your journey in life. Every encounter will be an invitation to embrace some aspect of your power and control imprints and conditioning. Every encounter will be an opportunity and Divinely sent message to benefit you and help you break those worn-out patterns that don't serve you any longer.

Uncovering Your Personal Animal Totem

The long and short of harnessing the power of the solar plexus is to open, balance, and, most of all, clear this chakra. You will need to be aware and recognize situations of power and control, ultimately asking yourself, "Is this my ego pulling the rope in the tug-of-war, or is this Divine guidance at play, giving me an opportunity to untwist the strands?" To do this takes a lot of bandwidth and guts, and that is what your totem animal for your solar plexus will ultimately be assisting you with. Be open to all the signs from nature this month, as they will be especially influential in helping you play with your fire. Even your foot, root, and sacral totems can be harbingers for these very experiences. Most of all, enjoy the journey, trust your gut, and embrace the opportunities to play with your fire.

Welcoming Your Totem Animal

You have now traveled another twenty-eight-day cycle of the moon, and another animal totem has arrived to be a part of your ever-evolving world. This animal will play an intricate role in helping you manage your power and control from a physical, emotional, and intellectual perspective. Think of your totem as a teacher who will help you recognize Aesop's fable about the sun and the wind in yourself and others, that kindness and gentle persuasion have a greater effect than brute force and severity. I hope your experiences this month have directed you to a new level of awareness that will bring a renewed and graceful essence to your playground. Please don't forget to acknowledge the guidance you have received, especially any from your foot, root, or sacral totems. Also, try not to forget that the more gratitude you have for the guidance, the more guidance you will be graced with.

This is the part of the ritual where you honor and welcome the company of your new guide. This is when you can review your journal and bask in those defining moments that guided you. This is also a time to look at those aspects that seem deep-seated but are also beacons for change. These can be those age-old beliefs that cause you to react and really don't serve you anymore. Throughout your journey in life, Divine guidance will always be there to rally your actions and help divert your reactions. Below is a prayer to welcome your solar plexus totem animal. Light a candle and allow the energetic flames to warm your solar plexus chakra as you welcome your solar plexus animal totem guide into your world.

SOLAR PLEXUS TOTEM ANIMAL PRAYER

I now reflect on the journey with my solar plexus totem animal. I have tremendous gratitude for its assistance and guidance. I honor how this animal has unveiled itself to me in so many delightfully spirited ways. My solar plexus totem animal will assist me in overcoming the impulses of my defensive ego that cause me to react. My solar plexus animal will help me recognize the destructive and limiting habits that cause me to control or be controlled. My animal guide will show me how to hold my power in ways that help me execute responsible actions. My solar plexus animal will guide me to the infinite realm of choice, where my talents, abilities, and greatest potential become my true choice. For it is here that I will find my true nature and the strength and courage to follow it, because I know the ego leads to a place of wallow. I have faith in the Divine process and allow its guidance to help, lead, and support me on my journey. I now welcome my solar plexus animal totem to assist me on my walk in life.

AMEN.

CHAPTER 12

THE HEART CHAKRA TOTEM

What's Up with This Chapter

∞ Uncovering Your Heart Chakra Totem Animal
∞ What Is a Heart Chakra?
∞ Let's Get Physical
∞ Honoring Your Heart
∞ The Heart Chakra Totem
∞ Connecting with Your Heart Totem
∞ Welcoming Your Heart Totem Animal

Uncovering Your Heart Chakra Totem

Congratulations! You have made it to the center of the chakra system and have finally reached the heart chakra, the gateway to the Divine. You are halfway through uncovering your complete personal animal totem. How 'bout that? Hooray! Theoretically, the heart chakra separates the three lower chakras from the three higher chakras. While this might seem like a moot point, it is significant when it comes to understanding the chakra system. The three chakras below the heart are all part of your personal walk in the physical world and can be referred to as your lower self. The three chakras above the heart are more connected to the Divine or the spiritual realm and are sometimes referred to as your higher self. Your heart chakra is considered the mediator of these two very diverse realms, and it's fascinating, magical, and enchanting to see how its energies can orchestrate various methods to open, improve, and stimulate a dialogue between the two realms. But that's what a mediator does. I find this even more captivating because the heart chakra is the place where your spirit resides when all is well. You know it is there by the dance in your step, the tweedle-dee in your tweedle-dum, and just by the magical way life flows for you. However, if you are feeling that all is not so well, chances are your ego has stepped in to play a little game of tug-of-war. If you remember from last month's journey, your spirit doesn't like to play tug-of-war, so it ties its end of the rope to your heart and goes to a place where all is well, leaving you in the playground with those spoiled brats and bullies of the lower self who tug on your heartstrings, so to speak. So how do you keep your ego from doing that? Well, for starters, the animal totem that comes to you will assist your heart in its gigantic job of mediating the higher and lower realms. Second, your totem will assist you with what's near and dear to your heart. And third, your totem will guide you to ensure that your spirit is an everlasting resident in your heart. For all this to happen, you need to be aware and recognize situations where your ego is causing your spirit to be a flight risk. No worries—again, your animal totem will help you do this. The nice thing is that with all the fire you worked with last month, you have warmed your heart up for this month's journey.

What Is a Heart Chakra?

The heart chakra is the fourth chakra in the chakra system. As you would imagine, it is associated with your heart and has to do with love. Because of its central location, right in the middle of the chakra systems, and primary responsibility as the mediator of the higher and lower realms, the key aspect of the heart chakra is balance. Fundamentally, the heart functions as an energy transformer for giving and receiving love. You'll learn more about how that works later. The symbol for the heart chakra is a twelve-petaled lotus, and, just for the record, should not be confused with those cute little less-than-three, sideways-heart-shaped symbols (<3) you see on Facebook or other social networks, usually posted when you're feeling schmaltzy and/or alcohol has been involved. Throughout history the number twelve has been associated with some pretty significant symbolism—months in a year, signs of the zodiac, apostles, inches in a foot, numbers on a clock, and my favorite, the dozen, especially donuts. Much like the ten petals of the solar plexus lotus are associated with the ten ego states we must overcome, the twelve petals of the heart chakra lotus are associated with the twelve states we must rise above to be able to not just love, but love unconditionally, compassionately, and forgivingly.

The heart chakra is linked to the seven-year cycle spanning ages twenty-two through twenty-eight. This is the time in our life when we usually form deep, loving relationships that capture our heart. In a perfect world, we would be able to sustain the amazingly euphoric ride of falling in love. However, when you throw in your multipurpose task team, your survival imprints, and the patterns and conditionings in your belief and value systems along with the twist of the ego's influence, it's a wonder we even come equipped with a heart at all. Well, we do, and the heart has some pretty big pants to fill in terms of its huge responsibility as a mediator for the higher and lower realms, and, of course, keeping you alive.

As the mediator and gatekeeper for the higher and lower realms, it's important that your heart chakra be sensitive and impartial to the needs of both parties. The lower realm is represented by the ego and its free will, and the higher realm is represented by your spirit and Divine will. The ego and its free will tend to be a real button-pusher and more or less try to dominate the heart. Your spirit, on the other hand, wants no part of this button-pushing dominance, hence it's pretty much always a flight risk. Now, you're probably thinking, how on earth does my poor spirit get a leg up with this incessant alpha-dog ego at play all the time? That's a very good question; you get a pretty pink heart sticker for that one. While this may seem like an untenable circumstance, there is a thing called divine justice at work all the time on the playground. Divine justice helps the heart to open, and it improves and stimulates the dialogue between the two realms by putting the ego in the state of shame or humility. It can be something as simple as the lifeguard saying, "Hey, you in the pink polka-dot bathing suit, *out* of the *pool*! Yes, *you*!" or someone pointing out the three sheets of toilet paper stuck to the heel of Little Miss So-Smug as she exits the bathroom. Essentially, anything that gets the ego running for cover is a huge opportunity for your spirit to get a leg up. One of the primary roles of your heart chakra animal totem is to help facilitate the heart in taming down the ego and wilding up your spirit so you can embrace and enjoy your true nature.

Let's Get Physical

The heart chakra is essentially superimposed over your physical heart, and like the heart, it is armored in the thoracic cavity. In this birdcage framework of bones, you will find the collarbone and shoulders is the heart chakra's roof; the ,ribs, and breastbone are the walls; and the diaphragm is the floor. In case you didn't know, the breastbone is shaped like the capitol letter T, reminding you that there is indeed a treasure in your chest. Inside your armored chest, you'll find your heart, which holds the treasures of your true nature and all its desires; the lungs, which blow air into that nature; the trachea, which allows the air passage; the esophagus, which bring nourishment down to energize your true nature with all its desires; and the thymus. The thymus lives between your heart and your breastbone and is responsible for producing T cells. T cells are a powerful group of cells that I like to call warriors because they have names like *helper*, *killer*, and *suppressor* and their job is to go in search of specific foreign invaders and destroy them. Much like foreign policy, but you didn't hear that from me. The heart chakra is associated with this endocrine gland, I think mostly because the heart can use all the help it can get in protecting your true nature from the ego, and words like *helper*, *killer*, and *suppressor* really send a message to it. At the bottom of this birdcage framework lies the diaphragm. The diaphragm separates the thoracic cavity from the abdominal cavity. Its job is to transport air, and unfortunately, sometimes a lot of it is hot air from our ego.

So I'm guessing by now you've figured out that the element associated with the heart chakra is air, being that pretty much everything in the thoracic cavity draws on it. Back in chapter 7, Setting the Ground Rules, I gave you information on the two types of breathing styles, so you might want to grab a Tic Tac and go back and read the second ground rule, on being conscious about breath. This will really help set the tone for working with the element of air, the diaphragm, and your heart chakra.

The element of air is everywhere. In fact, there are hundreds of ways to harness it. There is the air alert, airbag, air ball, air bubble, air chamber, air compressor, air conditioner, air duct, air express, airhead, and my favorite, the air guitar, to name a dozen (just to keep things aligned with the twelve petals of the heart chakra lotus). Air is, above all, necessary for all living things, and it's free. You can use as much or as little as you want. Air is so abundant that we all pretty much take it for granted until we need it, then we just can't get enough. Anyone who has ever hang glided, had any type of respiratory problems, or had to chase the dog around the house to remove from its mouth one of the new black suede pumps one's wife just bought knows the dreadful feeling of a lack of air. Besides keeping you alive and being free, one of the major benefits of air is that it can be the catalyst to align you with the very core of your true nature and the wonderful infinite world of guidance. Last month you became aware of how to manage your fire, especially when it is tied to the ego. This month you will learn how being conscious of air can blow your dominating ego right out of the water and allow you to jump over the river into the heart chakra without all the anger, resentment, drama, fear, despair, or other negative emotional or mental habits and tendencies, which all come with our attachment to the ego.

Let's talk about how to get over that bridge. A bridge is a structure that allows you to the other side of something, whether it's a river, road, opinion, or gap in your teeth. The purpose of a bridge is to provide passage over the obstacle. Consider your ego the obstacle and your diaphragm the bridge. The diaphragm's job is to pull and push air in and out of the lungs. So it makes a very good candidate for pushing and pulling your ego out of the way, which in turn allows the heart, the center of your being, to relax with ease and grace and not have to focus on being the mediator. You're probably thinking, if your diaphragm is pushing and pulling your ego around, why is it so hard to span the bridge into the heart and just stay hanging out with all that ease and grace? That's a brilliant question, if I do say so myself.

It sounds like a simple task to span the bridge; however, there is a catch. The diaphragm acts like a drawbridge, the kind that protects and defends a castle in the event of an attack. In your case, the castle is your heart. If you know anything about drawbridges, they open and close based on the will of the castle's resident. If you remember from back in chapter 2, What I Am Is What I Am, the perk of our human existence here on the earthly plane is that we have free will, and with that comes the choice of following guidance or not following it. So again we come face to face with your will versus Divine will. If we go back to your diaphragm, its function, and the two types of breathing techniques—chest and diaphragm—you can get a better understanding of how to keep your spirit and the Divine forces of guidance in residence. Chest breathing is shallow, using only the upper 10 percent of your lungs. When you're in chest-breathing mode, you are more than likely not conscious of your breathing, probably preoccupied with the external world, and blocked from the full force of assistance from Divine guidance, which is your free will, of course. When we are in my-will mode, our gaze is on our lower self and the outer forces at play, our drawbridge is up, and our mental and emotional habits and tendencies drive how we interact and react with others and to the events of our life.

In diaphragmatic-breathing mode, we are tuned into our breath and utilizing the lower 10 percent of our lungs, which packs the most punch for oxygenation. We consciously allow the flow of air to totally fill our lungs and abdominal cavity. Our abdomen houses the internal fire that heats our passions and desires but also dissolves patterns that disconnect us from our wholeness and infinite guidance. Our gaze is on our higher self, which always allows nourishment, nurturing, and loving kindness to emerge. When we close our eyes and breathe into this space, a sense of peace and calm begins to reside in our awareness and creates a portal to our true nature. It is at this place that our drawbridge is down and we are open to merging our passions and desires with Divine will, and cocreations come to light. This is the place where we allow ourselves to dismantle the strands that create separateness in the lower realms, and then weave together the two wills. When your will merges with Divine will, you are connected and in an open and expanded space that always allows guidance to flourish. You know you are there because you feel it in your heart. The animal totem that presents itself to you will help you stay linked to the Divine and all the universal forces that are there to infinitely guide you.

Honoring Your Heart

So far, all I've done is just plain gossip about the ego and its double-crossing shenanigans. I have affronted it as a renegade, bully, drama queen, and selfish heathen chasing your spirit off. By the way, gossip is an ego state. Nonetheless, the ego means well and is sort of working with your heart, even if it seems in a mildly sadistic kind of way. The truth of the matter is, though, as we travel through life, through all those seven-year cycles of chakra experiences with our multipurpose task force and a bit of our own personal teachings, we have all come up against some pretty crappy circumstances that have resulted in suffering, sadness, grief, sorrow, despair, you name it. And all these things make your heart wanna just shut the door and block out the cruel world. This is why your ego has so much power; it just jumps in during these vulnerable times and tries to help your poor little wounded self with its own ideas to get your needs met. You see, your ego has its own little plastic jerry-rigged drawbridge and stakes its claim on what can enter and exit your heart based on all those negative circumstances of the past. Unfortunately, the ego gets us in a lot of trouble because its only view on life is in the past, and its guidance just brings us back to the past, which is where all those heartaches reside, and that closes down your heart even more. So you just get more of what you don't want when you follow your ego, because it's just a loop. If you ever watched the TV drama series *Lost*, consider your ego a distress call, a plea for help, much like the French woman Danielle Rousseau's recorded signal that had looped on a specific frequency for sixteen years. Once the survivors figured that out, they pretty much just let it go and moved on with trying to get saved. Your heart chakra animal totem will be instrumental in helping you recognize the ego loop and, more importantly, helping you let it go so you can move on with embracing your true nature.

As you honor your heart chakra this month, give yourself permission to heal and forgive. Allow yourself to begin the process of witnessing and honestly examining the current state of your heart without judgment, fear, guilt, regret, resentment, hurt, or any of those lower energies that tend to anchor themselves downstairs in those lower chakras and make you feel downhearted. When you initiate this process, you allow your adult self to observe your negative past events as teaching mechanisms that have elevated you to a higher level of expanded awareness. All the challenging aspects of our life bring us to an expanded place of awareness that brings greater clarity and leads us to healthier people, places, and things. We could not possibly have come to these people or experiences had we not gone through the struggle. Every one of us comes here with a specific charter to embrace our true nature, and every brokenhearted experience moves us to a realm that brings us into alignment with experiencing the joy and pleasure of our true nature.

Give yourself permission to release the pains of the past and reawaken a new expression of you. Look at each strand of that braid of your lower self—the strand of your root chakra connected with your survival fears, the strand of your sacral chakra connected with the pain and suffering of your wounded inner child, and the strand of your solar plexus connected with power, control, and the monkey mind of the ego. As you honor the current state of your heart chakra, allow your higher self's perspective to assist you in illuminating the heavy shadows in those lower chakras. Allow this healing and forgiving light to weave a new, illuminated strand into each one of those lower chakras, giving you the freedom to finally renounce the snippets of your life that no longer serve you. As you focus on these new, illuminated strands of the lower self, you begin to gracefully fuse the higher frequencies of the universal forces into your being. As you continue to shed each shadow, you begin to change your personal vibration, which in turn changes your physical frequency. Trust that these higher frequencies in your personal vibration will always lead you to the place that is right for you, and the place that is right for you will always be shrouded with attractions that bring joy, laughter, and love into alignment with you. It is only through these higher vibrations that you notice the good in all things and what it means to be connected to the unlimited spiritual connectedness of oneness and Divine wholeness and the continuous feelings of lightheartedness.

Ways to Honor Your Heart

Start a gratitude journal
Rent the movie *Pay It Forward*
Practice balancing giving and receiving
Surprise someone with an unexpected gift
Volunteer or be of service to someone in need
Read the book *All I Really Need to Know I Learned in Kindergarten*
Soak in a bath with one pound of baking soda and one pound of Epsom salt
Rescue a lonely betta, also known as the Siamese fighting fish, from
your local pet store

The Heart Chakra Totem

Keep in mind that your heart chakra balances the physical realm and the spiritual realm. Your heart chakra totem animal will help you be aware of that balance. The more you work to clear the blocks in the lower chakras, the more you are able to allow the higher realms to influence your walk in life. If you were to envision a teeter-totter, the heart would be the central pillar and each realm would have a side. The physical realm, with its psychic weight of resistance and the heavy blocks of emotional burdens, would hold up the graceful, weightless side of the spiritual realm. Psychic weight—whether it's physical belongings or emotional or mental clutter—is heavy. The more you diminish and eliminate the weighty aspects of the physical realm, the easier it is for the spiritual realm to come into alignment and help you balance and clear the pathways of the heart, thereby creating a lightheartedness and more effective channel to the spirit realm.

Your heart chakra totem animal will be instrumental in helping you recognize the psychic loads that weigh down your lower self and cause your heart to be heavy. Your totem animal will assist you to make choices that allow you to release those heavy burdens on the physical side of your teeter-totter that keep the spirit realm suspended and really not supporting you. Heavy lower energies come in the form of judgment, resentment, envy, anger, hatred, jealousy—the list goes on and on, and all these energies are associated with feelings of being above or below someone or something. When you allow yourself to recognize these energies, and also investigate why you are harboring them, you activate both the healing and forgiveness process, which in turn clears the lower chakras of the obstacles inhibiting the higher realms from coming into alignment with your walk in life. As you take responsibility for both recognizing and making choices to eliminate these negative energies, your drawbridge begins to lower and the path to the heart opens. Trust and faith in this process are the two components that keep the bridge to the heart in an open state, allowing you to channel the spirit realm and accelerate healing and forgiveness. The moment you drop the ball and allow the lower energies to appear and engage with them on your playground, you put weight on your teeter-totter. The drawbridge to the heart begins to rise, trust and faith quickly shift to fear and anguish, and the ego steps in to run the show. Then ease and grace begin to slither away, and a rocky start to a bumpy road emerges. As you become fluent in understanding this process, you will learn how to get to the place of least resistance as quickly as possible to stay in alignment with the spiritual realm. Your animal totem will be most beneficial in these scenarios, as its presence will either keep you in the flow of Divine guidance or prompt you back in the stream.

Your heart totem animal's mission will be to help you stay tuned to the wonderful treasures the heart possesses when it's not heavy with the shadows that make it dark and cold. A warm, light heart is where kindness, compassion, love, and the infinite possibilities of the Divine universe are ever-present. This is where the high-vibrating energies of joy, happiness, unconditional love, understanding, generosity, and loving oneself in a sincere and nonegotistical way are compassionately projected. Most of my students find, as do I, that this totem is very elusive, much like the process of keeping the drawbridge to the heart open at all times. However, once you are conscious of this animal's presence, its significance becomes profoundly right on target. The path through the heart always leads to peaceful neutrality abundant in grace. It is through this center that you learn to embrace your true nature, and your animal totem will guide you in that task.

Meditation

As you go within this month, reflect on where you may be carrying a heavy heart. What grief, pain, suffering, turmoil, sorrow, or sadness are you holding that may be inhibiting the spiritual realm from nurturing you with its infinite healing and abundant joy that bring compassion, love, and kindness flowing into your life? Where has your discomfort removed you from comfort? Where has apathy removed empathy, abhorrence removed love? Symbolically, see each one of the vibrating low-level frequencies as an obstacle to your heart's drawbridge being perpetually open. This month, allow the fire you generate in your solar plexus to burn off all those adverse energies in the lower chakras. Let your fire warm your heart to permit your spirit and true nature to become new, permanent residents within. Identify the places where your giving may outweigh your receiving, or your receiving may outweigh your giving.

In the heart center, there is no difference between giving and receiving. We all come to this physical plane with numerous gifts. As we become aware of our true nature, these gifts begin to blossom, allowing us to create and experience abundance. Through the practice of sharing our gifts, we receive enjoyment, appreciation, pleasure, thanks, and gratitude. This generates a natural loop that replenishes what has been depleted. One of my spiritual teachers powerfully brought my attention to the act of balanced giving and receiving. I had a habit of going overboard with giving, whether it was my time, resources, money, or efforts. If someone gave me something, I had to return the giving with something greater or comparable. It was completely uncomfortable for me to receive something without some type of compulsion to give back. I was essentially blocking my own ability to receive and was quite good at dismissing its gestures. Giving yourself permission to receive is by far one of the biggest gifts you can give to the spirit of yourself. Your ego doesn't like it. Giving and doing for others puts you in the driver's seat, allowing you to call the shots and have some sense of authority over the situation. However, it's really just a smoke and mirrors game. What is happening is a massive blocking of abundance from the physical, emotional, and mental aspects of life that keeps us bound to situations of power and control and lacking the ease and grace of true compassion.

One of the simplest ways to determine if you have balanced giving and receiving is with your breath. As you take in a breath, see how far down you can get the air into your lungs; as you exhale see how much air you can get out. As you follow this rhythm, determine if your inhale is greater than your exhale and vice versa. If you are giving too much of yourself, your inhale will be shorter and your exhale will be longer. Your body knows your truth and will always clue you in if you ask. Allow yourself a few minutes to really take in the breath of life deep down into your lungs. As you continue to give yourself that deep breath, you will begin to notice little pockets of resistance that seem to just float out of the way and permit you to bring more of this self-nurturing therapy into your being. Mother Meera was once asked while giving a Darshan blessing—a bestowal of love, light and grace—"How can I thank you for what you are giving me?" She replied, "You are receiving. That is thanks. That is a great thing." Your heart totem animal will possess the medicine you need to practice balanced giving and receiving. Allow it to work its magic and you too will see that, as Mother Meera said, that is a great thing.

As you carry out your meditation this month, bring in the breath of life to each one of your lower chakras and allow yourself to discard the luggage that pulls heavily on your heart. Just as you monitored your inhale and exhale above, witnessing the balanced breath in your heart center, do the same for each of your lower chakras. Focus on your root chakra, and continue to take breaths in and out until you have a balanced flow. Continue the same practice for the sacral and solar plexus. When you get to your heart, determine if you still have balanced breath, and bring it back into alignment, if necessary. Allow yourself to receive the wonders of breath and its extraordinary capacity to bring wholeness, healing, and balanced love and happiness into your being.

This heart chakra meditation is a simple technique to release sadness and fear and to bring compassion and love into your life, especially if you are feeling alone or anxious, stressed, or tense. Sit in a comfortable position and practice the breath exercise as much as possible. Allow yourself to set the tone for your true nature to emerge. Continue to carry out your meditation three days in a row to allow yourself to be open to the frequencies of your heart totem.

HEART CHAKRA TOTEM ACCESSORIES

CANDLES	Use candles to help stimulate the heart chakra and invoke your connection with your heart animal totem. Candles can create a relaxing ambience and stimulate peaceful essences to warm your heart. Select candles with green tones to aid in connecting to the heart chakra vibrations. Allow yourself to experience any colors or scents that awaken your senses, engaging your heart's desires and passions, as these too will stimulate a heartwarming experience. When shopping for candles, allow yourself to experience all their pleasing aspects: their shapes, number of wicks, colors, scents, and even their names. There are many candles on the market specific to the heart chakra with names such as Healing, Forgiveness, Love, and Compassion. Rose scents also stimulate love and compassion.

INCENSE	Use incense for clearing any space and calling upon your heart chakra animal totem. Incense adds a wonderful tone to your clearing rituals. Scents such as rose, lilac, lavender, and geranium add a nice touch to your meditation or relaxation sessions. Incense helps connect you to the element of air when you follow its wispy trail of smoke. Engage your breath work when you use incense. There are many blends of incense on the market specific to the heart chakra. Allow yourself to experiment with the different types—incense comes in cone, stick, powder, rope, and pellet forms. Using incense can be a pleasurable way to expand your sacred ritual when opening, clearing, and/or balancing your heart chakra.
CRYSTALS	Use crystals for their color and energy qualities. Several crystals can benefit the heart chakra. Aventurine has a strong connection with the nature spirits and therefore evokes all elements and vibrates at unconditional love. It promotes compassion, empathy, and healing and especially benefits the thymus gland. Emerald is a spectacular gemstone, known as the "stone of successful love." It's an excellent crystal for the heart chakra and is used for healing the systems in the thoracic cavity. Peridot is one of my favorite stones. There are so many benefits to this gem, from helping you release old baggage to alleviating jealousy, resentment, anger, and spite. It's perfect for healing disparities in the solar plexus and heart and is ideal for keeping your drawbridge to the heart open. Pink calcite is also a wonderful crystal for the heart. I use it as part of my chakra stone set. It has tremendous loving energies and is great for accelerating forgiveness.
AROMA-THERAPY	Essential oils can be used for healing, relaxing, invoking, clearing—you name it. They are a perfect way to enhance your home spa while utilizing the water element. Their therapeutic properties can boost diffusers, vaporizers, humidifiers, bathtubs, and fountains to create a botanical utopia in all your environments. Remember that essential oils are very highly concentrated, volatile, aromatic essences of plants. I suggest buying them at Whole Foods or all-natural stores whose experienced personnel can guide you in their proper use. In my ultrasonic aroma diffuser, I use bergamot, jasmine, rose, tangerine, neroli, and ylang-ylang. Most stores that sell essential oils will have reference books on display with a tremendous amount of therapeutic information about each oil. Invite yourself to open your heart up to this kind of nurturing .

Connecting with Your Heart Chakra Animal Totem

Your heart chakra animal totem will help you tremendously with opening, clearing, and balancing your heart chakra. This animal will help you be aware of any imbalances in your lower chakras., This animal will help you learn to give and receive without fear, guilt, shame, power, control, or the need for approval. Unfortunately, these are the things that can sometimes blind us and make it difficult to see our animal totem. I remember when I was uncovering my heart chakra totem, I was literally at war with it. The pigeon is my heart chakra totem. During the cold, wintry days of January, I was

Uncovering Your Personal Animal Totem

diligently trying to determine what my heart chakra animal totem could possibly be. I'd constantly monitor the perimeter of my home from the windows in what I perceived as being expectantly open to my animal. As I gazed out, I became frustrated that the pigeons had learned how to tip my bird feeder and spill out the feed within minutes of my filling it. They would actually work as a team to accomplish it, literally lining up on the roof edges from out of nowhere every time I came out to fill the feeder. Not only did it make if difficult for the smaller birds to eat, the pigeons seemed to show up in flocks. I had never seen so many pigeons at my feeder, never mind lined up, gazing at me from the rooftops. I remember thinking I just wanted wildlife to show up, and how in the H-E double hockey sticks was I supposed to see my heart totem animal with these pigeon roosting all over the place, chowing down on all the seed? I was not feeling very giving toward them and wondered where on earth they were all coming from. I'm almost embarrassed to say just how frustrated I became before it finally dawned on me that the abundance I was experiencing with the pigeons was not only the call from my heart chakra totem but a message of how abundance comes in strange packages and can sometimes be right in front of your eyes. Oh, how I laugh about it now, and the pigeon has truly become a beloved totem guide and messenger for me.

Our heart is where we ultimately come to the awareness of a need to balance our lower self. It's the place where you learn how to give or receive without attachment. In one way or another, we all have been conditioned to a hodgepodge perception of giving and receiving with varying nuances of fear, guilt, shame, and a need for some kind of approval. However, when we learn to embrace giving and receiving without our conditioning tied to it, we move to a balanced state in the heart called unconditional love. Our heart is balanced with an unconditional love of self and an unconditional love of others. This is the place that we become aware that peace, love, abundance, joy, and happiness are present in each moment, even when a storm is brewing around us. As we become accustomed to navigating in this magnificent state of being, the tightly wound braid strands of the lower chakras become disentangled and no longer invite the negative polarities that drive our separateness. Each totem representing your lower chakras will be actively involved in assisting you to shed the armor inhibiting the compassion and kindness of balanced giving and receiving from the heart. Allow the opportunistic visits of the lower chakra totems to support the opening of your heart chakra this month. One of the fastest ways to get to an open heart state and increasing levels of clarity and unconditional love is through, gratitude, prayer, and forgiveness. When we find ourselves in the midst of suffering, chaos, and drama, the magnificent trinity of gratitude, prayer, and forgiveness washes them from the forefront and magically replaces them with what we need. One of the teachers in my sunrise yoga practice always ends the session with these words, which I love and are derived from Buddhist virtues: "Go, beings, into the world, free of suffering and the causes of suffering. Go, beings, into the world and find happiness and the causes of happiness." I find these words tremendously powerful in setting the tone for my day. However, when I do forget them, I am invariably graced with a visit from a pigeon.

Welcoming Your Totem Animal

Can you believe it? You've completed another month, and another animal totem has arrived to be part of your journey through life. This animal will play an intricate role in helping you draw on the things that will warm your heart. More importantly, it will help you release the shackles that keep you bound to the belief patterns in the lower chakras that inhibit heartwarming moments from regularly taking place in your life. Kindness, joy, love, and compassion can only be felt in our hearts. Remember that our past hurts, anger, grief, pain, and suffering are the motivational factors that allow our ego to take control and construct major roadblocks to the bridge into the heart. Your heart totem animal will lead you to the people, places, and things that foster you in forgiving, letting go, and healing those old wounds that obstruct peace, happiness, love, and joy. Your heart totem animal will help you put an end to the mud-slop game of tug-of-war your ego likes to play and allow you to embrace opportunities to clear the path to the heart. Begin to welcome your totem with one of my favorite poems from Shel Silverstein.

>I will not play tug o' war.
>I'd rather play hug o' war.
>Where everyone hugs instead of tugs,
>Where everyone giggles and rolls on the rug,
>Where everyone kisses,
>and everyone grins,
>and everyone cuddles,
>and everyone wins.

This is the part of the ritual when you honor and welcome the company of your new guide. This is the time to review your journal and bask in those defining moments that guided you to the areas that warmed your heart. This is also a time to look at those aspects that seem deep-seated but may also be beacons for change. These can be those age-old stories of suffering, grief, and pain that armor your heart in its heavy state. Trust that Divine guidance will always be there to assist you in things that heal, mend the heavy heart, and bring joy and peace, creating a light and warm heart. Below is a prayer to welcome your heart totem animal. Light a candle and allow the energetic flames to warm your heart chakra as you welcome your heart chakra animal totem guide in your world.

HEART CHAKRA TOTEM ANIMAL PRAYER

I now take the time to look at my journey this month with my heart chakra totem animal. I honor how my heart totem animal has unveiled itself to me in so many heart-warming ways. My heart totem animal will assist me in my journey to seek balance and allow the spiritual realm to guide my physical realm toward love and joy. I know that this magical and enchanting way of life flows with ease and grace. My heart totem animal will assist me in recognizing when my ego is trying to run the show and is in the process of disconnecting me from my source of infinite possibilities. My heart totem animal will lead me to the center of my heart, where the portals of unconditional love, compassion, and true abundance reside. My animal totem will help me recognize that disruptive situations and circumstances help me awaken to my true nature and lead me to my greatest potential. My totem animal will teach me that my will is a breath away from Divine will, and that one breath can bridge the gap that separates me from infinite love. I am not alone. When sadness, grief, or any kind of suffering emerges, my animal guide and the Divine forces of the universe will be there to lift me up and out of the chaos. My heart chakra totem animal guide will help me open, clear, and balance my heart chakra, which directs me to forgive, heal, and love unconditionally. I have faith in the Divine process and allow its guidance to help, lead, and support me on my journey. I now welcome my heart chakra animal totem to assist me on my walk in life.

AMEN.

CHAPTER 13

THE THROAT CHAKRA TOTEM

What's Up with This Chapter

∞ Uncovering Your Throat Chakra Totem
∞ What Is a Throat Chakra?
∞ Let's Get Physical
∞ Honoring Your Throat
∞ The Throat Chakra Totem
∞ Connecting with Your Throat Totem
∞ Welcoming Your Throat Totem Animal

Uncovering Your Throat Chakra Totem

Hip-hip hooray, raise your voice! Congratulations! You've made it to the other side of the chakra system, the great abutment to the higher realms. This is the pivotal point where you embrace the phrase, "As above, so below." The throat chakra is the center of communication and corresponds to how we speak and sing out to the universe. The throat chakra permits our spirit to sing and channel the loving sounds and vibrations in our hearts out into the universe. The vast, infinite universe, in turn, speaks back with its gifts. However, to receive these wonderful gifts, it is essential that we listen. Our voice permits us to drone on and echo the habitual conditioned prattling and chatter of the ego. In this case, the throat chakra represents our own personal little game of truth or consequences. How we voice our choices and listen to what is being said are key aspects of our self-expression, communication, and free will, and all have been primed into the familiar tones corresponding to our evolution through our lower chakras. Every conversation we have either enhances or depletes the energy to this center.

In last month's journey through the heart chakra, you learned that when you make the leap over the ego's frame of mind, you can tap into what it means to bring love and peace to your own heart as well as the hearts of those around you. When we are in this wonderful place of harmony and blissful stillness, our soul sings our serenity to the universe, and in those moments, the universe returns some of the most amazingly magical messages to feed our spirit and the spirits of those around us. I've heard it said that the throat chakra is the chimney for the heart chakra, and what we feel in our hearts we express through our throat chakra. In this month's journey you will learn that whatever comes up the flue of that chimney and out of your mouth reveals how much power and control your ego has over your true nature. Your throat chakra animal totem will assist you in identifying the areas of your life that might be causing you to strike the sour notes, the source of those unpleasant chords you receive from the universe. When I was growing up, we'd say, "Sticks and stones may break my bones, but words will never hurt me." However, I think Robert Fulghum said it best: "Yelling at living things does tend to kill the spirit in them. Sticks and stones may break our bones, but words will break our hearts." So mind your Ps and Qs this month as you learn how they can gracefully invigorate or dreadfully deplete the function of this energy center.

What Is a Throat Chakra?

The throat chakra is the fifth in the chakra system. It's centrally located in the throat and has to do with what we swallow. Fundamentally, the voice is what inhibits our truth. We use our voices to express ourselves in relationships with our families, coworkers, friends, close companions, and even strangers. Our ability to speak, the tone of our voice, and the words we utter all influence the way we communicate and how we express our right to be heard. The most powerful essence of this energy center is that it allows you to express and heal all of your needs, feelings, and thoughts trapped in the caverns of the lower chakras. Keep in mind that as we travel up the chakra system, the vibrational frequency of each chakra increases. In order to hold the higher frequency, you must be a clear channel of the higher frequencies. The more you clear, open, and balance the channels of the lower chakras, the more you are able to connect to and sustain the higher vibrations of the higher realms for longer periods of time. This powerful energy center has a great capacity to either build or destroy every type of relationship in your life. Your throat chakra permits you to engage in the high frequencies of joyful, loving, kindhearted gestures, which results in the delightful development of adoring and devoted relationships. On the other hand, dousing yourself in the low frequencies can bring about great destruction with expressions of anger, hate, judgment, jealousy, greed, and gossip. Every day we apply our voice to communicate what is going on in our lower chakras based on our imprints and conditioning. The majority of us have no awareness that these impressions are constantly sent out by the vibrations of our own voice. The throat chakra is linked to the seven-year cycle spanning ages twenty-nine through thirty-five. This is the phase in our life when our self-expression communicates our independence, inspirational drive, and perceptions of our world.

While most folks believe that the throat chakra is all about our voice, it has just as much to do with our ears. What we hear or choose not to hear certainly impacts how open, clear, and balanced this chakra is, but more importantly how effectively we relate to one another. The throat chakra is the indicator of how well we are balancing having our say while allowing others to have theirs. Communication, at the very least, requires two parties and involves listening just as much as speaking. When you hold back from speaking or stop listening to those you are relating with, you essentially block this powerful energy center. The same is true when you bulldoze over someone without hearing their input. Devoid of listening, it is virtually impossible to follow your intuition, let alone have honest and genuine relationships. Your throat chakra animal totem will assist, support, and aid you in the listening and speaking aspects of your life. These two key critical facets, when not balanced, hinder your connection to the higher realms and inhibit true authentic communication in all relationships. Your totem animal will be instrumental in helping you stay tuned to hearing the higher realms, speaking your truth, and healing the areas in the lower chakras that contribute to your physical health and wellbeing, your emotional happiness and contentment, and your mental peace and tranquility. This, in turn, will allow you to embody continued ease and grace with balanced and spirited wholeness.

Let's Get Physical

It doesn't take an Einstein to know that the throat chakra is located in the neck. This bottleneck region of the body separates the torso or core of your body from what I like to call your squash, or more familiarly, your head. The neck can be thought of as a pillar of strength and support. It houses a highway of muscles, nerves, veins, arteries, and organs that transfer information and matter between your upper and lower being. That's why the throat chakra makes a great representative for the higher and lower realms. This is the place where you essentially walk your talk. Bear in mind that the fuzzy concept of walking your talk was introduced to you about five months ago at the foot chakra. Do not despise those small beginnings, as you are now at the place where the actions of your feet merge with the actions of your mouth and permit the oneness of the higher realms to take shape. The upper perimeter of the neck unites 60 percent of our intuitive abilities in the form of clairaudience, or clear hearing; clairalience, also called clairscent, or clear smelling; and clairgustance, or clear tasting. The throat chakra plays a role in all of these abilities. When this chakra is open, clear, and balanced, these miraculous intuitive senses can expand the profundity of your consciousness to amazingly higher levels. Strange as that sounds, this is especially true when you work with the element of ether.

The element associated with the throat chakra is ether. Now, I'm not talking about the ether that doctors once used for anesthesia or that fluid you spray into the carburetor to turn over that old jalopy decaying in the garage. I'm talking about the esoteric ether. As I mentioned above, it doesn't take an Einstein to know that the throat chakra is in the neck; however, it does take an Einstein to understand the theories and philosophies of the space and matter of ether. So get yourself a comfy seat, fluff up a pillow, and try to stay wide awake while I attempt to make understanding ether easy for you.

When I was a teenager, I had a ragweed allergy. It was so bad that I underwent immunotherapy to help ease some of the symptoms. My doctor made this statement, which has been applied to many fields of endeavor, including sports, military combat, politics, and finding a parking spot in Boston: "Darlene, a good offense is the best defense, and most importantly, just try avoiding ragweed if you can." Okay, I thought, but what is ragweed? I asked the doctor, and she answered, "Oh, it's everywhere. It's all around this building." I remember looking at all the greenery as I left the building that day, wondering which one caused my body to stage this armored defense. Back then, there was no such thing as an Internet search. Regarding ragweed, the general consensus was that it was everywhere, but no one could readily point it out. At that time, I was an avid runner and had entered the Falmouth Road Race, a huge seven-mile race in Cape Cod. I was doing some stretches and starting to feel my allergies emerging. I remember saying to my running pal, "Oh no, my allergies are starting to kick up." My friend said, "What are you allergic to?" My response: "Ragweed!" She said, "Wow, that's everywhere." I said, "So I've heard, but I don't know what it looks like." She pointed to a large clump of a weed growing up from the signpost I was holding onto as I stretched my quadriceps and said, "That's ragweed right there." When I looked at it, I gasped, "Oh my God, that's everywhere!" Yes, indeed, ragweed was everywhere; I'd been literally ensconced in it without ever knowing. Anyway, that was back then, and today, I am happy to say, I am no longer allergic to ragweed. Good thing, because it's everywhere.

So you're probably wondering, what in the heck does this little story have to do with ether? Well, for starters, ether really is everywhere. I think the only difference between ether and ragweed is that the first frost will essentially destroy ragweed and literally nothing can stamp out ether, as it's literally everywhere. Ether is omnipresent, meaning that it is always present everywhere, simultaneously, all the time. Really, it is. In Sanskrit the word for ether is *akasha*, defined as space, sky, or that which is beyond this material world. If you are still with me, this is where it gets deeper, although everything sort of comes together in terms of what it means for the throat chakra.

The Throat Chakra Totem

If you go way back to chapter 1 when you were being groomed about creating space, I talked about space being boundless, vast, limitless, almost indefinable or unconfinable and its very essence being essentially cosmic emptiness. You would get a feel for what I'm saying here if you were to scale the top of the Swiss Alps with an alphorn, howl at the top of your lungs—Ri-co-la!—and then blow that horn. What arises from that projection into space is an echo, a reflection of sound waves that infers that the property of akasha is sound. More importantly, akasha is considered the space between the spaces, where polarities can join together. That means light and dark, masculine and feminine, Red Sox and Yankees, Republicans and Democrats—you name it, the sky's the limit. A variety of traditions, beliefs, and philosophies base their teachings on ether as the first element, as it created the space for the other elements to fill. What a co-inky-dinky; sound is the very thing that gets projected out of your mouth—or piehole, as I like to call it—to express all the elements of your lower chakras into space. The organ that allows this to happen is the larynx. The larynx houses your vocal cords, which essentially function through vibration. The thyroid, shaped like a cute butterfly, is the gland associated with the throat chakra. If you look at the top two wings of this butterfly, they appear to almost embrace the larynx. Energy healers consider thyroid dysfunctions to be associated with the fifth chakra being closed, blocked, or imbalanced; in essence, one's not being able to speak a personal truth. The thyroid is one of the largest glands in the endocrine system, which I find a little odd, because there's a lot of stuff piled into the neck, and that's where I would least expect one of the body's largest glands to be located. Even more so when you consider the pituitary gland in your head is the size of a pea, and that's not an insult to you specifically, it's true for everyone. Basically, the thyroid's job is to regulate the body's energy. Energy and vibration are the two inner forces that work together to help you create your greatest potential. However, for this great potential to be catalyzed into your highest and best potential, it must be purified. The throat chakra, being the center for self-expression and purification, allows you to harness this wonderful energy and vibration. Nonetheless, it must be purified, and the throat chakra allows you to do just that very thing.

The throat chakra is known as the great purifier. Everyone can experience this by bringing the lower chakras, those physical, energetic aspects of self, into alignment with openness, balance, and harmony. As we dedicate ourselves to this practice, the tone vibration emanating from our self-expression becomes increasingly purer and pulsates into akasha, which, in turn, echoes back to us to receive its goodness. The symbol for the throat chakra is a sixteen-petaled lotus flower; each petal represents one of the sixteen vowels in Sanskrit language that are symbols for sound. Within the throat chakra symbol is an upside-down triangle with a full moon, which can sometimes be depicted with the cosmic symbol for sound. One of the coolest things I discovered while studying the anatomy of the larynx is that it looks exactly like the upside-down triangle depicted in the center circle of the throat chakra symbol. The larynx in its open position allows for breathing, and the vocal cords create a perfect V that looks exactly like the upside-down triangle. The circle of the trachea below it looks like the full moon, which represents psychic energy connected to communication without words, as when we are in a state of listening. Isn't that neat? So, as you can see, there's a lot going on in this bottleneck section of your being. When you close your eyes and breathe into this space, you allow yourself to be open to the universal vibrations available for purifying your inner being. The animal totem that presents itself to you this month will help you balance the aspects of the habitual patterns in your communications. As you become faithful to the process of balancing this center, you will begin to witness your communication touchstones shift to harmonious qualities.

Honoring Your Throat

Working with the throat chakra and allowing the powerful energies of this center to work for you will require that you speak your truth. The first step in the passage to speaking your truth is to honor the current state of your throat chakra. Like all the chakras, your throat chakra has an overactive side and an underactive side. It really doesn't matter what end of the spectrum you think you fall into. Allow yourself to gaze at each side, as we usually navigate to both based on our patterns and conditioning. On the underactive side, some individuals may seem shy or reticent in unfamiliar settings, yet in familiar settings they can swing to the overactive side, triggering aggressive and overpowering energies and narrow-mindedness. You might not have noticed these potential shadow sides of yourself until now. Overactive imbalances of the throat chakra in their most aggressive form are arrogance, dogmatic control, and overbearing dominance. These self-righteous tendencies come from voices that bully, gossip, judge harshly, and are prone to critical negative talk. The underactive imbalances of the throat chakra in their most submissive form are usually the shock absorbers for the overactive imbalances. These come with a struggle to express personal needs and wants, excessive shyness, and a strong degree of secretiveness and unreliability. These timid and withdrawn tendencies appear with voices that may appear weak, stutter, withhold words, or are basically incapable of speaking up.

Of course, these are all extreme examples. However, when strong disagreements do emerge in our dealings, the forces of these propensities can surface quite swiftly and without restraint. When you become conscious of these forces, consider it an auspicious moment to honor that which is ready to be released. The evolution through each of your lower chakras has taught you to learn through a human-influenced sense of self; the fruition of that evolution through your upper chakras is an "unlearning" through the divinely inspired essence of your true nature. Honoring your throat chakra opens

The Throat Chakra Totem

the floodgates, allowing the powerful forces of the universe to assist you in speaking your truth while allowing the lower chakras to begin to come into complete alignment. The throat chakra is the center for purification, and as we travel up the chakra system, the vibrational frequencies increase with each chakra. If the lower chakras are not cleared, opened, and balanced, not a whole lot of good vibration will spew out of your mouth. Make no mistake about it, the throat chakra is located between your heart and third eye for a very good reason, as your mouth becomes the battleground between the two of them. This is where your wishing heart, eager to express your true nature, clashes with those perceived imprints that spout out of your ego mind. Einstein said, "We cannot solve our problems with the same thinking we used when we created them." If we want to produce different results in our life, we have to think differently and nurture a different mindset than the one we were trained to follow. This involves listening and speaking contrary to our conditioning.

I have a friend who is a spiritual teacher and former Catholic nun who felt her soul and true voice were trapped in the patriarchal system of the church. Thirty-three years after her vow to the church, she renounced her contract and went in search of the voice of her spirit. Paradoxically, her decision to leave the church did not come with hospitable embraces or well wishes. Those who were part of her once devoted and caring circle of peers bluntly distanced themselves from her and shunned her. Her isolation and loneliness were heartrending and mournful, yet amazingly eye-opening. She asked herself, "How could this place I called my devotional, faithful home for thirty-three years demonstrate such condescension and disdain for something that called to my spirit's voice?" You teach best what you need to learn, and the road to her voice put her on a wonderful journey of self; she now teaches workshops on voice empowerment. We laughed at lunch as she told me of a ninety-two-year-old woman who finally learned to say no as part of her voice empowerment teachings. This once meek little senior now pops off like a bold child who's just learned a new word. No! No! My friend said in her wonderful New Zealand accent, "I believe the staff at her residence is quite annoyed with me. You never know how much you hold inside until you let your spirit free, and when you do, you feel like you've finally found home."

It's never too late to learn to speak your truth. Some people live their whole life trapped in a place called home listening to the voices of others and never really hearing their own. The animal totem that comes to you this month will surely have a powerful influence on helping you speak your truth. As you honor your throat chakra, allow yourself to move beyond the limitations of those imprints that don't always speak to your true nature. Now you learn to unlearn those confines of your mold and surrender to the Divine forces waiting to guide you to the sound of your new voice, leaving the echo of the old one behind.

Ways to Honor Your Throat

Pray aloud
Listen to the sounds of nature
Only listen to good things being said
Sing along with your favorite songs
Practice saying nice things to strangers
Listen to a seashell or the sound of the waves
Say sweet things to yourself throughout the day
Record your voice with something that makes you laugh

The Throat Chakra Totem

Your throat chakra totem will help you with all forms of your communication, whether it is the way you listen or speak or the actions you take to communicate with the visible or invisible world. Every creature of nature, whether subtly or obviously, offers opportunities for you to be informed with great messages. You can see them appear metaphorically in your life in those awkward moments that create a frog in your throat or cause you to clam up, in a disappointment that makes you not want to give a hoot, in an incessant talker who rattles on, in an aping friend who parrots or mocks, or even in your fuming boss who roars like a lion. The list can go on and on. The animal that presents itself will provide valuable guidance to help you exchange information in the most empowering and respectful ways. This animal will help you honor your highest potential, which holds the truth of your own voice.

Our communication styles are not just limited to our mouth and ears. The throat chakra is also connected to a network of nerves that control our hands, wrist, arms, and shoulders.

These parts of our body are always at play when we are communicating. Our inflections and gestures say just as much, if not more, than what comes out of our mouth. People use hand gestures when talking on the telephone, to express anger when cut off in traffic, or even to hitch a ride. Our inflections and gestures not only communicate a message to the listener, but also reflect our attitude. The animal totem that comes to you will hold tremendous teachings to assist you with your communications, especially the ones that tend to lean toward the shadow side. Our shadow side holds the words, gestures, and inflections that expose the areas in our lower self that need healing, clearing, and balancing, and most of the time we are unaware of them.

The Throat Chakra Totem

Animals communicate through gesture, scent, and sound, whether by listening or through vocalizations. Animal communications are some of the most fascinating displays to observe. Male fiddler crabs actually wave their claws to attract a female, much like saying, "Yoo-hoo! I'm over here!" Elephants stomp and scream and flap their ears when threatened. And skunks set their boundaries by, well, you know, pretty much just showing up. Communication is an adaptation that helps animals survive. Just like animals in the wild, our communication is an adaptation that helps us survive, although everyone's conditioning varies its style.

Your throat chakra totem animal's mission will be to help you look at your approach to communicating, not just with others but also yourself. How you communicate with yourself speaks to the universe, and the universe gives you just what you ask for in the form of your thoughts. This is where the proverbial "What goes around, comes around" comes back to bite you. Your expressions, whether good or bad, have consequences you might not really like the taste of when they're served back to you. Your throat chakra totem animal will help you stay tuned into those so-called awful expressions and help you transform them into the wonderfully vibrating energies that always bring the sounds that soothe your soul.

When you mindfully allow yourself to become aware that the words you choose to communicate and the manner in which they come from you can have destructive effects on you, as well as others, you allow the purification process of the throat chakra to take hold and the higher vibrating energies to flow through you. These are the vibrational frequencies that keep you in alignment with Divine guidance. It is through this chakra center that you learn to speak your truth in the most honest and loving manner, because it benefits and connects you to your truth and others who will support it. Your throat chakra animal will warn you and prompt you to return to Divine guidance. It is through this chakra center that you learn to speak your truth, and your throat totem animal will support you as you get a real taste for making that happen.

Meditation

As you go inward this month and connect with your throat chakra totem animal, reflect on the power of your voice and the serenity of your listening. This will help accelerate the clearing of this chakra. Ask yourself if the power of your voice reveals the fear, guilt, shame, and grief of your lower chakras. Or, instead, does it channel gratitude, patience, acts of kindness, and forgiveness that come from the graces of the higher realms? Allow yourself to look at where your shadow voice may cause hurt or unhappiness and where the warm voice of your spirit heals and brings about cheerfulness. Give yourself permission to look at where your ego may wind you up with vehemence and wrath, causing you to react and block the voice of guidance whispering in your ears. In the heart chakra, there is no difference between giving and receiving, as it is always balanced with love. In the throat chakra, there is no difference between speaking and listening, as it is always balanced with understanding. Meditation is the great peacemaker that helps calm the ego mind. As you meditate this month, surround yourself with the sweet sounds of nature and ask for guidance with the blocked and unbalanced aspects of your voice. Take your meditation outside and gaze at the blue sky, allowing the unconditional vibrations of the universe to purify any imbalances. Enjoy the quiet place of stillness, and allow yourself to hear the answers that are delivered. Give yourself permission to set the tone for your true nature to emerge. Continue to carry out your meditation a minimum of three days in a row, allowing yourself to be open to the frequencies of your throat chakra totem.

	THROAT CHAKRA TOTEM ACCESSORIES
CANDLES	Use candles to help stimulate the throat chakra and invoke your connection with your throat chakra animal totem. Candles can create a relaxing ambience that allows you to listen your inner voice. Select candles with blue tones to aid in connecting to the throat chakra vibrations. Allow yourself to experience any colors or scents that awaken your senses and engage your voice to speak your desires and passions. When shopping, allow yourself to experience all the candles' pleasing aspects: their shapes, number of wicks, colors, scents, and even their names. There are many candle scents on the market specific to the throat chakra. Candles can have wonderful throat-chakra-invoking names, like Thankful Thoughts, Quiet Listening, and The Sound of Flames. Pay attention to each description's words.
INCENSE	Use incense for clearing any space and calling upon your throat chakra animal totem. Incense adds a wonderful tone to your clearing rituals. Scents such as wisteria, eucalyptus, rosemary, thyme, sage, and lavender stimulate the throat chakra and add a nice touch to your meditation or relaxation sessions. Incense helps connect you to the element of air when you follow its wispy trail of smoke. When using incense, you can pray aloud, chant, or practice toning. There are many blends of incense on the market specific to the throat chakra. Allow yourself to experiment with different types of incense, as it comes in cone, stick, powder, rope, and pellet forms. Incense can expand your sacred ritual with opening, clearing, and/or balancing your throat chakra. Listening to the very subtle crackling or sizzle of the resins is a wonderful way to enhance your clairaudience.

CRYSTALS	There is literally a crystal for every expression of your voice. Many crystals benefit the throat chakra. Blue lace agate is a wonderful stone with soft blue tones throughout. It is great for healing and activating the throat chakra. I have just been turned on to blue kyanite, a wonderful stone for opening up all communication channels. It helps strengthen your telepathic skills and acts as a great bridge between two people who have a hard time communicating. I use lapis lazuli for my third eye; however, it is a wonderful stone for balancing the throat chakra and healing the throat, larynx, and thyroid. Siberian blue quartz is a radiant crystal that helps activate the throat chakra. This crystal stimulates and eases communications for public speakers and helps refine information received, making it a powerful tool for psychics and mediums. I use blue calcite as the throat chakra stone in my personal chakra crystal set. This stone is great for amplifying energies, particularly in the area of communication. It helps you express your views calmly and with tact, and helps stimulate decision-making. Allow yourself to experiment with different crystals. See which ones attract you. Hold them in your hands and examine any subtle connections you might feel, as these are your intuitive expressions responding.
AROMA-THERAPY	Essential oils can be used for healing, relaxing, invoking, clearing—you name it. They are a perfect way to enhance your home spa while utilizing the water element. Their therapeutic properties can boost diffusers, vaporizers, humidifiers, bathtubs, and fountains to create a botanical utopia in all your environments. Remember that essential oils are very highly concentrated, volatile, aromatic essences of plants. I suggest buying them from reliable vendors or all-natural stores whose experienced personnel can guide you in their proper use. Essential oils can be used for healing sore throats, added to a compress for neck injuries, or as a calming component when stressful communications emerge. The following are some essential oils that work well with the throat chakra: chamomile, spearmint, peppermint, eucalyptus, lemon, clove, and frankincense. Of course, I am speaking for myself here; you should voice whatever essential oils speak best to you.

Connecting with Your Throat Totem

Andy Rooney once said, "If dogs could talk, it would take a lot of the fun out of owning one." I'm not sure I agree with that statement. I think it would be kind of interesting to learn their views on that unconditional love they seem to have the corner on. Your throat chakra animal totem will be guiding you in the very nature of that task. Every creature has a unique way of communicating that can play an important role in teaching you how to communicate and relate in an unconditionally loving manner. I grew up in an environment where hollering was part of the everyday format. In fact, no one ever gave it a second thought in my family. My mom hollered out the window to call us inside, yelled from the kitchen when dinner was ready, and shouted when you had the audacity to test her reign. That hollering part of her conditioning became a hollering part of my conditioning. It was a long time before I recognized that this shadow part of me that shouted out to the world was intimidating, aggressive, and worked quite well to get my needs met from those who would not openly dispute it and basically crouched in silence. This yelling pattern exposed itself in every one of my lower chakras. I utilized it when my survival fears popped up in my root chakra, when the emotions of my inner child emerged in my sacral chakra, and as part of my ego's technique to wield power and control in the daily routines of my solar plexus chakra. Sound intense? Not really. We all have these so-called demons that rear their ugly heads when it comes to our communications and trying to express ourselves and our needs. While in family dynamics it can be totally unseen and just a familiar way of interacting, to an outsider it can be a hair-raising experience.

When I began my personal journey to open, clear, and balance my chakras, I started to notice a part of me that reacted to life with this madcap hollering. As I committed myself to really look at this part of me, I began to see it mirrored all around me. My family, my spouse, my coworker, my friends—they all seemed to employ this same approach of expression when a dislike emerged, which totally miffed me. At the same time, it gave me a sense of curiosity that encouraged me to seriously move toward really looking at this part of me and addressing it. I didn't want to be one of those holla-back girls. When you move toward shifting behavioral patterns, spirit will always give you ample opportunities to get it right, and your totems will present themselves to you with great frequency.

One of the funniest ways I got control of my holla-back attitude was when I was on my way to an appointment with someone whose challenging receptionist reminded me of a cross between a barracuda and a vicious wolverine. Symbolically, of course, but I'd watched her antics a number of times, and it seemed she got a certain amount of pleasure out of getting people riled up. On my way there, I saw my throat chakra totem—the hawk—soaring in the sky above the highway. I said to him, "I know why you're here. Don't worry, I'm on to her. I'm not going to take that bait and let her get to me," as she had always seemed get the hair up on my back in the past. No sooner did I get there than she snapped at me that there was no appointment in my name on her schedule.

I didn't come to see you, I thought, and I could see myself starting to fall into defensive-linebacker mode as she rattled on about how she couldn't reschedule me sooner because I actually didn't have an appointment. I pulled up the e-mail on my cell phone confirming the appointment time and date and tried not to be terse. As I mindfully showed her the e-mail on my phone, she shouted, "I can't see that! You don't have it on paper?" I could feel myself starting to react and said, "No, I don't. I didn't know I would need objective evidence to reserve my appointment." I took a breath to get myself centered, remembering my hawk episode on the way there, and asked, "Do you want me to send this to you?" I could feel my tone becoming snappish, and I could feel a negative expression on my face as I looked at her. She said, "Why don't you just sit over there and let me see what's going on here!" She looked at her screen, paused, then looked up and said, "You're lucky. There's an opening at ten o'clock." I thought to myself, Why, you little—that's my appointment time! I could feel my hair-trigger response simmering, but I could also feel that part of grace in me that wasn't going to take the bait on that hook.

Feeling myself teetering at strike or resist, I gawked at her, then down at the magazines on the table in front of me so she wouldn't know I was agitated. I caught sight of my hawk on the cover of a wildlife magazine, which really grounded a refinement of grace into me at a much-needed time. I picked it up, smiling, and gazed over the magazine at her. I smiled kindly as she tapped on her keyboard. Needless to say, she got up and just seemed to disappear, and I was called in for my appointment at ten o'clock, as scheduled. Later that day, as I was out walking my dog along the river, I reflected on how grateful I was to have followed the guidance and not taken the reaction hook to bulldoze over her and make a stink and marinate in the soup of dissonant energy. As I passed a bunch of oak trees, I heard a loud screech, and there on one of the limbs stood a red-tailed hawk, just screaming its head off. Its mouth made an O, like in Edvard Munch's painting *The Scream*. I couldn't believe it. I had never heard such a powerful scream coming out of a hawk. I had heard that hawks could scream, but I'd never seen one so close up and so animated. I burst out laughing, so grateful for the wonderful amusement and humbled by the magnificent messages I'd received that day that had warned and guided me and now so amusingly affirmed my personal achievement of not being a holla-back girl. This majestic creature has been an astonishing guide for me over the years and continues to support me with some of the most magical and enlightening counsel.

When your throat chakra totem comes to visit, it will invariably be an invitation from the powers of Divine grace to behold some message. The spirit guidance that emerges will be an opportunity to listen, laugh, speak, sing, pray, and make an active commitment to quality communication. The throat chakra is the place where you learn to express yourself with harmonious tones that bring peace, love, abundance, joy, and happiness to yourself and others. Alice Walker said, "*Thank you* is the best prayer that anyone could say. I say that one a lot. *Thank you* expresses extreme gratitude, humility, and understanding." I couldn't agree more with her. Your throat chakra totem animal will be the guiding force that connects you to the wonderful expressions of the Divine, and the only thing you really need to do is show an expression of thankfulness.

Welcoming Your Throat Totem Animal

Hail to another animal totem becoming part of your Divine team of guidance! This animal will play an intricate role in helping you sing the magnificent glories that are part of the personal expression of you. To do this you must put a voice to the things that you no longer wish to carry and release them from your resonance. Then allow that hollow void to be filled with the fruits of harmonious vibrations that echo the true joyous expression of you. Your throat chakra animal totem will help you create the sounds that call forth the people, signal the places, and activate the things that will foster a symphony of harmony on your path. It will be up to you to use your voice to sing the praises that summon the universe to echo back the peaceful, loving vibrations that come with your efforts to speak words of gratitude, forgiveness, and prayer. These precious vibrational frequencies are the vital source that opens, clears, and balances each one of your chakras. This is the part of the ritual where you honor and welcome the company of your new guide. This is the time to review your journal and bask in those defining moments that guided you to speak up and be heard. This is also the time to look at those areas where you didn't make progress and should have, for these areas are now beacons for transformation. Trust that Divine guidance will always be there to assist you with voicing your true nature and will help you express it in every possible way. Below is a prayer to welcome your throat totem animal. Light a candle, put on some music, and sing a song of praise to welcome your new guide into your world.

THROAT TOTEM ANIMAL PRAYER

I now take the time to review my journey this month with my throat chakra totem animal. I honor how my throat totem animal has unveiled itself to me in so many expressive ways. My throat totem animal will assist me in the journey to speak my truth and allow the spiritual realms to guide my physical realm toward balanced harmony in all my expressions. I know that comforting and peaceful harmony flow with ease and grace, and to sustain these vibrations in me, I must grow. My throat totem animal will assist me in my growing process to speak the truth of who I am. As I awaken to my true voice, it opens the portal that fosters kindhearted understanding that bring things harmoniously together for me. My animal totem will help me to embrace challenging situations and circumstances, as they will help me awaken to my truth and the voice that shines on my true nature. My throat totem animal will lead me to the places where the soft, gentle sounds of nature will nourish my soul when the going gets rough. My throat totem animal guide will help me open, clear, and balance my throat chakra, which guides me to speak and sing the words that forgive, heal, and love unconditionally. I have faith in the Divine process and allow its guidance to help me, lead me, and support me on my journey. I now welcome my throat chakra animal totem to assist me on my walk in life.

AMEN.

CHAPTER 14

THE THIRD EYE CHAKRA TOTEM

What's Up with This Chapter

∞ Uncovering Your Third Eye Chakra Totem
∞ What Is a Third Eye Chakra?
∞ Let's Get Physical
∞ Honoring Your Third Eye
∞ The Third Eye Chakra Totem
∞ Connecting with Your Third Eye Totem
∞ Welcoming Your Third Eye Totem Animal

Uncovering Your Third Eye Chakra Totem

Well, look at you! I see you have added a wonderful new animal totem to the incredible forces of your guidance team. At the end of this month, you will have a deeper perspective of what that means, as you have now reached the sixth chakra. I like to call it the vision center; it's also referred to as the brow, third eye, or ajna chakra (pronounced aj-nah). This is the chakra where you view your world and the powers of your guidance team through some of the most amazingly unique and unparalleled learning experiences. It is through this chakra that you illuminate the path deep into the inner world that shines your light from within. Each one of your animal totems will assist you to see your way to the treasure, the pearls of wisdom that are the very source of your light and the gateway to your true nature. As you embark on uncovering your third eye animal totem, you will also activate a new command over your path that will permit you to follow the compass needle of your own inner vision. The third eye center gives you the unique perspective of seeing your thoughts manifest into the physical forms that are the expression of you and are ultimately fondly shared by those around you.

149

In last month's journey through the throat chakra, you became aware of how the inner and outer voices in your life play an essential part in the expression of you. Through a committed practice of exposing yourself to higher vibrational frequencies that resonate peaceful harmony and joyful love, you not only clear and bring balance to the throat chakra but also allow the lower chakras to clear and come into alignment. However, to uphold this guiding principle, you must see what is going on around you. The sixth chakra is where you learn the art of adjusting your focus on all those images around you to bring true clarity. The animal totem that presents itself to you this month will assist you in bringing clarity to your vision, which will help you develop a true assessment of all the imagery at play around you.

What Is a Third Eye Chakra?

The third eye is the sixth chakra in the chakra system. It is located in the middle of the forehead, slightly above your two physical eyes. We use our eyes to perceive the physical world around us, and we use our invisible third eye to give us perceptions beyond our ordinary sight, which connects us to our insight and intuition. Your third eye center works very closely with the higher realms and is always available to illuminate guidance at any given moment. Much like your throat chakra is the crux of you speaking your truth, the focal point of the third eye is seeing truth in your vision. Your ability to see clearly in life is enhanced enormously with the help of the third eye. This powerful energy center is the portal to the infinite realms, allowing you to see the past, present, and future through the subtleties of what appears to be an invisible multidimensional universe. The third eye is the lens of the Divine gift of clairvoyance, which focuses on our inner vision, telepathy, intuition, and paranormal forms of knowing. Through this vantage point, you are able to see the nonlinear universe, devoid of polarities such as good and bad, right and wrong, peace and war, beginnings and endings. This is where the chaos of opposite realities melts into the neutrality that renders our true nature without any distortions.

In order to illuminate the gifts of this powerful center, you must be willing to shine a spotlight on the perceived landscape you are viewing. This landscape is the backdrop that maintains our patterns, habitual conditioning, beliefs, and unconscious behavior that blur our vision. Last month you noticed how your self-expression either enhances or depletes the energy of your throat chakra; this month you will see how the way you perceive life will either bring clarity or obscure the vision through your third eye.

The third eye chakra is linked to the seven-year cycle spanning the ages of thirty-six through forty-two. Interestingly enough, this is the time in our life where our outlook starts to refocus from an early adulthood point-of-view, which is sometimes bombarded by an ego's perspective, to the natural progression of mature vision, which is geared more toward wisdom and understanding. Unless, of course your outlook changes and you make a trajectory to the nearest off-ramp, what some may refer to as midlife crisis. In that case, the backdrop becomes a radical, chaotic scene as the ego searches for its mojo in the material world of spray tans, sports cars, impressing younger lovers, or skirting responsibilities. This would be where the ego really goes hog wild to puff itself up. This is also why the third eye is referred to as the center of illumination, because if you have ever seen someone in the throes of a midlife crisis, it can be pretty illuminating.

The third eye center gives you the opportunity to look at your reality and ask yourself what the famous television commercial featuring Ella Fitzgerald did when she shattered a glass with her voice as it was recorded to a Memorex audio cassette. The tape was played back, and the recording also broke the glass, begging the question, "Is it live, or is it Memorex?" This is called the world of illusion, where you take command of how you truly see life. I mentioned earlier, the third eye chakra is also referred to as the ajna chakra. In Sanskrit *ajna* means to command or control. It is through our vision that we take command or control of our thoughts and the role they play in the theater of the lower chakras. These are the very actions that we carry out on a daily basis through the physical aspects of our lower self. This is where we engage with the images of our thoughts, dreams, fantasies, and intuition and essentially navigate through the fields of live or Memorex. The third eye chakra is the center of consciousness. Within this center you will find the blueprints for fostering the awakening of your true nature. The animal totem guide that presents itself to you will be instrumental in helping you navigate through what may appear to be a foggy web of illusions to realize what is true in your field of vision.

Let's Get Physical

Any ambiguity you may have about the third eye can be summed up with the question "Is it live, or is it Memorex?" There are a few reasons why I see it this way. One is because the third eye is known as the invisible eye. However, if it's invisible, how do you know it's really there? Another aspect up for debate is which endocrine gland, if any, is associated with the third eye. Is it the pineal or the pituitary gland? While both of these glands are planted deep in the middle of your cranium and associated with the brain, each plays a specific role in the vital functions of our physical body. From a spiritual, mystical, metaphysical, or occult premise, each has its own perceived functions as well.

When I teach my animal totem classes, I tend to lean toward the pineal gland being associated with the third eye. I'll explain why, and at the same time, I'll give you an opportunity to consider for yourself which one applies best for you. Just know that when it comes to the third eye, there are no right or wrong answers. If you were to research the pineal gland, you would find that, among other names, the pineal gland is called the third eye. The pituitary gland, on the other hand, is by no means called the third eye. It is referred to quite simply as the pituitary gland. Hold on, because here is where the slope becomes a little slippery. If you looked at an enlarged cross-section of the brain, you'd see the pineal gland actually looks like the Eye of Horus. Also known as the all-seeing eye, the Eye of Horus was a powerful symbol of protection in ancient Egypt. This eye can be broken down into six parts that correspond to the six senses—the five basic ones of seeing, hearing, smelling, touching, and tasting, and the sixth sense of thought. Again, this fits quite nicely with the third eye/ pineal gland theory, as the third eye is the sixth chakra and considered the motivating force of what we call sixth-sentient beings. Now, if you were to look at the location of the pituitary gland, interestingly enough, it too is located right in the center of your brain. To get to it, you would have to travel up your nostril and then proceed straight back; just below the crossing of your optic nerves is your pea-sized pituitary gland. Again, this is not a personal insult to you; everyone's pituitary gland is the size of a pea. Because this pea gland is so close to the many nerves that operate your vision, it is not uncommon for physicians to check the pituitary gland's function, not the pineal's, when patients complain of blurred vision, loss of peripheral vision, or double vision. As you can see, both glands can be connected to our perceived vision of reality. Physiologically, the pineal gland is responsible for our light and dark sides, so to speak. I'll try to make this simple, but I will warn you that a can of Red Bull or a double-shot of espresso might be warranted for this technical information.

Biochemically, the pineal gland is what I will refer to as a little sweatshop deep in the middle of your cranium that controls your dreamtime world and your waking world. It does so by utilizing tryptophan, an essential amino acid, which, in case you didn't know, cannot be produced in our bodies so we must get it from food sources like turkey, cheese, eggs, nuts, seeds, a variety of vegetables, or a Big Mac value meal. Tryptophan functions as a biochemical precursor for serotonin and melatonin. A precursor is something that comes before something else and leads in the development of another something. For example, a thoughtless snide remark can be the precursor to an argument with an overly sensitive spouse. I only use this example because serotonin and melatonin are connected to mood regulation, and thoughtless snide remarks can certainly affect someone's mood. Serotonin and melatonin help you sleep better and maintain Zen-like mind states where everything is wonderrrrrrful. The precursor to melatonin is serotonin, and within the pineal gland serotonin is acetylated and then methylated to yield melatonin. *Acetylated* and *methylated* are fancy words that chemists use when they stand in front of their little glass test tubes doing chemical stuff, which is basically what is going on in your pineal gland, only on a smaller scale. If you are starting to feel moody, hungry, or sleepy right now, it might not necessarily have to do with what you're reading. It's probably your serotonin or melatonin levels doing it for you. Melatonin is considered the hormone of darkness and will not come out in the light. That's because it is stimulated by darkness and suppressed by light. Basically, your pineal gland is the eye that senses light, which plays a role in regulating your personal rhythm of day and night.

The third eye is known as the chakra of perception and self-realization. It is through the vantage point of this chakra that you awaken to the unfolding of your true nature. The symbol for the third eye chakra is a two-petaled lotus flower. The two petals represent two polarities that are always trying to maintain a balance within all aspects of our reality. Each petal gives way to a channel of life-force energy that assimilates into blissful neutrality with our focused awareness. One petal represents the feminine lunar energies that are passive, nurturing, nourishing, and purifying, while the other petal represents the masculine sun energies that are active, productive, physical, and hold great dynamic vitality. In the center of this chakra's symbol lies a downward-facing triangle, in which the sacred syllable *om* stands. The downward-facing triangle represents the universal energies of creation flowing down into our being to help us see our true nature, which is beginningless and endless, with no wrongs or rights and no ups or downs. Only illusion, delusion, and denial blocks the truth in our vision and inhibits our ability to unite the two polarities into the harmonious neutrality that carries the essence of our true nature.

These forms of self-deception create what is called the web of maya. Maya is much like a spider's web, a sticky mesh that traps the creature's prey. As we hold fast to our conditioning, beliefs, and habitual thought patternings, we too become stuck in this web of illusions. The more we engage with these forms of self-deception, the more stuck we become in our habitual ways. Change, expansion, flexibility, and illumination of the path to our true nature become difficult, and our unconscious conditionings inevitably cause us to become more caught up in the tangled web. The third eye is the vision center, to help you learn to see clearly. When we focus our vision on the patterns of the web we are weaving with our habitual thought patterning, conditioning, and beliefs, we soon find that the sticky threads of resistance keep us fixed, stuck, and caught up in the maze of disorder and chaos. It is through focused awareness of the web's patterns that we are able to perceive the subtle, nonsticky silk threads that allow us to easily navigate to and from our desires without resistance. The totem animal that presents itself to you will be your visual aid, guiding you to see clearly the ultimate nature of your reality, and will lead you to the nonsticky silk threads of embracing your true nature.

Honoring Your Third Eye

To enter into the portal of the third eye and allow the powerful energies of this center to shine, you must look very closely at the truth of your vision. To do this, it's important that you honor what you see with open curiosity, no matter what that landscape may look like. This practice will give you a new perspective to see what is true and allow the guiding forces to surround you and lead you forward in a way that heals, empowers, protects, and encourages your true nature. As you take on this mission to look, see, and watch, give yourself permission to be the critic who creates the true review of the theatrical production known as your life. Allow yourself to look for denial, delusion, or illusions that result in dramas that obstruct the view of your true nature. When you give yourself permission to see what is true, the complicated contradictions begin to clear and the lens of your third eye becomes transparent. As you gaze at the scene and the script of your world, see if you can find any forms of denial. Denial is the place where we fall short of seeing what is true. Allow yourself to go deep and seek out areas that might be fraught with delusion. Delusions are those beliefs or conditions we maintain even when there is strong evidence to the contrary. Illusions are the demon of the third eye, aspects that deceive or mislead us with notions, dogmas, or a system of beliefs that keep us bound, limited, and restricted from the spirit of our true nature. Your third eye animal totem will be instrumental in helping you see the truth of the web that you weave. Your animal will help you remove the web's flimsy traps and snares that keep you bound to its patterns. Your animal will lead you to see the beauty and exquisite perfection of the web's silken threads that hold the essence of your true nature. Your third eye animal totem will be the benevolent gatekeeper, assisting you in seeing your way to your true nature.

Ways to Honor Your Third Eye

Stargaze with a telescope
Go to a museum or art gallery
Go bird-watching with binoculars
Play games, especially with children
Carry out visualization meditations
Take a different way home from anywhere
Take pictures while walking in your neighborhood
Allow yourself to daydream; use your imagination often

The Third Eye Chakra Totem

As humans we sometimes tend to lose sight of what matters most to us. Your third eye animal totem will help you focus in on all the aspects of your exterior world for observation and evaluation in your interior world. This animal will help you fearlessly bear those shadows cast by the unconscious dispositions of your lower self connected with your ego and bring them into the light to be gracefully transmuted by your Divine higher self. Your animal totem, through its keen eyesight, flexible adaptation, or innumerable other unique characteristics, holds exceptional gifts for you in those areas where you will need truth of vision. Animals' eyes work in all kinds of ways that allow them to see as well as protect their continued existence. Many of the prey animals—those with hooves, such as cattle, goats, sheep, antelope; and even octopuses—have horizontal pupils that give them increased peripheral vision. These animals have a visual field of up to three hundred thirty degrees, as opposed to humans, who generally only see in a field of about one hundred eighty degrees. Some predator animals—such as lions, snakes, lizards, sharks, and foxes—have vertical pupils, which give them great depth perception, useful for capturing what's in front of them. Whether your totem animal's pupils are circular, oval, slit, crescent, W-shaped, or pearl-shaped really doesn't matter. What matters is the excellent depth perception your totem animal will lend you when it's time to stay focused in the field of vision of your true nature.

My third eye animal totem is a ferret, and while I had my own domestic ferret, it was the black-footed ferret that actually presented itself to me and sealed the deal. However, my domestic ferret played an immense role in that confirmation. It is not unusual for our domestic pet companions to arise as one of our animal totems. No matter what species, it will manifest in a way that will make it clear to you. Ferrets generally sleep eighteen to twenty hours a day, but when they're up, they are up! I remember how my little guy just seemed to shift and suddenly be awake all the time. He went out of his way to get my attention with his crazy antics. He had this boundless curiosity where everything was something to investigate. I wondered if he had found a way to tap into the coffee beans, as his sleep time seemed nonexistent—really odd for ferrets. If he wasn't under my feet as I walked around the house, he was scratching my legs or biting my toes to pick him up as I worked at my desk. When I heard something smash downstairs, I'd say, "Oh no, what is he into now?" No matter how much attention I gave him, it didn't seem to be enough to settle him down. I wondered if he was suffering from an adrenal problem often found in ferrets and made an appointment to have him checked. However, what I discovered was that all that time, he was just trying to get me to look at him and make the connection. He'd scratch on the door, intent on getting in, when I was doing my meditation. When I was out running errands, I got a wonderful affirmation of a black-footed ferret, and it finally dawned on me that the ferret was my third eye totem. I couldn't wait to get home to thank my little guy for all his hard work. When I arrived, I found him belly up, in a deep sleep stupor in my ski hat. How metaphorical. I can still remember him being out for days. Never underestimate the connections your pets have to the spirit world. Whether it is a goldfish in a fishbowl or hamster on the exercise wheel, they all can bring great gifts of vision from the forces on the other side. The question is, will you see it for what it's worth?

Your third eye vision will not only aid you, but also support those close to you. When you mindfully allow yourself to become aware of what you choose to look at or not to look at, it opens the portal to your third eye and allows for the insights required to see your way through the apparent appearances at hand. These come in the form of higher vibrational frequencies that manifest in everyday life as pictures, symbols, or something put right in front of your eyes that keeps you in alignment with Divine guidance. It is through this chakra center that you will learn to see truth in your vision in the most honest and accurate way, benefiting you and connecting you with what is essential in seeing your way to your true nature. Helen Keller once said, "The only thing worse than being blind is having sight but no vision." Your third eye animal totem will help you take a nice peek at what you're seeing.

Meditation

As you go inward this month to connect with your third eye chakra totem animal, allow the powerful sensory organs of your hyperalert eyes to turn inward and guide you out of narrow thought patterns and into the infinite, an expansive openness that awaits you with its wonderful insights. Set an intention to allow yourself to look at everything in your field of view with new eyes. Investigate every image with that live-or-Memorex curiosity. The third eye is capable of seeing beyond the density of the ordinary and into the subtler realms of the extraordinary when you hold your focus and redirect your vision to it. As you meditate this month, seek out new ways of bringing vivid colors to your looking within. Try a guided meditation from the Internet, or practice your own visualizations to help bring clear vision to the third eye. Devote the time you need to enjoying a quiet place of stillness, and allow yourself to see what messages are delivered to you. Give yourself permission to observe the truth in your vision, as it will always lead you to the path of your true nature. Carry out your meditation as you normally do, and allow yourself to open up to the wonderful frequencies of your third eye chakra totem.

THIRD EYE CHAKRA TOTEM ACCESSORIES

CANDLES	Use candles to help stimulate your third eye chakra and invoke your connection with your third eye chakra animal totem. Candles can create a relaxing ambience and stimulate your imagination and daydreaming, which really helps you get into the gap when meditating. Select candles with dark blue indigo tones to aid in connecting to the third eye chakra vibrations. Allow yourself to experience any colors or scents that awaken your senses to engage your imagination and springboard you toward thinking about your hopes, desires, and passions. When shopping, allow yourself to experience all the candles' pleasing aspects: their shapes, number of wicks, colors, scents, and even their names. Many candle scents on the market are specific to the third eye chakra. Candles can have wonderful third-eye-chakra-invoking names, like Intuition, Inner Knowing, Clear Thinking, Clear Vision, Absolute Light, and Ajna. Read the candle's description and take note of its packaging.
INCENSE	Use incense for clearing any space and calling upon your third eye chakra animal totem. Incense adds a wonderful tone to your clearing rituals and inspires the imagination to connect with your intuition. Scents such as sage, eucalyptus, cedar, myrrh, frankincense, and holy basil stimulate the third eye chakra and add a nice touch to your meditation or relaxation sessions. Incense helps connect you to the element of air when you follow its wispy trail of smoke, good for visualizing your intentions, desires, and passions or practicing clairvoyance. Many blends of incense on the market are specific to the third eye chakra. Allow yourself to experiment with the different types; incense comes in cone, stick, powder, rope, and pellet forms and can be a pleasurable way to expand your sacred ritual while opening, clearing, and/or balancing your third eye chakra. Give yourself permission to be allured by the smoke trails' wispy shapes and see where they guide you.

(Continued)

THIRD EYE CHAKRA TOTEM ACCESSORIES (Continued)

CRYSTALS	There is literally a crystal to help activate, enhance, heal, and clear any kind of psychic energy in and around this center. Several crystals can benefit the third eye chakra. Though I mentioned lapis lazuli for the throat chakra, I use it primarily for the third eye. It aids in opening this chakra; stimulates psychic abilities, enlightenment, and meditation journeys; and helps connect you with your spirit guides. Sapphire is another wonderful stone that can be used for the third eye. It's known as the wisdom stone, as it enhances psychic awareness and supports confidence in one's own intuition. It also helps calm the mind and opens you up to receive heavenly messages. Ametrine is an awesome and powerful stone, as it combines both amethyst and citrine. Its dual action helps connect the higher realms with the lower, as well as unite masculine and feminine energies. It helps eliminate fears by revealing the hidden powers of the warrior that can be found in us all. Tourmaline has many beneficial metaphysical properties and comes in a variety of colors. Purple-violet tourmaline aids in raising your consciousness, stimulates the pineal gland, and helps remove illusions. It helps you tap into your creative insights and stimulates your intuition. Amethyst is an amazingly powerful stone with a very high spiritual vibration and can be used for both the third eye and the crown chakra. The list seems endless when it comes to this stone's attributes and healing properties. It's great at transmuting negative energies, which makes it an excellent stone to use with meditation journeys, lucid dreaming, or tapping into your intuition or psychic gifts. Allow yourself to experiment with different crystals. See which ones attract you, hold them in your hands, and examine any subtle connections you might feel, as these are your intuitive expressions responding. Look at the physical characteristics of the stone, like its veins, clusters, points, shapes, colors, and layers.
AROMA-THERAPY	Essential oils can be used for healing, relaxing, invoking, clearing—you name it. They are a perfect way to enhance your home spa while utilizing the water element. Their therapeutic properties can boost diffusers, vaporizers, humidifiers, bathtubs, and fountains to create a botanical utopia in all your environments. Remember that essential oils are very highly concentrated, volatile, aromatic essences of plants. I suggest buying them from reliable vendors or all-natural stores whose experienced personnel can guide you in their proper use. Essential oils can be used for healing, especially when it comes to the eyes. You can make eyewashes, eye pillows, or compresses that can be used for sleep, meditation, or stress reduction. The following are some essential oils that work well with the third eye: frankincense, lavender, chamomile, lemon, clary sage, and eucalyptus. Take a look at the reference books and see if any oils catch your eye.

Connecting with Your Third Eye Animal Totem

I like this Jonathan Swift quote: "Vision is the art of seeing what is invisible to others." He sums up the phenomenal powers you can experience when you connect with your third eye animal totem. As you begin to open and clear this chakra, you will take command of the powerful resources of the third eye, which will assist you in seeing what is invisible to others. Your third eye animal totem will help you evaluate past experiences and look at the bumps in life with a different perspective. This has the power to heal suffering from past wounds, support change and balance in the present, and encourage clear and insightful vision as you travel future landscapes. Every creature on earth possesses this unparalleled approach to assisting you in learning and living your true nature. The animal that comes to you offers you a unique and exquisite gift to help you see the essence of your true nature. It is not necessary that the animal have great eyesight either. Ferrets have horrible vision; in fact, they can only see a few feet in front them. However, the essence of my true nature is found in this animal's character. Ferrets love to play. They are incessantly curious and immensely entertaining. As pets, they are referred to as nature's clowns. They are very dexterous and inquisitive and will explore every crack and crevice without fear or worry. They will climb to great heights fearlessly and maneuver into places you thought were impossible for them to reach. Their silly antics and frisky frolics can bring laughter and joy to even the most solemn and somber environments. My third eye chakra animal totem is a constant teacher of how play can expand my awareness and help me remove the narrow-minded paths of limited patternings. This soft furry little guide teaches me how to play in my playground without fear of survival, to guiltlessly create with the humorous synchronicities of the universe, how to be empowered and empower without shame or feelings of unworthiness, to love without expectations or conditions, and most of all, to express myself with a madcap weasel war dance and a little dook-dooking, which is a sound that ferrets make when they're excited.

When your third eye chakra totem comes to visit, it will invariably be an invitation from the powers of the Divine to expand and find truth in your vision. The spirit guidance that emerges will encourage you to use that truth to build some of the most wonderful, harmonious creations that can only come with clear vision and a focused command of the powers of the third eye. The third eye is the place where you learn to see the peace, love, abundance, joy, and happiness within yourself and turn it outward to shine into the world of those around you. Ellen DeGeneres once said, "If we're destroying our trees and destroying our environment and hurting animals and hurting one another and all that stuff, there's got to be a very powerful energy to fight that. I think we need more love in the world. We need more kindness, more compassion, more joy, more laughter. I definitely want to contribute to that." Me too, Ellen! The third eye holds that very powerful energy, and your third eye animal totem will show you how to harness it to see your way to embracing your true nature.

Welcoming Your Third Eye Animal Totem

I will end this section the way I began this chapter, and I'm sure you now have a much deeper perspective of what it means to see. So I'll repeat: Well, look at you! I see you have added a wonderful new animal totem to the incredible forces of your guidance team. This animal will play an intricate role in helping you see that the Divine light is everywhere and in everyone if you choose to focus the lens of your perspective. Allow your third eye chakra totem animal to be your personal phototaxis indicator. *Phototaxis* is a technical term that biologists use to define the movement toward or away from light. Moths, flies, cockroaches, earthworms, and many insects have these light sensors for their basic survival. Even the greenery that makes up our Mother Earth uses light to survive. Your third eye animal totem will be your phototaxis sensor and will lead you toward the light and away from the darkness. Welcome your new totem animal by lighting a candle and basking in its illumination. In the words of William Wordsworth, "Come forth into the light of things, and let nature be your teacher."

THIRD EYE ANIMAL TOTEM PRAYER

I now take the time to reflect on my journey this month with my third eye chakra totem animal. I honor how my third eye totem animal has unveiled itself to me in so many illuminating ways. My third eye animal totem will assist me in my journey to see the truth in my vision and help me see that the spiritual realm will guide my physical realm toward balanced harmony. My third eye totem will lead me to see that comforting, loving, peaceful harmony flows with ease and grace, and just by turning my eyes inward, nothing is ever out of place. My wonderful totem animal will lead me to see that things all around me are helping me to be me. My animal totem will teach me to grow and to know that the truth in my vision has a spectacular mission. As I work with my totem, it's not hard to see how my true nature is awakening in me. The colors are vivid when my vision is clear; when I follow my totem, I've nothing to fear. I have faith in the Divine process and allow it to help me, lead me, and support me on my journey. I now welcome my third eye chakra animal to assist me on my walk in life.

AMEN.

CHAPTER 15

THE CROWN CHAKRA TOTEM

What's Up with This Chapter

∞ Uncovering Your Crown Chakra Totem
∞ What Is a Crown Chakra Totem?
∞ Let's Get Physical
∞ Honoring Your Crown
∞ The Crown Chakra Totem
∞ Connecting With Your Crown Totem
∞ Welcoming Your Crown Totem Animal

Uncovering Your Crown Chakra Totem

Alleluia! Hallelujah! And woo-hoo! Congratulations are in order—you've finally made it to the top of chakra system! This is that amazingly exquisite place where you awaken to pure consciousness. This is the place where you will find the answers to all those questions your soul wants to ask: What is my true nature? What do I want out of life? What is my purpose? The crown chakra is where you link *you* to the Divine, which is connected to all things, without the illusions of separateness, contrast, or resistance. It is through this chakra that you unite all things, visible and invisible. Just as you began this journey with your foot chakra and moved to the root chakra, forging your connection to Mother Earth, the crown chakra wraps up the journey by showing you your connection to God, Our Father in Heaven, Great Spirit, the Universe, Source, your Higher Power, or whatever you want to call the Divine forces guiding you through this journey. The crown chakra links you, the individual, to the universe, which is in everybody, every place, and everything. It is no coincidence that each of your animal totems has played a key role in your journey here, to this place, at this time. As you embark on uncovering your crown chakra animal totem, you will also activate a new kind of awareness that travels far beyond your physical perceptions to examine your self-realizations. Your crown chakra gives you the passport to the unlimited, infinite, all-knowing—referred to as omnipresent, omnipotent, and omniscient—consciousness of the Divine.

In last month's journey through the third eye chakra, you became aware that what you see is not always the truth and how you see it is not always with clarity. By changing the lens by which you view the aspects of life and adjusting your focus to bring true clarity to whatever that depth of field may be, you essentially allow yourself to let go and move beyond the dramas of pain and pleasure and those filters that eschew your true vision. This act of letting go prepares you for the final step in your journey through the chakras and embracing your true nature. For this act of letting go permits the act of letting God, the universe, source—those amazing Divine forces—provide you with the wonderful essences of ease and grace. The crown chakra is where you learn to have both faith and trust as you let go and let the universal forces masterfully unite you with your true nature and anything else in your walk through life.

What Is a Crown Chakra?

The crown chakra is the seventh and final chakra in the major chakra system. While there are more chakras above the crown, it can be considered customs or the border protection agency responsible for safeguarding your passage to those other chakras. Not everyone can visit these chakras without doing a tremendous amount of deep soul work, and once the journey begins, it is doubtful there is any turning back. The crown chakra is the door to the cosmos, or the universal energies that work on your behalf to awaken you to higher states of awareness. There are a few theories on whether the crown chakra is located within or above the top of the head. Whichever the case, I will tell you what one of my spiritual teachers told me: "Darlene, just trust the feeling of it, and try not to get hung up on its positioning." I can tell you from my own experience that sometimes it feels like it's within my head and sometimes it feels like it's above my head. And so, my friend, I advise you to simply trust the feeling of it.

The crown center vibrates to the vibrant color violet and the purest color of vivid white, which contains all the wavelengths of visible light. A phrase sometimes associated with the crown chakra is "I see the light." This phrase has been tossed around in a variety of ways, from Bible-thumping religions to folks who finally understand something clearly to individuals who have had a near-death experience (NDE). Seeing the light can be experienced through meditation, prayer, song, or just by sitting in the airport waiting for a delayed flight. Seeing the light has no boundaries, which is what you become conscious of when you immerse yourself in the energies of the crown chakra. The crown chakra turns on the lights in the lower chakras so you can see what's going

The Crown Chakra Totem

on and shifts the channels to our advantage. Much like a moving company transports your personal possessions from one place to another, the crown chakra assists you in moving your lower chakras from one place to another as it energizes you to awakening to your true nature. The crown chakra essentially sparkles its Divine light on the whole chakra system. It shines on what you see with your third eye, what you speak with your throat chakra, what you love with your heart chakra, what power you put into your solar plexus chakra, where you find pleasure in your sacral chakra, and how you survive in your root chakra, lighting your footsteps along your path. To experience the exotic nectar created by this Divine light only requires that you ask to see the light. As spirit beings functioning in a human body, we sometimes forget free will, one of the basic facets of life here on the earthly plane. Our free will is the main obstacle to our receiving the gifts of this Divine light. However, when we ask, its brilliance emerges. We see the light and experience the union with its source.

The crown chakra is linked to the seven-year cycle spanning the ages of forty-three through forty-nine. By this time in our life, we have traveled and experienced each one of the lower chakras. These travels have educated each of us with our own personal wisdom that can sometimes have effects that keep us blocked and/or jaded. To move beyond the trained impressions of our individual experiences requires that we release and detach from the fixed concepts that emerge from the "all about me" and bring them into the light of consciousness. The crown chakra is where you unite your aloneness with the all-oneness of the unified field of consciousness. The only thing that separates aloneness from all-oneness is one L. Use that L to represent the lower self; when you shine a light on that one missing L and unite it, its new wholeness becomes the all. The crown chakra is where the all-knowing, all-seeing, all-powerful aspects of the Divine come to light. Muhammad Ali said, "A rooster crows only when it sees the light. Put him in the dark and he'll never crow. I have seen the light and I'm crowing." The animal totem that comes to you will help you see the light on the path to your true nature and all the joys that lead to that enlightenment.

Let's Get Physical

Even though this has probably been drilled into your head by now, I'll repeat that the crown chakra completes the major chakra system and is located on the top of your head. I won't go into details as to where on the top of the head to allow you the wonderful phenomenon of experiencing its exact whereabouts on your own. However, I will give you this small piece of information that might cause you to further ponder the crown's location. I still remember my first experience holding a newborn baby when I was a kid. The first warning that came out of my mother's mouth was to be careful of the soft spot. I remember staring at that diamond-shaped divot on the top of the baby's head as I sat there frozen, afraid to make a move, fearful that the delicate contents of that part of the baby's head could possibly be damaged by one false move. To this day, any time I hold a newborn I will invariably gaze at that diamond-shaped soft spot that I now know is called a fontanel. Fontanels enable the skull to flex while the baby travels through the birth canal to arrive here on this wonderful earth plane. This area is believed to be the opening of the crown chakra and allows the Divine force energy to enter the body. While you're busy pondering that, it will give me an opportunity to bring back to mind the pineal/pituitary gland debate. Last month I gave you some examples of why I thought the pineal gland fit nicely with the third eye as an endocrine gland associate. This month I will continue in that same fashion, only now, with the pituitary gland on the radar, I'll allow you to make your own hypothesis of how the chakra/endocrine association works best. As I mentioned last month, both of these glands are planted deep in the middle of your cranium and are associated with the brain, so, at the very least, it should put you in a heady state of agreement whichever side of the debate you tend to keep in mind.

The pituitary gland is sort of an oxymoron when you think about, as this pea-sized gland is also referred to as the master gland. Get it, pea-sized master gland, oxymoron? Anyway, the pituitary gland controls many of your bodily functions, as well as some of the other endocrine glands, by releasing a ton of different hormones that are usually referred to with capital letters like GH, TSH, FSH, and ACTH. There are nine hormones produced in the pituitary gland, and interestingly enough, based on many alternative medicine practices, imbalances such as over- or underactivity of the chakras can be correlated with deficiencies in certain hormones. Which is another great reason to keep working at balancing your chakras and perhaps avoid having more capital letters thrown at you with comments like "Maybe it's PMS." I'll use a few more capital letters and guide you through the same GPS route from last month to get to the location of the pituitary gland. Travel up your nostril, then proceed straight back and just below the crossing of your optic nerves and you'll find your pituitary gland. The pituitary gland gets its marching orders from the hypothalamus. I'll try to make this simple, without getting into a whole lot of physiological and biological jargon, but, again, I'll warn you that a can of Red Bull or a double-shot of espresso might be in order to help you stay alert for this pseudotechnical information.

The hypothalamus has the endless and thankless job of keeping your body happy as a clam. Temperature, hunger, water, sex drive, emotions—you name it, the hypothalamus has a sensor on it. The hypothalamus is basically a bridge between your nervous system and your endocrine system. This is the place where your sensory central, the hypothalamus, meets your master gland, the pituitary. While sensory central makes its own hormones—which requires a quick turnaround because it is so busy with its unappreciated, gargantuan job of monitoring the nervous system—it also does some outsourcing to the master gland, which specializes in those endocrine hormones with the capital letters I mentioned earlier. Sensory central sends supersonic text messages to the master gland to giddy-up and make some hormones. Simply put, sensory central and the master gland are highly complex systems that receive a continuous barrage of information from various sources in your body to keep you as cozy and comfortable as a flea on a bird dog.

By now you're probably wondering where I'm going with all this blah-blah hypothalamus and blah-blah pituitary gland stuff and just want me to get to the point. As my younger sister Debbie would say when asked if she had done something yet that had totally dropped off her radar, "I was just about ready to do that." So here goes. With all those myriad metabolic processes going on inside you that control your interior comfort and wellbeing, the majority of them are happening without your even being consciously aware of them. Which, by the way, is how many of us navigate through life. However, you personally don't need to start, finish, control, or manage any part of how those metabolic processes get done. The master gland with messages from sensory central has it all covered and under control. You need only go peacefully and joyfully about your business because a higher source within your very own being knows how to handle your interior comfort on its own. This is one of the primary reasons I believe the pituitary gland makes for a great association with the crown chakra. Your little pea-sized gland called the master gland provides a perfect metaphor for what it means to be connected to a source bigger and greater than yourself.

The crown chakra allows you to be the master gland and rest in the knowledge that everything is just as it should be and there are many things happening for your wellbeing that can't be seen, felt, or found within the moment. By allowing yourself to ally with the greatest of Divine source, which you can metaphorically call sensory central, you allow yourself to become outsourced to the pea-sized master gland. Allowing the universe to support each and every step you take will help you in each one of your chakras to see, to express, to love, to empower, to find pleasure, and to joyfully live your true nature. Trust that the great Divine source knows how to handle all that you do not know how to handle better than you ever can. The crown chakra is where you learn to become conscious of trust, to let go of the phrase "my way," and to invite a better way to unfold. A way that might look very different than what you might have thought, yet better than anything you could have possibly imagined on your own.

The crown chakra is known as the chakra of consciousness. When you connect to the core of this chakra, you anchor your being to a unified axis of unlimited assistance. You awaken your being to your purpose and the infinite gifts of your true nature. These gifts light the way and work to align you with extraordinary passageways that lead to a greater connectedness to the Divine source. This is where you and the Divine unite into a common field of blissful wakefulness.

The symbol for the crown chakra is a lotus flower with a thousand petals emanating from its center. Each one of these glistening petals possesses a gift that holds the essence to your true nature. The crown chakra is where you unlock the limits of the mind and become conscious to the blueprint of your true nature. The crown is the place where everything unites. Even the two petals that represent the polarity of masculine and feminine energies of the third eye unite at the crown and create the transcendence of both. The crown is where you birth the unmanifested aspects of what is possible into the wonderful manifestations of what is possible. The animal totem that comes to you this month will provide the guidance that will lead you to a rich exploration of what is possible. The only thing you will ultimately need to do to make anything possible is to be conscious of the messages and guidance that come, be detached from how it will become possible, and allow the higher powers of source to formulate the plan that will unfold more spectacularly than anything you could even begin to fathom.

Honoring Your Crown

For the last eight months, you have traveled through each of the chakra centers, learning what it takes to ultimately harness the energetic forces of these chakras to connect to the Divine forces of the Universe. The crown chakra is where you take inventory of each center and invite the all-providing source of infinite prosperity and unconditional love into your being to assist you in releasing anything that is not part of your true nature. To do this requires that you honor every belief, imprint, conditioning, or whatever habitual behavioral patterns you have carried with you up to this place and time in your life. Honor how each of them—whether you think they are good or bad, pretty or ugly, right or wrong, funny or sad, liked or disliked—have helped you to survive, cope, and manage and, in the end, have protected you from the blows of life. By honoring these temporary structures, you begin to become consciously aware that they are just provisional pointers that have helped direct you to your true nature. As you become more consciously aware that these features are no longer serving your wellbeing, you in effect invite the Divine presence to intervene and work on your behalf to put in place the true nature of your identity. This Divine support creates your very own rite of passage that leads you to the people, places, and things that support your wellbeing and your true nature.

As you honor the current state of your crown chakra, look back in your journal and pay tribute to the animal guide associated with each chakra. The crown chakra is where everything unites into oneness and there are no separate parts. As you bring the parts that separate you from oneness , you join the natural world with its synergistic properties that always work together for an effect greater than the sum of the individual parts. The ingredients of this synergy branch out to brighter paths that powerfully and magically light the way, benefiting all. Your crown chakra totem animal will hold the synergistic properties for bringing those separate parts of your life harmoniously together to a greater effect than those individual pieces could have ever accomplished on their own. As you honor your crown chakra, you release yourself of those separation phantoms of the chakras that manifest as the tears of fear, the filth of guilt, the shame of blame, the thief called grief, the lies that buy, the confusion of illusion, and the hindrance of ignorance. As you detach yourself from these sources of adversity, the true nature of you emerges. To quote Arthur Golden, "Adversity is like a strong wind. I don't mean just that it holds us back from places we might otherwise go. It also tears away from us all but the things that cannot be torn, so that afterward we see ourselves as we really are." The crown chakra is where you find the help to move beyond those phantoms that hold you back from the places you might otherwise go.

Ways to Honor Your Crown

Pray
Meditate
Go to a kirtan
Walk a labyrinth
Convene with nature
Visit a sacred temple
Honor your sacred space
Attend a different kind of spiritual service

The Crown Chakra Totem

One of the most important things your crown chakra animal totem will help you overcome can be summed up in the expression "Can't see the forest for the trees." Viewing the big picture is by far one of the trickiest fishnets we can get ourselves tangled in. When we are up close and personal with those people, places, and things in our life, we sometimes need to take a step back to get a better perspective of those details we are focusing on. We can get so caught up in the particulars of life that we fail to see the overall picture. When we get too intimately close to our personal conditions, we tend to hunker down and seal ourselves off instead of stepping back and creating more space to get a panoramic view of the scene. When we deliberately choose, or are forced to choose, to step back and rise above those pickets that have us fenced in, we soon begin to notice the whole forest that we failed to see because of our limited viewpoint.

As humans, we sometimes tend to lose our perspective of the forest, especially when we surround ourselves with those metaphorical trees of attachments that are made of a belief system that is based on old experiences that keep us small. Our attachment to those trees surrounding us can block us and cut us off from realizing the universe's infinite gifts. Your crown chakra totem will act as your personal periscope, inviting you to see above the shallow bunker that keeps you boxed in. This limited perspective causes us to cling to those separate aspects of ourselves that necessitate our attachments and induce resistances that keep us trapped in a muddle. Your crown chakra totem animal will help expand your consciousness from the safety of the foxhole and move it to a space offering a vast, unlimited perspective that is the pinnacle of each of the crown chakra's thousand petals. Your crown chakra totem will function like a conductor who directs the orchestra's performance with his or her visible cues. It will help you unify those separate instruments, strike the right tempo, and direct your path with the right tones. The crown chakra is your direct connection to the Divine and those universal forces of infinite guidance and possibilities. The animal that presents itself to you will help you tap into this celestial network offering unlimited channels of divine live streaming, this place of clear, pure consciousness, your personal HDTV network.

One of the most magical and extraordinary parts of uncovering my personal animal totems was that I never really knew what animal lurked around the corner to greet me and ultimately become an intimate part of my personal walk. The supernatural enchantment that accompanies this divinely guided process astounds me more and more each day. My crown chakra totem is the panther. I call it the great shape-shifter. When I was uncovering my crown totem, I could feel this creature's tremendous vibration around me as I meditated. Its frequency seemed so strong; I could feel that this animal possessed great, powerful guidance. I remember seeing an inordinate number of black cats at that time. Some hung around my house, which was strange, as our dog considered them sport if they came remotely near our property. I found it especially hair-raising when the cats would dart out from between the cars as I drove or jump out from behind a fence as I walked. I'm not really a superstitious type, but it was really starting to give me the willies. Every time I ventured to conclude my totem was a cat, I was led to yet another animal that would coax me to question my cat conclusion.

It was funny when this totem's essence finally emerged. I was working a late-night shift, sitting in my cubicle, waiting for the technicians to finish a sanitation task upstairs in one of the lab suites. A technician came down to ask a question and stood with his arms outstretched, holding onto the top of each side of the cubicle's entrance.

The Crown Chakra Totem

This husky guy wore a totally color-coordinated outfit, and right there, in the center of his sweatshirt, was a big, black panther poised to pounce. The way the technician stood, with his arms wide apart, made it look like this panther was coming through the cubicle toward me. It was then that it dawned on me that the panther could very well be my totem. That night, on the way home, I spotted another black cat running down the sidewalk. The next day I began to do some research on the panther. There were so many things about this animal that rang true for me. However, I knew this totem needed to pick me, and I needed more validation before I could confirm my totem as the panther. Deep down I knew that if the panther was indeed my totem, Spirit would make it clear. Spirit is always way ahead of the game, and it wasn't long before I received a phone call from the contractor renovating our house next door asking me to let some carpenters in who were on the way over. I went next door to open up and thought I'd check out how things were coming along. When I got to the top of the second floor stairs, the whole room was filled with batts of insulation. The most amazing thing was that the Pink Panther peered out at me from every one of those packs of insulation. There was my affirmation of the panther— pretty in pink. What an incredible validation it was for me. Since its inception, my panther has been an amazingly powerful guide. I feel tremendous joy when the black cat crosses my path, as I know it is my great shape-shifter with a message that spirit will be calling upon me in some extraordinary way. The crown chakra is the portal where infinite possibilities emerge, and the extraordinary animal that comes to you will offer amazing guidance to assist you in trusting and believing that wonderful possibilities can come true. Saint Augustine said, "Faith is to believe what you do not see; the reward of this faith is to see what you believe." Your crown chakra animal totem will guide you to have faith in what you believe, so you will undoubtedly see what you believe.

Meditation

As you go inward this month, set your intention to believe, and let that intention flow down into each one of your chakras. Believe in the Divine light of your true nature. Believe in the clarity of your true nature. Believe in the expression of your true nature. Believe in the compassion and unconditional love of your true nature. Believe in taking the actions to create your true nature. Believe in the pleasures and delights that stem from your true nature. Most of all, believe that it is your mission to have the strength and courage to live your true nature. Set your intentions to connect to the source of each one of those thousand petals of light and believe in the infinite potential that will flow through you, bearing the gifts of peace, joy, wisdom, and unconditional love. Trust that your animal totem will be the beacon that directs you to this wonderful Divine source of light that will balance, heal, and transform your walk in the most magical and enchanting ways. While it may appear that this is the last stop in your journey to uncover your personal animal totem, the truth is your journey is really just beginning. Allow yourself to reawaken to the elements of space, air, fire, water, and earth in your world in a whole new way.

Give yourself permission to let that little light in you shine and your animal totem will come alive to illuminate the road with spectacular guidance. By now, you know the gig—carry out your meditation in the manner that works best for you and allow yourself to open up to the wonderful frequencies of your crown chakra. It will truly be enlightening.

CROWN CHAKRA TOTEM ACCESSORIES	
CANDLES	Use candles to help stimulate your crown chakra and invoke your connection with your crown chakra animal totem. Candles quickly connect you to the Divine realms and enhance your meditation. Select candles with purple and/or violet tones to aid in connecting to crown chakra vibrations. Allow yourself to experience any colors or scents that awaken your senses. This will engage your imagination and springboard you toward connectedness with spirit and your true nature. When shopping for candles, allow yourself to experience all their pleasing aspects: their shapes, number of wicks, colors, scents, even their names. Many candle scents on the market are specific to the crown chakra. Candles can have wonderful crown-chakra-invoking names, like Crown Bliss, Violet Light, Self-Realization, Divine Light, or Sahasrar. Set an intention for where your candle might lead you, and invite the unknown vibrations to make their way into your life.
INCENSE	Use incense for clearing any space and calling upon your crown chakra animal totem. Incense adds a wonderful tone to your clearing rituals and inspires your spirit to connect intimately with the Divine. A variety of scents from different regions of the world can enhance your meditations. Scents like frankincense, myrrh, camphor, and cedar work nicely for the crown chakra. There are also many incense blends specific to the crown chakra, with names like Enlightenment, Unity, and Angelic Journey. Allow yourself to experiment with different types of incense, which come in cone, stick, powder, rope, or pellet forms and can be a pleasurable way to expand your sacred ritual of opening, clearing, and/or balancing your crown chakra. Permit yourself to follow the smoke trails' wispy shapes and see where they guide you.

CRYSTALS	Use crystals for their color and energy qualities.. Many crystals can activate or enhance the crown chakra. While diamonds are supposedly a girl's best friend, they are also a symbol of purity. The diamond's pure essence brings our life into a cohesive wholeness, brings love and clarity to partnerships, and bonds relationships. White sapphire offers another extremely pure energy and aids in removing obstacles to the spiritual path. Selenite is a wonderful stone to bring clarity to the mind and stimulate the crown to higher consciousness. I keep one with my other crystals, as it helps keep them energized. Telepathy is enhanced when this stone is held in your hands, especially when meditating. Seraphinite is a great stone to use for self-healing and aids in spiritual enlightenment. It can also be used in conjunction with the third eye when meditating to stimulate meditative journeys. Amethyst is by far the most widely used crystal for the crown chakra. It is a powerful and protective stone, with a high spiritual vibration. It can be used for calming, healing, and clearing and helps balance all levels of the auric fields. Many psychics and healing practitioners will have large ornamental geodes in their offices; they are great for removing negativities from the environment. Ask crystal practitioners what they can recommend for you. Many will read your energies and recommend a crystal specifically for you.
AROMA-THERAPY	Essential oils can be used for healing, relaxing, invoking, clearing—you name it. They are a perfect way to enhance your home spa while utilizing the water element. Their therapeutic properties can boost diffusers, vaporizers, humidifiers, bathtubs, and fountains to create a botanical utopia in all your environments. Remember that essential oils are very highly concentrated, volatile, aromatic essences of plants. I suggest buying them from well-known vendors or all-natural stores whose experienced personnel can guide you in their proper use. Essential oils that work well with the crown are frankincense, jasmine, rosewood, and sandalwood. Sage is always great for clearing, especially for meditation journeys. There are many blends available specifically for meditation and that can invoke dreamtime.

Connecting with Your Crown Animal Totem

Ralph Waldo Emerson said, "What lies behind us and what lies before us are tiny matters compared to what lies within us." As you allow your totem animal to lead you to inhabiting the energies of your crown chakra, your true nature will emerge with an amazing unfolding of freedom that is bigger and wider than anything you could have ever imagined. Your crown chakra totem will lead you to a new paradigm free of the confines that come from the blocks in the lower chakras—fear, guilt, jealousy, greed, lack, limitation, selfishness, ignorance, arrogance, etc. For it is through the crown chakra that you will be guided by the Divine light that transmutes those tears of fear into joyful anticipation, the filth of guilt into fresh innocence, the shame of blame into graceful acclaim, the thief called grief into compassionate unconditional love, the lies that buy into truthful tranquility, the confusion of illusion into blissful clarity, and the hindrance

Uncovering Your Personal Animal Totem

of ignorance into Divine wisdom. As you tap into this infinite source of delightful possibilities, only your true nature can emerge from this wonderful Divine soup for your soul.

Your crown chakra totem will enable you to connect those dots of your life journey, creating a wonderful illustration of your true nature. Each dot you connect represents an outpouring of healing, seeking, growing, serving, and sharing a piece of your true nature to the world. Every creature on earth possesses this amazing medicine as part of its true nature. The animal that comes to you will assist you in connecting all those dots, for its primary responsibility is for you to realize your wholeness, which is shrouded in the essence of your true nature.

One of the major messages connected to my crown chakra totem, the panther, is to reclaim what is rightfully mine. I have spent a great deal of my life seeking to accomplish that very task. As a child, my true nature became buried in a shield of defense that safeguarded me from the turmoils of an abusive, alcoholic stepfather and a mother who struggled to both survive and endure with the hope of new beginnings time and time again. My panther has not only helped me go back in time and reclaim and heal what was rightfully mine, but has also taught me to take comfort in darkness, as tremendous new strengths and influences are about to be awakened in me. Your crown chakra totem will give you not only the medicine best needed for your journey, but also the medicine that aids you in clearing out all the major and minor ailments that inhibit that liberating freedom essential to the path of your true nature.

When your crown chakra totem comes to visit, it will be a wonderful invitation from the Divine for you to become aware of the those people, places and things around you that set up hurdles on the path to your true nature. These are the snags that keep us trapped in the metaphorical chains of attachments that hinder our freedom to heal, grow, explore, share, and serve. Your crown chakra animal totem will assist you in becoming conscious of the shackles that hamper your freedom to live your true nature. Your animal will also help you hold a spirit to let others live their true nature as well. I think Nelson Mandela, who spent over a quarter of a century in prison, said it best: "To be free is not merely to cast off one's chains, but to live in a way that respects and enhances the freedom of others." The crown chakra is where you become aware that everything works together and there is no freedom in separateness. Your crown chakra totem animal will awaken you to that freedom, for that will be where you will find your true nature.

The Crown Chakra Totem

Welcoming Your Totem Animal

Congratulations! You have unveiled the final animal of your personal animal totem. This animal will play a significant role in helping you emulate the spirit of your true nature. As this new nature of you unfolds, it will ultimately separate you from your previous self and unite those parts into the true nature of you. Your crown chakra totem will be the catalyst to unifying the energetic forces of the lower chakras. Each one of those animals holds a critical strand of the web woven of your past, present, and future. Your crown totem, along with Divine timing, will lead you to discover that embedded in the center of this web lies a chrysalis, that place of struggle that is transmuted into the birth of a beautiful butterfly that explores all the wonderful colors, smells, sounds, and tastes of the ever-blooming and flowering world. You are that butterfly. Your crown chakra totem will lead you to these wonderful moments that connect you to the all-providing infinite source of the constant Divine presence. This is the place where time merges with timelessness, where lessons will always be revealed with blessings, and living in the moment will always disclose a surprised "Aha!"

Welcome the crowning-glory totem animal of your chakra system by lighting a candle and musing on the wonders of your journey. I will top off this chapter with an anonymous quote: "All of life is a journey. Which paths we take, what we look back on, and what we look forward to is up to us. We determine our destination, what kind of road we will take to get there, and how happy we are when we get there." I will add that you, my friend, have a wonderful group of animals that will certainly make the journey amazingly worthwhile.

CROWN TOTEM ANIMAL PRAYER

I now take the time to reflect on my journey this month with my crown chakra totem animal. I honor how my crown totem animal has unveiled itself to me in such astounding ways. This animal will help me be aware of the marvels of connectedness. My crown chakra totem is a symbol of unity and will help unite each animal in my personal totem into the phenomenal oneness that is garnished with Divine guidance. While my totem may appear independently, I know that its guidance will be an opening to the portal of connectedness that leads me to the infinite possibilities of the Divine realm. My crown chakra totem animal will anchor the essence of my spirit to the Divine forces of the universe that only come with ease and grace. This animal will assist me in being aware of the gifts and blessings that will continually connect me to my true nature. My crown totem animal will guide and assist me to be aware of any separateness and that Divine guidance is ever-present in my journey to bring everything lovely together. The only thing I will need to do is notice, and it will lead me to the opportunities that align me to my true nature, which flows richly with the highest and best potential for my soul's journey. I have faith and trust in this Divine guidance and give my crown chakra animal totem permission to assist, lead, and support me as I travel my road in this life. I now welcome my crown chakra totem animal to be a part of my walk.

AMEN.

PART III

All Together Now

Okay, so you have uncovered your person animal totem. Now what? This section will lead you from the courtship phase of your relationship with your totems to a more developed, maintained, and defined relationship that will continue to grow and mature. While each totem has its own specific medicine that will guide you independently, the team working together will add a new level guidance to your landscape. This section offers you an opportunity to work on building your own personal oracle from these trusty messengers who have come to assist you in reclaiming and preserving your true nature.

CHAPTER 16

WORKING WITH YOUR MOTLEY CREW OF CRITTERS

What's Up with This Chapter

∞ Anchors Aweigh!
∞ Ahoy, There!
∞ How Guidable Are You?
∞ Plane Sailing

Wow! Look at you with a brilliant colorful nature that reflects your new guidance team! Congratulations are in order; you have unveiled the complete version of your very own personal animal totem. You should be very proud of yourself, as uncovering your personal animal totem is quite an accomplishment. When I teach my totem course, the last class of the journey always seems to offer a cathartic passage to the bittersweet. The students finally get to see the completed version of their personal animal totem in its picture form, the tribe reminisces about the funny episodes and humorous aspects of how their totems appeared throughout the journey, and then ultimately the scene shifts to that farewell feeling when it's time to say good-bye. Much like an end to wonderful vacation, as you pack to go home, you try to savor as many of your travel moments as you can. You have been on a nine-month journey that brought you to eight enchanting islands within your being. There, you discovered unique aspects of yourself that are all vital parts of the unfolding of your true nature. The good news, my friend, is that the journey never ends; it's actually just beginning for you. You and your motley group of critters are embarking on *le premier jour du reste de ta vie*. That's French for "the first day of the rest of your life." So buckle up and enjoy the ride!

Anchors Aweigh!

Now that your guidance team is on board, it's time to weigh anchor. That's the nautical term used when it's time to bring the anchor aboard a vessel in preparation for departure. Your ship is officially ready to sail with its talented crew and uniquely guided navigation system. When you began this journey to embrace your true nature back at the foot chakra, you anchored your feet to Mother Earth. Remember that your foot chakras are two split centers that are always linked and always work as a unified center. When you were born in physical form into this very physical world, you were given the great privilege of experiencing duality, polarity, or whatever you care to call those opposites that manifest as feminine/masculine, passive/assertive, rich/poor, good/evil, happy/sad, sickly/healthy, follower/leader, conscious/unconscious. Each one of these seemingly incongruous pairs tends to be forerunners of the storms in our internal world. Your foot chakra gives you the opportunity to encounter these aspects in unity, as opposites are really just two sides of our physical reality. It's much like a coin. The coin has a head side and a tail side, and its value does not change based on the side you are looking at, as its polarities merge into a oneness of its value. Every morning when your feet hit the ground, these two centers are your energetic anchor to unity, and your foot totem is your guide that leads you to embody it. The same is true for your crown chakra.

The crown chakra anchors you to the heavens, God, the Divine, Great Spirit, or whatever you call that grand, one power of all that is. This center of all that is has no separate elements, possessions, or aspects, as its essence is founded in wholeness, unity, and oneness. These two chakra centers, and the totems that symbolize their energies, help you bridge the physical obstacles in life in a way that heals, transforms, and ultimately connect you to your true nature. That connection is embodied in prosperity, health, unconditional love, and the creative juices required to share the beautiful gifts of your true nature to the world, cultivating oneness. Keep in mind that it is only the central pillar within each of us that carries those dissonant energies of separation. As you follow the guidance of your motley crew of totems, you invite the connectedness of the Divine to be a part of your internal world and mend those seemingly outwardly separate segments. This twenty-four-hour access is available every single moment of the day to guide you through whatever may come your way. So set your sails on those passions and desires, trust the process, and invite those nonphysical intentions and ideas that come to light in the crown chakra to become true physical manifestations. Know that it is what you focus upon with attention and intention that becomes real and takes physical form, and your foot chakra totem will guide you to opportunities to bring them into existence. Ultimately, it will be up to you to determine whether to sail solo or work with the crew.

Ahoy, There!

Over the past months, your focus has been working with each chakra totem on an individual basis. Now it's time to get your motley group of critters to work their magic as a tribe of faithful warriors, not forgetting that within this group of critters lies the very powerful energy centers of the chakra system. While your totems will assist you day to day with enchanting visits that bring various levels of joyful guidance, their main mission will be to help you clear and balance the mighty chakra centers that harbor the essence of your true nature and teach you to throw overboard any cargo that doesn't emanate from it. Though I have touched on the basics of each chakra center, it is important that I touch on the chakra system as a whole. Understanding the streams of energy that flow up and down the chakra system will not only open you to other levels of awareness, but will present you with a greater appreciation for your totem animals' abundant guidance for staying connected to your true nature. There is really only one thing to keep in mind on your expedition through life: You are the captain of your ship and ultimately command your earthly vessel. You alone are responsible for its safety, how you want to operate it, what cargo you want to carry, how and where you want to navigate, and whether or not to take guidance from your motley crew of critters. You can run a tight ship and do it all on your own, but I can guarantee you it will definitely not be as illuminated with the enchantment and magic that come with following guidance. Without guidance, sooner or later you will need to batten down your hatches and take refuge from those imminent storms. I hope you catch my drift here.

Although I touched on it briefly during your journey through each chakra, I will now highlight how energy changes as it moves up and down the chakra system. As you move up from the root chakra, the velocity of each spinning chakra increases. Likewise, as you move down from the crown, the spinning decreases. The physical plane vibrates much more slowly than the conscious one. That statement alone should give you a pretty good perspective on what it will take to get your passions, desires, or inspirations afloat in physical form and not have them run aground prematurely. While you might have these great visions, ideas, or designs floating around in your awareness, you must be able to work them through each of the chakra centers for them to manifest into physical form. You must remain focused on your desires and what you want to create in your life, while at the same time remove the obstacles that inhibit the delight, joy, and pleasures that emanate from your true nature. This will be one of your greatest challenges in life. However, when you train your conscious mind to recognize the symbolic messages communicated from your totems, your earthly vessel will continue to make headway no matter where the tides turn, as you will have the staying power to remain focused on your desired destination.

Uncovering Your Personal Animal Totem

When you traveled through each chakra and uncovered each totem, hopefully you became aware of some of the limiting beliefs and ingrained conditioning that filter your reality. As you navigate through the physical world, each chakra will emit a beacon to attract you to a port of call with opportunities specifically designed for the enlightenment of your true nature and the dismantling of your limiting beliefs. Your totems will help you fortify your sea legs and guide you to all kinds of invitations to create a little leeway, ensuring that in stormy seas you will hold an even keel and stay the course. As you become skilled at riding the waves of energy that flow up and down the chakra system, you will develop an absolute bearing of which chakra centers take the wind from your sails and send you adrift. Not to worry; as you navigate your vessel, your motley crew of critters will be there to buoy your spirits and guide you as the crow flies. They will be your trusty task force, guiding you to adjust your rigging and stay the course to the jollies of your desired marina. As you explore the depths of your inner world, I offer these two expressions of truth. Ponder them as you set the sails to your desires. The first is an English proverb: "A smooth sea never made a skilled mariner." The second is from a poem by Sarah Bolton, "Paddle Your Own Canoe."

Voyager upon life's sea,
To yourself be true,
And whatever your lot may be,
Paddle your own canoe.

How Guidable Are You?

When I was in the process of removing some of my own major energetic blocks, one of my amazing spiritual teachers, in the intensity of it all, looked me dead in the eyes and asked, "How guidable are you, Darlene?" I could tell by the way she looked at me that I was being asked a rhetorical question, that my homework would be to reflect on that very question, and that she would never require an answer. To this day I ask myself that very question when guidance comes, and I can tell you with great reverence that the guidance, when followed, has saved lives, healed grief, brought safety, extended unconditional love, and bridged enormous disparities. When your totems make their appearance, ask yourself that very question: How guidable are you?

It's essential that you greet each visit as an invitation to expand your awareness in areas where you are not aware. The message that accompanies the divinely guided visit does not necessarily conclude the moment you notice it. It can be what I call the usher syndrome, or the harbinger of a Divine appointment. Sometimes the message from your totem is intended to draw you to something that has nothing to do with your totem, much like an usher acts as an escort, leading you to a specific spot. When your totem makes an appearance, it is important that you notice any other symbols or totems that might be around, as your totem can initiate help from other sources. For example, if my blue jay were cackling in a tree, and just below a mockingbird was feeding, the message could very well be for me to pay attention to the mockingbird. A little later I might see a lone mockingbird just singing away on a telephone wire. The mockingbird has now come into my awareness, holding some form of a message for me. When I research the meaning of the mockingbird, I find it is right on target with guidance I needed to move forward in a certain area of my life. When you start to notice recurring patterns, know that your guidance team is knocking. No worries if your miss it; they will always give you another opportunity. Your team of Divine guidance is infinitely available to lead, assist, and support in every aspect of your life; however, you must be open to receive the way the guidance comes through in order to reap its blessings. The long and short of it is that your totems will initiate many enchanting and clever ways to gain your attention, but ultimately you will be the gatekeeper of how guidable you want to be. If you feel that your animals are not coming through with guidance, ask yourself the same question that my spiritual teacher asked me. How guidable are you? Because that's how much guidance you'll get.

Plane Sailing

Keep in mind that when you are working with your totems, you are blending two very different planes. One is our familiar physical plane, which consists of the visible reality of space and time with all its phenomena ensconced in what we know and how we live our life day to day. The other is composed of the not-so-familiar timelessness of the spiritual plane, which consists of subtle states of consciousness that transcend our known physical world. The second is the plane that marks what is real and eternal and ultimately what the "all that is" is all about. This is where the forces of our experiences merge with the Divine, where the most diverse polarities merge into the unity. This is the place where your internal peace and harmony surpasses any human understanding. Your totems' mission will be to guide you to this place of blissful synchronization and assist you in connecting to this place as much as humanly possible. As you become practiced at following the guidance of your totems, you will find yourself becoming quite skilled at navigating the physical plane. You will soon learn that to know the ropes of the spiritual plane is where the smooth sailing seas exists. Any time your totems presents themselves, you are being invited to connect with those heavenly synchronicities that lead you to the ease and grace of the wide blue yonder. As the captain of your vessel, you ultimately have the power to choose how you care to sail through the so-called waters of your life. The next chapter will steer you toward various examples and scenarios of your animal totem guides' day-to-day presence in your life. Your totems are always there, and if you find your totems are not making themselves present, the

Uncovering Your Personal Animal Totem

implication is you are not either. Your dedication and devotion to the guidance you receive will be directly proportional to the effort you put in—block the guidance, it blocks you; limit it, it limits you. Your totems will always send an invitation, which is basically an offer to engage with guidance and some kind of assistance in the most magical way. I will end this section with one of the poems I post daily with animal photos on my Uncovering Your Personal Animal Totem page on Facebook.

Sometimes our totems can give us a lift.
Trust it, it's all part of spirit's great gifts.
For our totems are always there to guide.
So just take a chance and enjoy the free ride.

CHAPTER 17

WHAT YOUR MOTLEY CREW OF CRITTERS CAN DO FOR YOU

What's Up with This Chapter

∞ Like, Duh!
∞ Who's Your Totem?
∞ What Goes Around, Comes Around
∞ Wake Up and Smell the Coffee
∞ I Can See Clearly Now
∞ Hallelujah, It's a Healing!
∞ Abracadabra!
∞ Sometimes You Just Gotta Let It Go
∞ If You Play Your Cards Right

This section is designed to give you insight into some of the most obvious aspects your totems will be helping you with, regardless of the chakra they represent. These are little pointers to let you know that guidance is always working on your behalf in some of the wildest and most clever ways. Use this section to help you tap into your totems for various types of guidance. While each totem visit will be for a unique purpose, these short examples will help you put a little reasoning around them.

Like, Duh!

Sometimes our totem visits state the obvious: "There is my totem!" The message can be they have just stopped by to say hi and let you know they're around for guidance. This type of visit can be a conduit to help you to tap into Divine guidance in that moment or in general. You can ask yourself which chakra center that totem represents.

Take the opportunity to do some soul-searching about what energies in your life might have something to do with that particular chakra center. A totem visit should always bring a smile and a feeling of comfort that all your needs are being and will be met. So celebrate and trust the visit.

The celebration of beauty is an invitation to ask your soul every day, "Mind if I join you?"
—Anonymous

Who's Your Totem?

Your animal totems will always be your animal totems and will offer significant guidance. However, that doesn't necessarily mean that no other animals can offer you significant guidance. If fact, the very nature of our animal totems is to escort us to amazing guidance, which, in many cases, is another animal or conditions beyond the depth of field of your animal totem. So always look at what's going on in the scene where your animal totem has appeared. Our totems can and often will function as an escort, ushering in other messengers as guides. If you are not aware of your totems' clever tactics, you can miss some very significant guidance. Your totems' delightful approach is a wonderful and enchanting way of teaching you to expand your awareness.

Where do consequences lead? Depends on the escort.
—Stanislaw Jerzy Lec

What Goes Around, Comes Around

No matter when you uncover your personal animal totems, you will sooner or later find that they have always been with you. I know this from both my personal experience and from the testimonies of clients and students alike. As your totems help you clear the blocked and stagnant energies of your chakras, this energetic deforesting of your innards makes way for the clear channel of viewing your past, present, and future. You suddenly get a glimpse of all the dots in your history where your totems played a part. As you become more adept at working with your totems, you will also learn to trust their connection to your future.

An orb spider anchors the first strand of its web by floating it into the wind to catch on a solid object, creating the foundation for its spiral web, a form that ensures its continued existence with the abundances of its catches. You too have dropped your own strands, creating the foundation of your web. The very strands of your past are now the anchors that will ensure your continued existence, allowing you to weave the path to the abundance of your catches. Our animal totems help us connect our past to our present, which ultimately allows us to capture our true nature and manifest the desires and abundance we yearn for in our future. The web we weave is a spiral, circling round and round, always giving us an opportunity to go back and add a supporting structure that will ultimately meet the needs of our future. Moreover, the personal web we have weaved will help us understand that our past deeds hold important strains for our future. Your totems teach you how to connect your past, present, and future, creating the wonderful states that hold the essence of our true nature.

> *You can't connect the dots looking forward; you can only connect them looking backwards. So you have to trust that the dots will somehow connect in your future. You have to trust in something—your gut, destiny, life, karma, whatever. This approach has never let me down, and it has made all the difference in my life.*
> —Steve Jobs

Wake Up and Smell the Coffee!

Our totems help us reawaken those parts of ourselves that, for whatever reason, appeared to be lost, forgotten, or even misplaced. As you work with each totem and become more familiar with being open to and following the opportunities your totems guide you toward, those forgotten or hidden parts of yourself will begin to emerge in sparkling new ways. Former talents, crafts, fashions, and knacks long forgotten will suddenly reappear with a spectacular authenticity that transcends their original value. This is when you unexpectedly find yourself immersed in an endeavor that propels you to awareness of the beauty of those long forgotten moments; you awaken to them in the most magical and enchanting way. You suddenly experience the moment with every one of your physical senses, and your consciousness stirs with the immense feelings of connectedness to all that is. You come away from these awestruck moments with a new understanding of the essence of your true nature and the spark of the Divine that lies within. You begin to trust and look forward to the places your totems will lead you, for you now know that it is to achieve your highest and best in life.

> *Once you wake up and smell the coffee, it's hard to go back to sleep.*
> —Fran Drescher

I Can See Clearly Now

Your totems teach you to trust what you already know—your intuition. I think the lyrics to Johnny Nash's song "I Can See Clearly Now" explain it best: "I can see clearly now, the rain is gone. I can see all obstacles in my way. Gone are the black clouds that had me blind. It's going to be a bright, bright, sunshine-y day." It truly is amazing how it unfolds, but our totems do help us pinpoint those obstacles that get in our way. They help us navigate through the black clouds that sometimes blind us, and they lead us to see those bright, sunny days. They teach us to trust in our own knowingness, believe in our own insights, and have confidence that the medicine they bestow upon us will work to our best advantage. Once you become versed at working with your totems, you will notice how they step in way before your doubts, worries, fears, and uncertainties start to emerge. Surprisingly, our totems tip us off to trouble beforehand, so we can get into the flow of trusting our own intuition above everyone else's. When your totems come to visit, examine what chakra they represent and check for the significance of the guidance for that particular chakra center. Learning to trust your intuition will require that you experience that trust in each one of your chakra centers. Your totem animals will lead you to the areas in your being that require more trust in your intuition. And they will ultimately lead you into believing in yourself and trusting what you already know.

The intuitive mind is a sacred gift and the rational mind is a faithful servant. We have created a society that honors the servant and has forgotten the gift.
—Albert Einstein

Hallelujah, It's a Healing!

Our totems heal those unseen and unknown energetic aspects of ourselves. Studies show that our conscious mind only represents approximately 8–12 percent of the brain's total capacity. It is concerned with or can hold on to only one single thought at a time. On the other hand, our subconscious mind takes up to 95 percent of our brain's capacity. Our subconscious mind has a perfect memory and can remember every experience, person, place, or thing. Everything that we have encountered from the time we were born, and even before, is present in your memory. Taking that a step further, I'm sure that bowl of everything you carry around in your subconscious holds many unseen wounds, grief, turmoil, suffering, disappointment, and all those not-so-good things that our conscious mind may dismiss, ignore, disregard, or just doesn't know about yet. The good news is your animal totems assist you in healing these unnoticed and unseen energetic aspects that, in a sense, are not yours to carry. In fact, many of my students and clients find their totem animals were either present or part of the scene at the time of an emotional episode. When their totem animal unveiled itself, an instant healing occurred, releasing emotional energetic aspects these individuals didn't even know they were carrying. No matter how long ago the emotional episode occurred, these folks remembered the incident as vividly as if it happened yesterday. Not only do our totems manifest the particular medicine we need to heal our past, they have exactly the right medicine to fortify our healing with the fortitude and empowerment essential to our true nature. The unveiling of your animal totems essentially initiates the process of healing. As you heal these unseen or unknown energetic aspects of yourself, you essentially begin to raise your personal vibration to a level that is in direct alignment with your true nature. The more you immerse yourself in these higher vibrational frequencies, the easier it is for your to connect with your guidance, experience increased healings, and awaken to the unfolding of your true nature.

Healing may not be so much about getting better, as about letting go of everything that isn't you—all of the expectations, all of the beliefs—and becoming who you are.
—Rachel Naomi Remen

Abracadabra!

Perhaps one of the most delightful aspects of uncovering your personal animal totem is the unexpected magical enchantment that suddenly emerges into your world in a fresh new way. Just seeing your totem appear out of nowhere, whether you're driving, walking, or sitting in your home—can bring joy, comfort, and soothing to your internal world. The dictionary describes magic as a conjuring of tricks and illusions that make apparently impossible things seem to happen, or the great power of influencing events by using mysterious or supernatural forces. Our totems seem to follow these mysterious lines of fantasy and trickery to grab our attention. They lead you to mesmerizing multiple worlds that encapsulate the wonders of nature, the powers of the universe, the adventure and exploration of discovering the beauty within and around you. They stir you to imagine with childlike curiosity no matter what circumstances abound as they honor your way of knowing. Every phase of our life offers us an opportunity to dance with and muse on the mystery and wonders of the world. Our animal totems give us an opportunity to really play with the spirit realm. They lead us to make connections we wouldn't normally make, to see things in bright new ways. They boost our mood, lighten our load, and make us laugh. We are not meant to ever grow up enough to stop playing, and our totems shepherd us into that very place of playfulness. Each day give yourself an opportunity to play with the magic of spirit. It's really quite simple—abracadabra!

We don't stop playing because we grow old; we grow old because we stop playing.
—George Bernard Shaw

Sometimes You Just Gotta Let It Go

If anything, your totems have given you the best examples of what it means to let go. During your journey to uncover your personal animal totem, you could not control when, where, or how your animal totems would take make their presence known to you. The wonderful and amazing surprises that accompanied each visit embodied the age-old proverb "Let go and let God." As you traveled to unveil each animal totem, you allowed yourself to be open to every possible way your totem might come through.

Uncovering Your Personal Animal Totem

Any notions or ideas you might have had gave way; you had no attachment to the outcome of the visit, you just waited expectantly. However, during its unfolding you got to experience the excitement, delight, and true appreciation of how your totem manifested itself. You experienced the very essence of "Let go and let God." In a sense, you consciously surrendered your free will to the will of spirit and got some pretty amazing results—eight totems, to be exact. Your totems will help you harness this let-go philosophy, and if you can mindfully put your arms around this practice and trust it, that excitement, delight, and true appreciation can continue to flow. It's much easier to comprehend a philosophical or spiritual concept in general terms than it is to practice it in everyday life, but you essentially did it when you uncovered your totems. Interestingly enough, it is exactly that unexpected connection with your totems that is the key to solving many of your challenges and-so called problems in life. If you adopt the practice of letting go and make use of the same mindset you employed when you uncovered your totems, when you find yourself burdened by conflict and confusion, you will find that the Divine will step in and with a result far better than anything your free will could ever create or solve. If you think about the crazy way your totems showed up during your journey to uncover them, at the very least that should give you the confidence to trust and have faith in the Divine to meet every single one of your needs and burdens. When I find my students and clients are too caught up in trying to control and manage the outcome of situations, I tell them this little joke/parable.

A man named Jack was walking along a steep cliff one day when he accidentally got too close to the edge and fell. On the way down, he grabbed a branch, which temporarily stopped his fall. He looked down and, to his horror, saw that the canyon fell straight down for more than a thousand feet.

He couldn't hang onto the branch forever, and there was no way for him to climb up the steep wall of the cliff. So Jack began yelling for help, hoping that someone passing by would hear him and lower a rope or something.

"Help! Help! Is anyone up there? Help!"

He yelled for a long time, but no one heard him. He was about to give up when he heard a voice.

"Jack, Jack!" the voice called. "Can you hear me?"

"Yes, yes!" Jack answered. "I can hear you. I'm down here!"

"I can see you, Jack. Are you all right?"

"Yes, but who are you, and where are you?

"I am the Lord, Jack. I'm everywhere."

"The Lord? You mean, GOD?"

"That's me."

"God, please help me!" Jack cried. "I promise if, you'll get me down from here, I'll stop sinning. I'll be a really good person. I'll serve you for the rest of my life."

"Easy on the promises, Jack," God said. "Let's get you off from there, then we can talk. Now, here's what I want you to do. Listen carefully."

"I'll do anything, God," Jack said. "Just tell me what to do."

"Okay. Let go of the branch."

"What?" Jack asked.

"I said, let go of the branch. Just trust me. Let go."

There was a long silence.

Finally, Jack yelled, "Help! Help! Is anyone else up there?"

When our totems come to visit, they will always hold a message and guidance that can release us and set us free from the predicaments that we humans sometimes find ourselves caught up in. In the end, what it all comes down to is, sometimes you just gotta let go.

The harder you fight to hold on to specific assumptions, the more likely there's gold in letting go of them.
—John Seely Brown

If You Play Your Cards Right

There are literally hundreds of different types of oracle cards and tarot decks on the market today offering any form of guidance you have a fancy or preference for. You name it, and there is literally an oracle deck that can guide you in it. There are angel, fairy, ascendant masters, goddess, animal, nature, color, wisdom, and healing cards, just to name a few. These are all tools of divination, as are systems like astrology, numerology, palmistry, the I Ching, tea-leaf reading, pendulums, and so on. It doesn't matter which you use; as the saying goes, all roads lead to Rome. Whatever route you take to Rome will offer its own panoramic view. Interestingly enough, the same effort you put into learning any of these different modalities can also be applied to building your own oracle with your animal totems. As you embark on a devotional practice with spirit, follow the guidance of your animal totems, and document each occurrence, you will find that there are common concepts represented by their visits. The more you work with your animal totems, the greater your connection will be with them. As you develop a strong working relationship with each animal, you will begin to understand its meaning with clear and profound insight. Your totem animals will help you create your own personal oracle; however, only you can decide whether you want to make a game of it.

Uncovering Your Personal Animal Totem

Life is like a game of cards. The hand you are dealt is determinism; the way you play it is free will.
—Jawaharlal Nehru

CHAPTER 18

AFTERTHOUGHTS

What's Up with This Chapter

∞ Afterword
∞ The End

In the years to come, each of your totem animals will herald a tremendous amount of guidance and play a significant role in helping you stay attuned and Divinely connected to the spirit realm, from both an exterior perspective and an interior one. In fact, in case you haven't noticed yet, helping you keep your connectedness to the spirit realm is the very mission and purpose of your totem animals. In the beginning, the nuances of this attunement might be quite subtle, like perhaps you just notice your totem. However, when you have a bear by the tail, you will be grateful for their appearance. As you become more versed and invested in working with each one of your totems, the subtlety of just noticing becomes more robust, with a knowingness about what the appearance actually means. The more you work with the characteristics of each animal in your totem, the more comprehensive your revelation of its sighting will be. Remember to pay close attention to the element each totem animal represents, as this too will play an important role in what is being communicated to you.

Remember the little seed you planted way back at the root chakra section? Every element nurtured its progress, for seeds grow from the earth, rain, sun, air, and space. Your totem visits will help you grow, for these gifts from the universe will always offer you the right elements to assist your growth. Learning to understand the role each totem plays in ensuring the balance of the entire totem team is the essential part of realizing your true nature. Allow your animal totems to be the great cultivators that feed each element of the chakra system, bringing you to your greatest, highest, and best in life. The only thing that you ultimately need to do is notice, as nature will always play its part. Lao Tzu encouraged his followers to take their time to observe and understand the laws of nature, thereby developing intuition and building up personal power. Lao Tzu urged them to use that power to live life with love, and without force. Your totems hold the very key to your experiencing the laws of nature. You need only show up.

> *Nature does not hurry, yet everything is accomplished.*
> —Lao Tzu

Afterword

When I set out to write this book, I went back and forth on what I would call it, *Uncovering Your Personal Animal Totem* or *Embracing Your True Nature through Nature*. The former seemed like a logical name to me; after all, it's what I call the course I teach on the subject, and *Uncovering Your Personal Animal Totem* is essentially what you are doing in the process. So why not call the book that? However, as I began to write about uncovering your personal animal totem, something much deeper and immensely greater started to unfold, and it began to change my perceptions of what I call the ordinary world. As an intuitive, I spend a lot time meandering in the realms of the unseen and unknown. There, my perceptions are guided to reveal my path as well as to aid my clients in their journeys. I am always humbled by these connections and the immense peace, solace, and love they prompt. However, what I did not know was that during the writing of this book I too would be astounded by the renewed magical essences my own totem animals would suddenly manifest. Sure, I work with my totems every day and it's magical and enchanting, but the shift that transpired during the writing of this book was astounding and transcended what I thought was my true nature in such an extraordinary way that it resulted in an immensely greater unfolding of my true nature. My little lower self had no idea of the powerful forces that would unfold in this journey, while my higher self knew exactly where I was being guided to take refuge.

My personal totems have always been there to magically guide and boldly lead me and to bring gentle comfort on my path, but this journey has certainly given me a greater appreciation of and humbling at their true nature and the magnificent forces they hold. Each chapter and section of this book holds the little pieces of the unfolding of my true nature too. Not only were my connection to the graces of my animal totems strengthened and reinforced, but I was also connected to the powers of infinite spirit in ways that surpassed any of my most awesome prior connections. Make no mistake about the powerful forces of your totems. The more you respect, honor, and have gratitude for the amazingly graceful guidance they present to you moment to moment, the more access you will have to the portal of expansion that will shift your paradigm in remarkably new and miraculous ways. So the long and short of it all is that while I

Afterthoughts

thought I was leading *you* to embrace your true nature, I was ultimately being led to my true nature. It has been my sincere pleasure to be your guide in this journey to uncover your personal animal totem.

All I have seen teaches me to trust the creator for all I have not seen.
—*Ralph Waldo Emerson*

THE END

Not really, it's just the beginning.
A little birdie told me so.
—Darlene Stout

The symbol of the little bird in each chapter is a silhouette of a picture I took of Spunk, an orphan house sparrow I rescued that was only a few days old. I thought it was dead. However, when I got a closer look, his barely formed mouth opened and let out a hardly audible squawk, letting me know he was still alive, though barely. I was in the midst of writing this book when he arrived, and every twenty minutes my writing was suspended to hand-feed him. A week later his eyes opened. Next, the shafts of his feathers began to emerge. And before long he began to actually look like a bird.

I had no idea what kind of bird he would grow into, and every day brought a new insight into who his family of origin could be. He soon learned to jump out of the cereal bowl kept him in on my desk during the day for his feedings. Rapidly, he began to explore more, and before long he was perching on branches I brought in from outdoors. He would boldly jump and practice his flight, and soon he was jumping from the branches to my shoulders, where he would scream for me to feed him. He knew I was his food source and caretaker, and it became clear that he had imprinted on me.

There is no doubt in my mind that spirit sent this little bird to me to help me gain a deeper knowledge of the powerful impact imprinting has on our true nature. Spunk has been an incredible master teacher for me in the writing of this book. The sparrow is one of the most common birds; it has thrived where other species have failed. The song sparrow's medicine supports the chakra energy awakening the heart and throat and reminds us to lovingly sing out our own song of dignity and worth. The sparrow demonstrates that even a common little bird can triumph, even when all looks bleak. Perhaps that is why sparrows are so abundant.

Uncovering Your Personal Animal Totem

*When the final format of this book was sent to my editor, Spunk removed himself from this earthly plane to returned home to that, all that is, place that sent him . I miss his powerful little spirit immensely and have great reverence and gratitude for his help in the creation of this book.

TIPS, TRICKS, AND DIVINE WISDOM

Carry out your meditation in your sacred space. Always clear your sacred space before you start. Perform your meditation three days in a row. Even if you think it isn't working, it is.

Let the animal appear, no matter what animal comes up. Every animal that appears is a powerful and masterful teacher. Even though a cockroach or rat may not seem desirable, they have abilities and skills that cannot be matched by any other animals. Be open-minded! There is a great reason why this animal has come to you.

Going within is a process of growing and learning to see ourselves truly. The animal that appears helps us to learn our true nature. When the animal appears in your meditation, continue to interact with it as much as possible. This will help you develop more vivid clairvoyance. Even if only a portion of the animal appears—for instance the head, foot, or wing—trust it!

Throughout the month, confirmations will come in a variety of ways—in your meditation, dreams, actual encounters, magazines, and art, and on television, radio, computer screens, bumper stickers, and Facebook. Confirmations can and will show up anywhere. Stay present!

You may also notice appearances of the animal's natural predator or prey in the wild. Remember not just the animal but the natural habitat of the animal is also key. Once you identify your animal, research it in its natural environment. Go outdoors and online, to sites like YouTube and National Geographic. Explore!

Visualize your animal in the chakra center you are working with, even if the animal has not appeared. This will really prime the pump to clairvoyance and initiate a welcoming sign. Again, don't underestimate the power of meditation and the power of your animal guide.

If you are having trouble connecting, it is usually because you are too much in your head, meaning you are thinking too logically about it. Spirit is not logical, and animals do not navigate by logic; they follow a natural flow of being in the moment and open to the moment.

Pray and ask for help. Surrendering means letting go and allowing. Prayer will always give way. Don't forget to use some accessories as part of your prayer ritual. Have faith!

MEDITATION

The following meditation can be used as a template each time you begin to uncover a new totem for your personal animal totem. You may also use any of your own meditations as a channel to bring your animals into your mind's eye. The Internet has some wonderful guided meditations that can help you receive clairvoyant or telepathic images of your animals too. Each time you begin to uncover a new totem animal, perform your meditation for three consecutive days. You can make this meditation more powerful by recording it and/or playing music along with it. Your personal voice will enhance the effects of the meditation. Use any of the totem accessories to enhance the journey and invoke a connection with your animal totem.

Animal Totem Meditation

You are now going to take a journey to meet your totem animal. Close your, eyes take a deep breath, and allow yourself to become perfectly comfortable wherever you may be sitting or lying. Concentrate on your breathing and follow it as it goes in, turns around, and goes out, much like a wave on a seashore. Now focus on your body and scan it from head to toe, consciously relaxing all those places that are not perfectly comfortable. As you breathe in and out, give yourself permission to do whatever you need to do to become peaceful and comfortable in this place where you find yourself at rest. Allow your body to relax to the rhythm of your breath, just like the waves on the beach on a warm sunny day flowing in and out. Notice how your body seems to release something every time you exhale, becoming more and more relaxed. Look for tension in your muscles, stiffness, any pain or soreness just being exhaled away as you breathe. Notice any tiny pockets of tension. Now bring your attention to the tips of your toes, removing all tension with every exhale as we move up your body. From your toes to your chin, thighs, and hips, exhaling all tension. Moving up into the abdominal area, up into your chest. Check your spine. Start at the tailbone, moving up the spinal column to the back of the neck and shoulders. Now come down the arm to the fingertips, releasing any tension you might feel with your exhale. Wiggle your fingers, removing all tension in the joints. Now

Uncovering Your Personal Animal Totem

come back up the arms, stopping at your shoulders, lifting and then relaxing them to remove any hidden tension. Move up into your head, your lips, jaw, nose, up to your forehead, removing any tension that might be tight between the eyebrows.

Notice how your body does begin to relax. Now allow yourself to detach from this physical present time and imagine that all the conditions and cares swirling around you are just melting away as you continue to become more comfortable in this quiet, safe, comfortable space. As you are sitting there in your quiet peaceful space with your eyes closed, you notice a little spark of light. It's very tiny, but as you focus on it, it begins to get bigger and bigger and begins to glisten and dance. As you relax you are captivated by this sparkling dancing light. As you watch this light, a beautifully lush meadow begins to unfold all around it. As you watch this meadow, it begins to expand and grow larger, almost as if it is being rolled out to you. The meadow is now all around, and you can feel the earth solidly under you. You smell all the fragrances of this meadow. The air is so fresh and refreshing and the sun so warm and cozy, like you have never felt it before. This beautiful meadow is so relaxing.

As you look into the distance, you notice a shadow moving across the meadow, as if cast by a bird. You watch this shadow move closer to you and all around you. As it circles you can feel the wind from its wings making the fragrances of the meadow deepen into your senses. Far off in the distance, you can see large, stately trees and the smell of forest starts to take over your senses. As you experience the wonderful smell of this far-off forest, you begin to see another shadow emerge that resembles the powerful presence of an animal. This animal seems familiar to you. As you wonder about this familiar animal, you notice out of the corner of your eye that off in another direction a crystal-clear river feeds into a beautiful and expansive crystal-clear ocean. The smell of the ocean air excites your senses as you watch all kinds of colorful fish glisten in the water. The subtle presence of a flying insect suddenly captures your attention as it hovers around the meadow flowers and majestically drifts through the blooms of the field. You feel its excitement and enthusiasm, as it seems to swim like the fish in this natural heaven of pleasure. Even the grass seems to be waving to this tiny little insect. You feel so connected to everything that moves, everything seems to stimulates your senses as if it were communicating to you in some indescribable but enchanting and magically wonderful way.

As you relax and enjoy this wonderland, the tiny glimmer of light returns and summons you to follow it past the distant mountains, up into the sky where the clouds swirl and the mountain air captures your senses. It is so amazingly peaceful as you float above it all. As you relax in this euphoric flow of pleasure, you can hear faint whispers that seem fairy-like but harmonize in the breeze. You too seem to be intrinsically harmonizing with the subtle nuances of the unseen essence of what seems to be an angelic rhythm. It's almost as if you can see, hear, taste, smell, touch, and feel a knowing connection to all that is. Suddenly, every animal and creature on earth is a part of you and you a part of it. You relax as the shimmering waves of this natural energy dance about you, allowing you to soar in the effervescent freedom of your true nature. As you ride the stream of your true nature, you see the tiny glimmer of light has returned, and you feel yourself starting to descend from this magical place. As you feel yourself getting closer to the meadow, you feel a groundedness that you have never experienced before. You can feel what every plant and tree feels as its roots extend deep into the heart of Mother Earth. As you lie there in the meadow, musing over this great journey you have just taken, you feel more alive and connected to nature than you have ever felt.

As you connect to your breath and start to feel yourself coming back to your world, a subtle movement catches your attention. As you breathe in and out, you notice that it's an animal, and you are brought back to a place of wonder because you realize it is one of your chakra animals. As you look into the eyes of this creature, you can feel its powerful energy and amazing essence. You can see your reflection in its eyes, and you know it's really the reflection of your true nature. As you gaze at this part of yourself, the tiny glimmer of light returns, and your reflection seems to merge with this creature and you feel its powerful nature. You feel your chakra tingle, and suddenly you feel an unknown empty space within your core being filled with the energy of your animal totem. You feel such gratitude and appreciation for what you have just experienced. Sit here with this energy for as long as you like. When it is time for you to return, follow the tiny glimmering light back to the meadow that will fade from your vision. Ride the energy back to the present, back to your breath, back to where you sit or lay, slowly wiggling your toes and fingers. When you are ready, you may open your eyes.

www.ingramcontent.com/pod-product-compliance
Lightning Source LLC
LaVergne TN
LVHW061217060426
835508LV00014B/1336